BIRNBAUM GUIDES

2010

Walt Disney World®

WITHOUT KIDS

Wendy Lefkon
EDITORIAL DIRECTOR

Jill Safro
EDITOR

Frieda Christofides
DESIGNER

Jessica Ward
ASSISTANT EDITOR

Alexandra Mayes Birnbaum
CONSULTING EDITOR

THE OFFICIAL GUIDE

D1057454

DISNEY EDITIONS
NEW YORK
AN IMPRINT OF DISNEY BOOK GROUP

ISBN 978-1-42311705-6

Printed in the United States of America

Other 2010 Birnbaum's Official Disney Guides:

FSC

Mixed Sources
Product group from well-managed forests, controlled sources and recycled wood or fibre

Cert no. SW-COC-002550
www.fsc.org
© 1996 Forest Stewardship Council

A Word from the Editor

When you stop to think about it, a Walt Disney World guide for grown-ups makes a lot of sense. After all, how many kids do you know who have been there alone? As it happens, Disney has been catering to adult sensibilities for a long time; the most obvious example is one entire theme park, namely, Epcot.

Of course, the rest of the World is by no means the exclusive domain of small fry. In keeping with the spirit of the World that Walt built, there are no age limits here. Disney's Hollywood Studios is a veritable haven for movie buffs. The Magic Kingdom sprinkles guests with pixie dust and transports them to the giddy, fantasy-filled days of their youth. Disney's Animal Kingdom, a lush celebration of all creatures great and small, is sure to lure the nature lover out of even the most buttoned-down sophisticate. Add to the above a hopping nightlife district and a sports complex, and you have proof positive that the World has expanded in precisely our direction. Chic resort hotels and restaurants, world-class golf courses, and sensuous spa treatments only add to the allure.

Editor Jill Safro consults with Minnie and Mickey, the ultimate Walt Disney World insiders.

PHOTO BY MICHAEL CARROLL

But there's also another, more subtle level on which Walt Disney World has always appealed to grown-ups. More than ever before, Disney's creative efforts are crossing over to the grown-up side of the street. Lots of adults are descending on the parks with notions that are vastly different from those of the parental persuasion.

This book, unlike *Birnbaum's Official Guide to Walt Disney World*, is by no means comprehensive. Rather, it skips the flat-out kid stuff and delivers the goods on the grown-up amusements Disney has to offer. And because this guide is updated every year, we have spent the past twelve months debating which of the attractions, hotels, and restaurants—both new and old—continue to merit special attention by adults. Final decisions were reached after making countless trips to Florida and putting everything to the test.

Even with research aplenty, this book would never have seen print were it not for the assistance of many other people. To begin, we owe a thank-you to the people who run Walt Disney World. It is their willingness to explain operations in the most accurate way possible that makes this the Official Guide. However, it is important to note that while the folks at Walt Disney World help us to ensure factual accuracy, they do not determine what we do and do not cover in the guide. All editorial decisions are made by the editor.

In the listing below, I've tried to acknowledge Disney staffers who contributed their time, knowledge, and experience to this edition.

For their key roles behind the scenes, we salute Nisha Panchal, Jennifer Eastwood, Diane Hodges, Jeff Titelius, Michelle Olveira, and Linda Verdon.

Special kudos to those for whom doing Walt Disney World research is truly a labor of love. The class of 2010 includes Irene Safro, Roy Safro, Amy Henning, Chris Henning, Avery Henning, Joy Weigel, Chris Weigel, Hayden

We Couldn't Have Done It Without . . .

Pam Brandon	Bebee Frost	Sarah Sinoff
Barbara Carroll	Richard Gregorie	Mark Peters
Mike Carroll	Karen Haynes	Rosely Piraino
Stacey Cook	Mark Jaronski	Frank Ritti
Craig Dezern	Kristi Koester	Anna Rivera
Debbie Dizon	Jason Lasecki	Laura Simpson
Christi Erwin Donnan	Frankie Lobono	Rick Sylvain
Mark Drennen	Alison Mahony	Dara Trujillo
Irene Ferdinand	Carrie Matson	Pamela S. Weiers

Weigel, Margaret Verdon, and Trace Schielzo.

Of course, no list of acknowledgments would be complete without a mention of our founding editor, Steve Birnbaum, as well as Alexandra Mayes Birnbaum, who continues to be a guiding light and a careful reader of every word.

Finally, it is important to remember that Walt Disney World is constantly changing and growing, and with each annual revision, we refine and expand our material to serve your needs even better. For the present edition, though, this is the final word.

Have a great visit!

Don't Forget to Write

No contribution is of greater value to us in preparing the next edition of this book than your comments on what we've written and on your own experiences and discoveries at Walt Disney World. Please share your insights with us by writing to:

Jill Safro, Editor
Birnbaum's Walt Disney World Without Kids 2010
Disney Editions
114 Fifth Avenue, 14th Floor
New York, NY 10011

Table of Contents

8 Planning Ahead

First things first: Lay the groundwork for an unforgettable vacation by timing your Disney visit to take advantage of the best weather, crowd patterns, and special goings-on. We set forth information about package and ticket options, offer time- and money-saving strategies, and present the keys to the World's transportation system. Our custom-designed sample schedules will help you plan your days and nights. And a round of specialized advice offers the promise of a hassle-free trip.

38 Checking In

Whether it's elegant, rustic, whimsical, or romantic digs you're seeking, you'll find them among Walt Disney World's 22-plus resorts and two island-bound cruise ships, themed as only Disney knows how. Choose from hotels whose architecture and ambience evoke such locales as Africa, New Orleans, Martha's Vineyard, Polynesia, or an early 1900s mountain lodge. Within our listings we explain the big draws and grown-up appeal of all the resorts located within Walt Disney World borders.

80 Theme Parks: The Big Four

Enchanting, engaging, entertaining . . . overwhelming. The Magic Kingdom, Epcot, Disney's Hollywood Studios, and Disney's Animal Kingdom can rekindle even the most sluggish sense of wonder. But where to begin? Right here. We've devised strategies to help you make the most of each day. We've also provided detailed theme park walking tours that highlight the most alluring stops for adults; a primer on Fastpass, Disney's time-saving service; and lists of touring priorities that rank every attraction. From "Don't Miss" to "Don't Knock Yourself Out," we've scoped out the grown-up fun quotient.

140 Diversions: Sports, Shopping, and Other Pursuits

Because the World's attractions extend way beyond the theme parks, so does our guidance. Here, discover the options, including first-rate 18-hole golf courses, tennis, boating, fishing, and biking. Shoppers will have a field day checking out our favorite shopping spots. For those who prefer soaking and sliding, we plunge into the water parks. Our in-depth report on romantic (and private) fireworks cruises reveals the creative

essence of this adult-minded retreat. We also visit the natural realms of Fort Wilderness and indulge in the sinful splendor of Walt Disney World's spas.

182 Dining & Entertainment

Here's your insider's guide to adult best bets for full-service restaurants and casual eating spots in the theme parks, resorts, and elsewhere in Walt Disney

World. We've found dining rooms with prime views, cheap eats, sweet treats, afternoon tea, wines by the glass, and hearty microbrews. After dark, you'll know where to go to watch the big game, hear R&B, join in a rollicking sing-along, and dance the night away, as well as how to navigate the newest Downtown Disney hot spots, find a dinner show, or catch a theme park spectacular.

Anyone can have a magical time at Walt Disney World with advance planning.

Planning Ahead

There are plenty of hotels, restaurants, and theme park attractions for everyone at Walt Disney World. So why sit down with a book to plan ahead? Because a little attention to detail beforehand—we like to think of it as shopping for fun insurance—pays big dividends once you arrive. Just ask the couple who had the foresight to book a table at the deluxe Victoria & Albert's dining room before they left home (not to mention all the other meals—the Disney Dining Plan is so popular that most eateries are doing a booming business). Or the friends who arrived with tickets in hand and avoided the line at the entrance to Epcot. Or the golfers who were able to snag a coveted mid-morning tee time.

Our point: You can't be assured of the vacation experience you want without knowing which of the gazillion ways to enjoy Walt Disney World most appeal to you—and how to make sure these potential highlights don't become missed opportunities.

This first chapter not only provides the framework for a successful visit, but also establishes a vital awareness that helps the information in subsequent chapters fall right in line.

On the following pages, you'll find insight on when to visit; advice on tickets, packages, reservations, and how to save money; information on how to get around the World; flexible touring schedules; and tips for older travelers, couples, singles, and guests with disabilities. In short, it's a handy guide to all the magic of Disney.

This chapter is a planner that you'll return to again and again—no doubt with greater purpose than the first time through, when you're still eager to learn about Disney's hotels, theme parks, dining, and nightlife. So go ahead and give it a quick skim if this is your first read, but don't forget to come back.

WHEN TO GO

Much tougher than the question of whether you want to visit Walt Disney World is the prickly matter of when. In addition to your own schedule, there is the weather to consider; you would also like to avoid the crowds, although you'd love to get a peek at the Christmas parade or that flower festival you read about in the newspaper. You want to experience Disney World at its best. But when?

Weather and crowd patterns are charted in this section, along with other factors, such as extended park hours, so you can see how possible vacation dates stack up. Timing your visit to meet all expectations may be impossible, but our experience does suggest certain optimum times. Mid-January through early February, late April through late May, September through early November (book well in advance if you plan to visit during Epcot's popular Food and Wine Festival), and the week after Thanksgiving through the week before Christmas stand out as good times to find oneself in the World. (Though you'll *never* be lonely at Walt Disney World!)

Taking things one step further, we like to underline the period from the Sunday after Thanksgiving to the week before Christmas as the best timing for a visit. This is a chance to savor Disney during one of its least crowded and most festive times of year.

WDW WEATHER

Average:	High (F)	Low (F)	Rain (inches)
January	72	50	2.4
February	74	51	2.3
March	79	56	3.5
April	83	60	2.4
May	88	66	3.7
June	91	71	7.3
July	92	73	6.2
August	92	73	5.8
September	90	72	5.8
October	85	65	2.7
November	79	59	2.3
December	73	53	2.3

If your travel dates fall outside the above-mentioned ideal, don't despair. Walt Disney World makes a spectacle of itself year-round. This listing highlights holidays and happenings that— for their fanfare, crowd-drawing potential, and, in some instances, accompanying package deals— are worth factoring into your vacation plans.

NOTE: We've provided 2010 dates where available, but the specifics may change. For details about events and vacation packages, call 407-W-DISNEY (934-

7639), or pay a visit to to *www.disneyworld.com/whentogo.*

Holidays & Special Events

WALT DISNEY WORLD MARATHON

(January 7–10): Marathoners lace up for a 26.2-mile race through scenic areas of Disney World on January 10. Disney characters inspire more than 14,000 runners to stay the course. There's a half marathon on the 9th and a 5K family fun run on the 8th. Call 407-939-7810, or visit *www.disneyworld sports.com* for information. Vacation packages are available. All marathon weekend events are extremely popular, so plan as far ahead as possible.

ATLANTA BRAVES SPRING TRAINING

(February–March): Some of Major League Baseball's greatest gather at Disney's ballpark to get a jump on the upcoming season. Tickets sell quickly. For details, visit *www.disneyworldsports.com,* or call 407-WDW-GAME (939-4263).

ST. PATRICK'S DAY (March 17):

On this day, impromptu shindigs sprout like shamrocks in the

All in the Timing

Consider the following WDW trends before settling on vacation dates. For details on park hours and attraction refurbishments, call 407-824-4321.

Shortest Lines, Smallest Crowds: The first week of January through the first week of February (with the exception of New Year's Day and WDW Marathon weekend); late April through late May; the week after Labor Day until Thanksgiving; the week after Thanksgiving through the week before Christmas.

Longest Lines, Biggest Crowds: Presidents' week; the third week of March through the third week of April, especially Easter week; June through Labor Day, particularly the Fourth of July; Christmas through New Year's Day. Marathon weekend draws big crowds, too. Weekends tend to be busy throughout the year. Consider a Sunday–Thursday stay to avoid the weekend influx of locals.

Potential Pitfalls: The water parks and certain WDW attractions sometimes close for renovations (most often during winter months). Spring break (between February and mid-April) lures many students, as do Grad Nites (weekend events in late April and early May).

Extended Hours: The two weeks surrounding Easter; summer; Thanksgiving weekend; Christmas through New Year's Day.

more spirited corners of the World. Raglan Road, Downtown Disney's Irish pub, is rather festive on this occasion.

EPCOT INTERNATIONAL FLOWER & GARDEN FESTIVAL (March 3–May 16): This flowery, annual event—a fragrant affair featuring some 30 million blossoms—not only makes a glorious perfumery of Epcot, but also allows gardeners to learn a trick or two from the folks who care for 10,000

rosebushes and then some.

In addition to character topiaries and elaborate display gardens, guests can take part in workshops, behind-the-scenes tours, dining, and a nightly concert series featuring acts from the 1960s and '70s.

EASTER (April 4): Extended hours—and monumental crowds—at the parks make for a hopping Magic Kingdom. It's one of the busiest times of the year.

STAR WARS WEEKENDS (select weekends in May and/or June): Galactic good times can be enjoyed as Disney's Hollywood Studios salutes the ever-popular *Star Wars* saga with celebrities and characters from the movies, autograph and photo opportunities, trivia contests, and more.

What to Pack

- Comfortable shoes (2 pair)
- Sunglasses and sunscreen
- A bathing suit
- Insect repellent
- T-shirts and shorts for day
- Casual separates for evening (jeans are usually okay)
- Lightweight sweaters or jackets for summer evenings and air-conditioned rooms; warmer clothing for evening (and often daytime), from November through March
- A jacket for men and a dress or comparable outfit for women for dinner at Victoria & Albert's
- Suitable togs and equipment for tennis, golf, fishing, jogging, or gym workouts (racquets, clubs, balls, golf shoes, and poles are available for rent)
- Lightweight rain gear and a folding umbrella

FOURTH OF JULY CELEBRATION

(July 4): Double-fisted fireworks at the Magic Kingdom, Epcot, and Disney's Hollywood Studios are a glorious salute to our nation's birthday. The parks often have extended hours to mark the occasion. But you pay a price: It's the busiest day of the summer.

CHILDREN'S MIRACLE NETWORK GOLF CLASSIC

(Fall): In this tournament, now in its 40th year and presented by Wal-Mart, top PGA Tour players compete alongside amateurs on two WDW venues: the Palm and Magnolia golf courses. The drama builds until the final day, when the Magnolia's fickle 18th hole has been known to twist the fates of more than a few players. At press time, the PGA Tour had not announced the 2010 fall schedule. For info, call 407-824-2250.

EPCOT INTERNATIONAL FOOD & WINE FESTIVAL

(October 1–November 14): The temptation to eat and drink your way around World Showcase is intensified by cooking demonstrations, plus samples of a host of exotic specialty dishes, international wines by the glass, and worldly desserts (about $2 to $7 per taste). Special five-course dinners sponsored by various vintners are also a highlight (to book this dining experience, call 407-WDW- DINE [939-3463]). There is a nightly concert series featuring musical acts from the 1970s and '80s, and a "Party for the Senses" each weekend.

Hot Tickets

Here are a few numbers to add to your pre-vacation Rolodex.

- Consider that a recent stretch brought such acts as Pat Benatar, New York Dolls, and Rusted Root to House of Blues. For information, call 407-934-2583 or visit *www. hob.com* a few months ahead.

- To make a sure thing of witnessing Cirque du Soleil at Downtown Disney, call 407-939-7600 or visit *www.disneyworld.com* for tickets up to six months ahead.

- Advance planning also pays off when ESPN Wide World of Sports complex hosts, say, the always popular Atlanta Braves. Call 407-939-4263.

FESTIVAL OF THE MASTERS
(November 12–14): One of the South's top-rated art shows, the Downtown Disney event draws upward of 200 award-winning exhibitors from around the country. It tends to be least crowded on Friday and Sunday mornings.

DISNEY'S MAGICAL HOLIDAYS (Mid-November through December): The whole wide World is positively aglow with holiday spirit, and it doesn't stop at decorations: There's a nightly tree-lighting ceremony at Epcot.

The Magic Kingdom celebrates

Cost-Cutting Tips

- Planning a trip during Disney's "peak" season? Be sure to check the rates at the Swan and Dolphin resorts. As business-oriented hotels, they tend to run incredible specials during some of Disney's busiest times of year.

- Consider accommodations with kitchen facilities to save on food costs, or stock your mini fridge (available free at deluxe and moderate WDW resorts or for a $10 nightly fee at value resorts).

- It's possible to stretch your dining dollar by purchasing the Disney Dining Plan. It is available only to guests staying at resorts owned and operated by Walt Disney World and must be booked with the room.

- Compare lunch and dinner menus. The same dishes may be cheaper by day.

- Buy a WDW resort mug good for unlimited refills (of soft drinks) at the hotel during your stay; save time, too—just swipe the bar code on your mug past the reader at the self-service dispenser and fill 'er up.

- Keep a refillable water bottle with you on steamy summer days.

- When choosing a place to stay, don't break the budget for a resort packed with amenities you won't have time to enjoy. Also realize that often the only difference between the least and most expensive rooms in a hotel is the view, and decide how often you'll be looking out that window.

- If you plan to make multiple visits to Walt Disney World within a year, get an annual pass. Ownership nets many discounts, including savings on meals, merchandise, and room rates.

- Membership in organizations such as AARP and AAA often come with a few Disney perks as well. Check with your member representative to see if there are any special privileges to which you are entitled.

- Disney Rewards Visa holders can take advantage of exclusive theme park discounts and money-saving opportunities.

- Take advantage of Disney's Magical Express—a free shuttle service to and from the airport for WDW resort guests (see page 21 for details).

the season with Mickey's Once Upon a Christmastime Parade and Mickey's Very Merry Christmas Party, a special-ticket event held on select nights from mid-November through the third week of December that includes hot chocolate and cookies, plus snow flurries on Main Street and fireworks.

Epcot invites guests to enjoy a Candlelight Processional, featuring a mass choir, 50-piece orchestra, and celebrity reading of the Nativity story (inquire about dinner and show packages: 407-WDW-DINE [939-3463]).

Disney's Hollywood Studios mesmerizes with the Osborne Family Spectacle of Dancing Lights—an enveloping display featuring millions of lights that twinkle to synchronized music. Vacation packages are available; for details, call 407-828-8101.

Animal Kingdom presents Mickey's Jingle Jungle parade.

NEW YEAR'S EVE CELEBRATION

(December 31): At least three of the theme parks—all of which are still decked out in full holiday regalia—are open after midnight, attracting huge throngs and presenting high-spirited fun and entertainment.

Many of the WDW resorts have special celebrations. Double-size fireworks are launched in the skies over the Magic Kingdom, Epcot, and Disney's Hollywood Studios. Downtown Disney has hosted special New Year's Eve celebrations, and La Nouba by Cirque du Soleil (Downtown Disney West Side) rings in the new year with a special finale.

"Extra Magic Hours"

Perk alert! The "Extra Magic Hours" program can give you additional hours of playtime in the parks—at no extra charge. If you're staying at a Walt Disney World owned-and-operated resort hotel (plus the Swan, Dolphin, or Hilton on Hotel Plaza Boulevard)—and have the right kind of ticket—you'll also have the chance to play in your favorite theme park *after* it has closed to the general public—for free!

In a nutshell, one park opens its doors an hour early or stays open up to three hours late each day for guests bearing a resort ID and the right park ticket. It allows you to visit some (but not all) attractions and hobnob with Disney characters.

What's the right kind of ticket, you ask? If you have a ticket with "park-hopping" privileges, you're in no matter what. If you have a Magic Your Way base ticket without the park-hopping feature, you must visit the park offering the "Extra Magic Hours" that particular day. Check with your lobby concierge for the "Extra Magic Hours" schedule and procedures, or visit *www.disneyworld.com*.

THE LOGISTICS
Should You Buy a Package?

Vacation plans put forth by Disney are known as Magic Your Way packages. The goal is to encourage you to tailor your vacation to your own needs, wants, and budget. The components of the base Magic Your Way package include accommodations at a WDW resort (any price category, excluding the Swan, Dolphin,

Ticket Tips

- All admission tickets and passes are nontransferable. The "Ticket Tag" system enforces it. (See page 19.)
- Multi-day tickets expire 14 days after first use—unless the "no expiration" option is purchased.
- At the end of your visit, note the number of unused days on a multi-day ticket. Write it on the ticket itself (provided, of course, that you purchased the "no expiration" option for the ticket).
- Most tickets can be upgraded within 14 days of first use (even if there are no days left). Tickets with the "no expiration" option must be upgraded within 14 days of first use, too. Adjustments must be made on WDW property.
- If you want to visit more than one theme park on a single day, you need to buy the Park Hopper option or an annual pass.

and resorts on Hotel Plaza Boulevard) and an upgradable Magic Your Way base ticket. Guests may also include the Disney Dining Plan (see page 190). There are such things as Magic Your Way Premium and Platinum packages, too. They come with many of the most popular add-on options, such as park-hopping, golf, fishing, water sports, admission to Cirque du Soleil, and more.

The Disney Cruise Line can combine a visit to Walt Disney World with a cruise vacation.

For details about Magic Your Way packages, contact the Walt Disney Travel Company by calling 407-828-8101 or visiting *www.disneyworld.com*. Note that you must pay for vacation packages in their entirety up front. *Cancellations must be made at least 45 days in advance in order to receive a full refund.*

Other operators with plans featuring WDW include American Airlines Vacations (800-321-2121; *www.aavacations.com*) and Southwest Vacations (800-243-8372; *www.southwest.com*). Online tour operators offering Disney World packages include GoGoWorldwide Vacations (*www.gogowwv.com*), Travelocity (*www.travelocity.com*), and Vacation

Outlet (*www.vacationoutlet.com*); 800-690-2210.

If you think you might be interested in buying a package, call for brochures. And keep in mind that the right package: (1) saves you money on the type of lodging, transportation, and recreation you want; (2) includes meaningful extras, as opposed to fluff like welcoming cocktails or so-called privileges that are really services available to all guests; (3) fits like a glove; no matter what the sale price, you wouldn't buy gloves that were too big, nor should you buy a package that encompasses more than you can enjoy.

Money Matters

A few points of interest related to green matter and its plastic counterparts: Traveler's checks, American Express, Visa, Master-Card, Discover Card, Diners Club Card, JCB, Disney's Visa Card, Disney dollars, and Disney gift cards are acceptable for most charges at WDW. While restaurants in the parks accept credit cards, some refreshment stands accept cash only.

Disney resort guests who leave a credit card imprint upon check-in may use their hotel ID card to charge meals at all restaurants and most food carts, purchases at shops and lounges, and recreational fees. These guests also receive the benefit of Express Check-out—an itemized bill is slipped under their door on the day of departure—a nice perk when that morning rolls around and last-minute to-dos await.

As for banking, there are a

That's the Ticket

Admission tickets may be purchased at Disney's stores at the Orlando International Airport, theme park entrances, Guest Relations at Downtown Disney, any WDW resort, any hotel on Hotel Plaza Boulevard, and the Transportation and Ticket Center (offerings vary at each location). WDW resort guests may charge tickets to their rooms. Cash, traveler's checks, Visa, MasterCard, American Express, Discover Card, Diners Club Card, JCB, and Disney's Visa Card are also accepted.

Multi-day tickets can be bought at some Disney Stores, by phone at 407-824-4321, online at *www.disneyworld.com* (allow two to three weeks for processing), or via mail order (allow three to four weeks). Get annual passes at theme park entrances, at a Disney store, through WDW's Web site, or by mail. To get tickets by mail, send a money order (including $4 for handling), payable to the Walt Disney World Company, to: Walt Disney World; Box 10140; Lake Buena Vista, FL 32830-0030; Attention: Ticket Mail Order.

slew of ATMs accessible for a $2 service fee. There are locations in all four theme parks; the Transportation and Ticket Center; Pleasure Island; Downtown Disney Marketplace and Disney West Side; and the lobbies of all WDW resorts. For full-service banking, there is a SunTrust opposite Downtown Disney Marketplace, at 1675 Buena Vista Drive (407-828-6103 or 800-786-8787); hours are 9 A.M. to 4 P.M. weekdays (until 6 P.M. Fridays), with drive-in teller service from 8 A.M. to 5 P.M. Monday–Thursday, 8 A.M. to 6 P.M. Friday (if you have an account with them).

Admission Options

With the exception of annual passes, all admission media are called Magic Your Way Tickets. They are available for one to ten days. The goal is to let guests custom-build their tickets, based on individual schedules, wants, and budgets. In brief: You purchase a Magic Your Way Base Ticket. The first decision you need to make? Number of days. After that, you have a selection of different "add-ons" to choose from (each one costs extra). They include: park-hopping privileges, a "No Expiration" option, and the "Water Park Fun & More" option.

You may add any or all of the aforementioned options as you purchase your base ticket. What's more, you may "upgrade" by adding one of these elements after you buy the base ticket, provided that you do so at Walt Disney World *within 14 days of first use*.

After a little number crunching, it becomes clear that the "per day" price comes down as more days are added to the base ticket. Note that there is no longer an advance purchase savings option. Keep in mind that all tickets are nontransferable.

NOTE: For the purposes of this section, the term *parks* means Magic Kingdom, Epcot, Disney's Hollywood Studios, and Animal Kingdom. Prices do not include tax and are likely to change.

"Water Park Fun & More" add-on options may include admission to Typhoon Lagoon, Blizzard Beach, ESPN Wide World of Sports complex, DisneyQuest, and more.

The following ticket prices were accurate at press time, but they seem to go up when we least expect it. Call 407-824-4321 or visit *www.disneyworld. com* for updates.

MAGIC YOUR WAY BASE TICKET:
Good for 1- to 10-day admission to one theme park per day only.

No park-hopping allowed. Days used need not be consecutive, but remaining days expire 14 days after first use. The cost for this ticket: $75 for one day; $149 for two days; $212 for three days; $219 for four days; $222 for five days; $225 for six days; $228 for seven days; $231 for eight days; $234 for nine days; and $237 for ten days.

NO EXPIRATION ADD-ON: Not sure if you will use all your theme park days? Consider purchasing the "No Expiration" option. Think of it as a kind of insurance. If you buy this add-on, it means any unused days on your ticket *never expire*. (Without this add-on, unused days expire 14 days after the ticket is first used.) It's not available for 1-day tickets, for obvious reasons. Prices for 2- to 10-day tickets are: $17 for two days; $23 for three days; $50 for four days; $70 for five days; $80 for six days; $110 for seven days; $145 for eight days; $170 for nine days; and $200 for ten days.

PARK-HOPPING ADD-ON: Allows you to "hop" from theme park to theme park within a single day (i.e., spend the morning at Magic Kingdom, hop on the monorail,

Disney's "Ticket Tag" System

As a means of enforcing the non-transferability aspect of all Walt Disney World tickets, Disney has devised a system to trace each ticket to its rightful owner while passing through the turnstiles at any of the theme or water parks. It's simple in theory: After signing the back of the ticket, you slip it into the machine at any park entrance. While the machine is crunching the data encrypted on that mysterious magnetic strip, you will be asked to press your index finger on a little gizmo perched on the ticket-grabbing device. Afterward, your newly personalized ticket should pop out the other side and give you the green light to enter. You'll have to do this every time you use the ticket. It slows the park-entering process—so allow extra time to get in. Note that guests no longer need to get a hand stamp to re-enter a park on any given day.

and spend the evening at Epcot). It's available for 1- to 10-day tickets for the flat rate of $50, regardless of the number of days on your base ticket.

WATER PARK FUN & MORE ADD-ON: This option provides admissions to water parks and places such as DisneyQuest and ESPN Wide World of Sports complex. It may be added to *any* base ticket (1–10 days) for $50. The number of admissions depends upon the number of days on the base ticket: a 1-day ticket yields two visits, while 2- to 10-day tickets yield the same number of add-on visits as park days.

THEME PARK ANNUAL PASS ($469; $429 for renewal): Valid for unlimited admission (during regular operating hours) to all four theme parks for one year from the date of purchase; includes unlimited use of Walt Disney World transportation and free parking at the theme parks.

PREMIUM ANNUAL PASS ($599; $549 for renewal): Valid for admission to the four theme parks, the water parks, ESPN Wide World of Sports complex, and DisneyQuest for one year from purchase date; includes unlimited use of WDW transportation and free theme park parking.

NOTE: Both types of annual passes may net discounts on Walt Disney World resort rooms (depending on the season and availability), dinner shows, and much more.

Medical Matters

Although medical care is readily available at WDW, travelers with chronic health problems are advised to carry copies of all prescriptions and ask their physicians to provide names of local doctors. Diabetics should note that Walt Disney World resorts will provide refrigeration for insulin. More generally:

• Report emergencies to 911 operators. Dr. Phillips Hospital (407-842-8801) and Celebration Health (407-303-4000) are two local hospitals.

• Each of the theme parks has a First Aid Center staffed by a registered nurse.

• Doctors On Call Service (407-399-3627) offers 24-hour house-call-only (non-emergency) medical service.

• Another non-emergency medical care option is Centra Care Walk-In Medical Care (407-934-2273); 12500 S. Apopka Vineland Rd., open 8 A.M. to midnight weekdays and 8 A.M. to 8 P.M. weekends.

• For referral to a pharmacy or to find out how to have medication delivered, call Turner Drugs: 407-828-8125. (It's located next door to Centra Care.)

GETTING AROUND

Before you can find your way around WDW, you must have a firm sense of where you are (and where you are not). Walt Disney World is about 22 miles southwest of Orlando in a smaller community called Lake Buena Vista.

The most important (and congested) highway in the Orlando area is I-4, which cuts through the southern half of Disney World. All the area's other major highways intersect I-4.

Among the more frequently traveled is Route 435 (or Kirkman Road), a route that links I-4 to the major hotel and business thoroughfare called International Drive, known locally as I-Drive.

Should You Rent a Car?

Will you need a car during your stay? It's a tough call. Most area hotels offer buses to and from Walt Disney World. Disney's own resorts and parks are serviced by buses, monorail trains, and boats, which provide efficient (though time-consuming) means of traveling within WDW borders.

This transportation is available to visitors staying at WDW resorts and those with a multi-day park ticket or an annual pass. However, if you plan on leaving Disney property or exploring the many WDW resorts—and the great dining opportunities they offer—we recommend a car, or committing some of your travel budget to taxi rides.

Disney's Magical Express

Flying to WDW via Orlando International Airport and staying at a Disney-owned-and-operated resort? Regardless of your airline of choice, you are eligible for "Disney's Magical Express"—a free service that allows guests to check their specially tagged luggage at their originating airport, skip baggage claim in Orlando, board a free shuttle bus to their WDW resort, and have their luggage delivered to their room free of charge. On the final morning of the trip, guests flying on participating airlines can bid adieu to luggage at their resort and get boarding passes at the same time. At press time, participating airlines included AirTran, Alaska, American, Continental, Delta, JetBlue, Northwest, United, and US Airways. Note: Airline luggage fees may apply.

Guests can be booked on any airline to get free round-trip shuttle service, though guests flying airlines other than those mentioned above must bring their luggage to the airport themselves. Buses aren't direct, so you may stop at a few resorts. (If you'd prefer door-to-door service, consider taking a taxi or a car service. See page 22 for details.) Since bags may arrive hours after you do, pack everything you'll need for that afternoon or evening in your carry-on. Expect to leave WDW three hours before your return flight time.

Note: Guests staying at the Swan, Dolphin, Shades of Green, or on Hotel Plaza Boulevard are not eligible for Magical Express.

Disney's transportation is reliable (departing from most areas every 20 minutes or so), but it can accommodate only limited spontaneity. If you decide to drive, note that parking at any of the theme parks costs $12 per day (it's free for WDW resort guests and annual passholders).

We find it's easiest to rent a car from one of the airport's on-site companies (Alamo, Avis, Budget, Dollar, and National). You can rent a car after you've arrived at WDW, too. Inquire at your hotel.

Once inside the resort, you can

Getting to WDW from Orlando Airport

During rush hour take the airport's South Exit, and follow the Central Florida Greeneway (Route 417) to State Road 536, which leads right to WDW; tolls total $2.25. The distance is about 22 miles. For the shortest route, take the airport's North Exit, head west on Route 528 (aka the Beachline Expressway) to I-4 west, and turn off at the appropriate WDW exit; tolls are $1.50.

- **Exit 64:** Magic Kingdom, Disney's Hollywood Studios, Fort Wilderness, Grand Floridian, Contemporary, Polynesian, Wilderness Lodge, Palm and Magnolia golf courses, or Celebration

- **Exit 65:** ESPN Wide World of Sports complex, Animal Kingdom, Blizzard Beach, Coronado Springs, All-Stars, Pop Century, or Animal Kingdom Lodge

- **Exit 67:** Epcot, Typhoon Lagoon, Old Key West, Caribbean Beach, Swan, Dolphin, BoardWalk, Yacht and Beach Club, Port Orleans Riverside and French Quarter, Saratoga Springs, Lake Buena Vista golf course, Bonnet Creek Golf Club, or Downtown Disney

- **Exit 68:** Resorts on Hotel Plaza Boulevard

- **For those without wheels:** A Selective Limousine, Inc., offers direct car service to Disney resorts. Mention this book and you'll get a special rate of $95 for a car for up to four passengers or $195 for a limo for up to 7 passengers; call 407-891-7503 or 800-730-0211. Florida Towncar will transport up to five people for $100 if our book is mentioned when making the reservation. Call 407-277-5466 or 800-525-7246. Both companies provide efficient, friendly, professional service to all Disney resorts and area hotels. Mears Motor Shuttle, though time-consuming and sometimes frustrating, is another option for guests staying in Hotel Plaza Boulevard hotels, the Swan and Dolphin, and area hotels that are not on Disney property. Mears serves area hotels at about $20 one-way or $33 round-trip, per person. For info, call 407-423-5566 or 800-759-5219. Taxis are also an option. Last, but certainly not least, guests staying at a WDW-owned-and-operated resort may take advantage of the most economical service of all: Disney's Magical Express. It's free, if not really express (see page 21).

rely on buses, the monorail, boats—or, in some cases, your own two feet—to get you wherever you're going. Not all destinations can be reached directly.

Our Take on Taxis

Disney's transportation system is vast and cost efficient. That said, it can also chew up time and, at times, be flat-out confusing.

Getting from a Disney resort to any theme park is a no-brainer. It's also relatively easy to "hop" (though not necessarily quick) from park to park. The options always include buses and choices such as monorail or ferry. However, as we've traveled the World over, we have come across a few trouble spots. In each case, we've solved our transportation woes by hailing a cab. The drawback? It'll cost ya.

Traveling between resorts usually involves at least one bus transfer. If you ask bell services to call a cab (they'll make sure it's authorized, with regulated fares), you should get to your destination in a fraction of the time. Trips generally cost about $7–$25 plus tip.

Cabs are also a means of getting to and from Orlando International Airport. Taxis can take up to nine passengers. Fares are generally in

Tips for Drivers

- Florida state law requires use of headlights in the rain or fog and at dusk.
- There are gas stations at the Magic Kingdom Auto Plaza, opposite Pleasure Island, and near BoardWalk. They are open 24 hours.
- Be alert to slippery roads when it rains, as a fine layer of oil accumulates between drizzles.
- It's legal to turn right at a red light anywhere in Florida, unless a sign is posted.
- Call 407-824-0976 for free towing at Walt Disney World. The Magic Kingdom Auto Plaza's AAA Car Care Center provides the service. Off-property, call Riker's Towing & Roadside for 24-hour towing (407-855-7776) and Riker's Automotive for repairs (407-238-9800), or call AAA if you're a member.
- For traffic, news, and weather reports, tune to 580 AM.

the $60 to $70 range, depending on the traffic and the integrity of the driver. (We've been taken miles out of our way on many occasions over the past several years.) What's more, many drivers do not have Sunpass (so you'll have to pay 55 cents per minute while waiting to pay tolls). Bottom line? Until there is a flat rate offered between the airport and WDW resorts, we are sticking with towncars, rental cars, or Disney's Magical Express.

DAY-TO-DAY SAMPLE SCHEDULES

A Day at the Magic Kingdom

- Plan to be in the parking lot at least 30 minutes before the park is scheduled to open.

- Pick up a park guidemap and Times Guide at the entrance. Take note of performance times for special entertainment such as parades, fireworks, etc.

- If you haven't booked a table in advance (never a good idea to arrive without reservations!), stop at City Hall to inquire about any restaurant availability.

- When the park opens, grab a Fastpass (see page 83) for your number one "must-see." Then head to Adventureland. After Jungle Cruise and Pirates of the Caribbean, move on to Frontierland. Do Splash and Big Thunder mountains before skedaddling over to the Haunted Mansion in Liberty Square. Follow it up with a cruise on the *Liberty Belle* Riverboat.

- Don't forget about your Fastpass assignment!

- About 20 minutes before the afternoon parade (daily at about 3 P.M.), either camp out on Main Street or skip it and head for Fantasyland to see key attractions—Peter Pan's Flight, The Many Adventures of Winnie the Pooh, Mickey's PhilharMagic, and It's a Small World—before the crowds swell back to normal after the parade.

- Phobic about long lines? The Walt Disney World Railroad, Tomorrowland Transit Authority, and The Hall of Presidents all tend to keep wait times to a relative minimum. And take advantage of Fastpass as much as possible.

- Breeze through Mickey's Toontown Fair. Then head over to Tomorrowland and take a jaunt through toyland on Buzz Lightyear's Space Ranger Spin and board a rocketship to outer space at the new-and-improved Space Mountain. This is also where you'll find the park classic, Carousel of Progress. If you haven't done so, take a trip on the Tomorrowland Transit Authority.

- Spend the rest of the day tying up loose ends on your touring checklist and perusing the shops on Main Street.

- If there are two runnings of the parade, aim to see the later one, when the crowds are apt to have dwindled and better viewing locations can be had. And do not miss Wishes—the nighttime fireworks spectacular.

A Day at Epcot

- Guests are often permitted to enter the park a few minutes before the opening time, though the attractions may not be running yet.

- Stomach growling? Slip into Sunshine Seasons in The Land.

- If you don't have reservations for lunch and/or dinner (see page 185), you can stop at Guest Relations to book a table at one of the restaurants of World Showcase. (You are more likely to snag a last-minute table for lunch than for dinner.)

- Fight the urge to see Spaceship Earth (the lines are lighter later on) and head to Soarin' inside The Land. Get a Fastpass for Soarin', then head to Mission: SPACE (the "less intense" non-spinning version is our preference), Test Track, the Imagination pavilion (don't miss Honey, I Shrunk the Audience), and finally, The Seas with Nemo & Friends pavilion. (Try to  catch "Turtle Talk with Crush.") Don't forget to head back to The Land during your Fastpass window for Soarin'.

- Before heading to World Showcase (it opens at 11 A.M.), visit Spaceship Earth and Innoventions—and anything else you want to see. (Future World usually closes earlier than World Showcase.)

- Know that most World Showcase pavilions have both table- and quick-service eateries. Several, including Chefs de France and San Angel Inn, offer annual passholder discounts.

- View the movie at the Canada pavilion. Then wander through the shops, gardens, and pub at the United Kingdom before fully exploring France. (There's a movie here, too.)

- Walk toward The American Adventure to catch the extraordinary live performances and the star-spangled Audio-Animatronics show, stopping to take in art galleries and other sights along the way.

- Fully explore the remaining pavilions, pausing for the occasional international treat or frosty beverage. Know that there are boat ride attractions within the Norway and Mexico pavilions.

- Don't forget about your dinner reservation!

- Get to the World Showcase Lagoon at least 30 minutes ahead to secure a spot to watch the evening's presentation of IllumiNations—Reflections of Earth. It usually happens at 9 P.M.

A Day at Disney's Hollywood Studios

- Arrive before the posted opening time, as doors often open early.

- Pick up a complimentary guidemap and Times Guide; many attractions have set showtimes, and some don't open until later in the morning. Study the layout of the park—it has been known to confuse even the most skilled navigators.

- Haven't had breakfast yet? Consider stopping by the Starring Rolls Cafe for a quick croissant and a cup of coffee.

- This plan assumes a quick lunch taken whenever your personal lunch bell rings (good bets include Sunset Ranch Market and Backlot Express).

- If you're up for some early morning thrills, head to The Twilight Zone Tower of Terror or Rock 'n' Roller Coaster, but be sure to do so before you eat. (Consider getting a Fastpass for one and waiting in the standby line for the other.) For something much tamer, you should try Toy Story Mania, followed by The Magic of Disney Animation, Walt Disney: One Man's Dream, and Muppet*Vision 3-D.

  - Stroll over to Pixar Place to go behind the scenes via the Studio Backlot Tour. Note: The Block Party Bash parade passes through each afternoon. Try to catch it.

  - Make time for Sounds Dangerous Starring Drew Carey. The Indiana Jones Epic Stunt Spectacular!; Lights, Motors, Action–Extreme Stunt Show; and Star Tours all merit a look-see—as do the Voyage of The Little Mermaid and Rock 'n' Roller Coaster (if you haven't done it yet, and provided that you're comfortable being flipped and shaken like James Bond's martini).

- Between attractions, check out the shops on Sunset and Hollywood boulevards. For a relaxing breather, slip into the Tune-In Lounge.

- Note when the Beauty and the Beast—Live on Stage takes place and be sure not to miss it.

- Get a spot for Fantasmic at least 60 minutes before showtime (on select nights). This evening spectacle wraps up the day nicely (though the bleacher-style seating can be tough on tired backs).

A Day at Disney's Animal Kingdom

- Arrive about 15 minutes before the park's posted opening time, and prepare to bond with others waiting to enter.

- Pick up a guidemap and Times Guide and check schedules for shows you may want to see, such as Flights of Wonder or Festival of the Lion King. Plan to arrive about 45 minutes before the Lion King show begins, and up to 30 minutes for Finding Nemo—The Musical.

- Resist the urge to conduct an informal wildlife census in the Oasis and head for the bridge to Discovery Island. The animals will be here all day. Minimal lines for your biggest priorities—Expedition Everest (for daredevils), Dinosaur, Kali River Rapids, and Kilimanjaro Safaris—won't be around for long. If possible, get a Fastpass assignment for Expedition Everest (or your favorite attraction) first thing in the morning. (FYI: Fastpass assignments for Expedition Everest may be gone soon after park opening.)

- Give the Tree of Life a quick glance before heading to the first brachiosaurus skeleton on your right. In DinoLand U.S.A., make the acquaintance of Dinosaur, a bumpy, bouncy thrill ride.

- Make your way to Camp Minnie-Mickey in time for the next Festival of the Lion King staging.

- Next, go to Asia and ride the drenching Kali River Rapids. Afterward, walk through the Maharajah Jungle Trek and explore the tiny village of Anandapur. While you're in the area, consider taking in Flights of Wonder (check a Times Guide for the schedule).

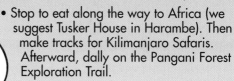

- Stop to eat along the way to Africa (we suggest Tusker House in Harambe). Then make tracks for Kilimanjaro Safaris. Afterward, dally on the Pangani Forest Exploration Trail.

- Now it's time for It's Tough to be a Bug in the Tree of Life. Be sure to check out the amazing animal carvings on and around the enormous tree.

- After you've done all your "must-sees," hop on the Wildlife Express to Rafiki's Planet Watch.

- No fireworks here (imagine the stampede). As an alternative, experience dinner as entertainment at Rainforest Cafe (or hop to Epcot for IllumiNations).

27

CUSTOMIZED TIPS
Guests with Disabilities

Walt Disney World has long earned praise from guests with disabilities because of the attention paid to their special needs. Still, familiarization with the World as it relates to one's personal requirements is essential, and to this end, the theme park guidemaps can be of tremendous help. And the *Guide for Guests with Disabilities* is certainly required reading, too. It is available at all wheelchair rental locations (as well as City Hall in the Magic Kingdom and Guest Relations at Epcot, Disney's Hollywood Studios, and Animal Kingdom). However, we recommend getting this publication before leaving home. To receive a free copy, send a written request, well in advance, to: Walt Disney World Guest Correspondence, Box 10000, Lake Buena Vista, FL 32830, or call 407-939-6244.

Those interested in guided tours should note: The Society for Accessible Travel & Hospitality (347 Fifth Ave., Suite 605, New York, NY 10016; 212-447-7284; *www.sath.org*) can provide a list of travel agents who are knowledgeable about travel for people with disabilities. To receive the listing, just call (there may be a $5 fee).

If you prefer to connect directly with a tour operator who specializes in travel for the disabled, consider Flying Wheels Travel (507-451-5005) or Accessible Journeys (610-521-0339). The following advice is an indication of WDW facilities and services:

• Accessible parking is available at the theme parks (inquire at the Auto Plaza upon entering).

• All monorail stations are accessible to guests in wheelchairs. All Disney buses are equipped with wheelchair lifts.

• Life jackets for guests with disabilities are available at the water parks.

• Resorts with "zero-depth-entry" pools have a few aquatic wheelchairs available. Such resorts include Animal Kingdom Lodge, Grand Floridian, Polynesian, and Saratoga Springs.

• Most theme park attractions are accessible to guests who can be lifted to and from their wheelchairs with the assistance of a member of their party, and many can accommodate guests who must remain in their wheelchairs.

Consult the *Guide for Guests with Disabilities* or a guidemap, or ask a host or hostess for additional guidance.

Note that all hotels listed in the *Checking In* chapter offer rooms specially equipped for guests with disabilities. Walt Disney World resorts are easily explored by wheelchair. While guestroom and bathroom configurations vary from hotel to hotel, lending themselves better to guests with certain needs, all resorts offer roll-in showers.

For assistance in selecting a Disney hotel whose public areas and rooms best serve your specific requirements, ask to speak to someone in the Special Reservations Department when you call Central Reservations (407-939-7807, voice; 407-939-7670, TTY). Confirm any special requests before you arrive.

Most Disney resorts have a very small number of free wheelchairs (with a $315 refundable

In the Evening Hours

Here's more than a week's worth of activities for your consideration. For more information on after-dark amusements, refer to *Dining & Entertainment*.

- Attend a dinner show. All require reservations, and the Hoop-Dee-Doo Musical Revue calls for more forethought than any other.

- For a relatively cheap thrill (about $8 or so per person) and an early night, take a wagon ride at Fort Wilderness. Or enjoy a slightly more extravagant carriage ride for about $45 for four people.

- Play the coolest tennis at Walt Disney World. There are a few courts lighted for night play.

- For dining as a special event, book a table at Artist Point, California Grill, Cítricos, Shula's Steakhouse, Victoria & Albert's, or Jiko—The Cooking Place.

- If ready-made nightlife appeals, go exploring at Downtown Disney—one stop, several options (we love Pleasure Island's Raglan Road). Or swing by the West Side to see who's playing at the House of Blues. Karaoke fans should seek out Kimonos, a sushi/karaoke bar in the Swan resort.

- Take a wine tour. California Grill at the Contemporary resort, Jiko—The Cooking Place at Animal Kingdom Lodge, and Cítricos at the Grand Floridian take crushed grapes seriously and pour wines both by the glass and in pairings suggested by the sommelier.

- Prefer the grain to the grape? Beer lovers' hangouts include BoardWalk's ESPN Club and Crew's Cup lounge at the Yacht Club resort.

- For a nostalgic evening, stroll the boards at BoardWalk, where everything from saltwater taffy to a dance hall and a sing-along piano bar awaits.

deposit). Request one when you check in. You may use the wheelchair across Disney property for your entire length of stay. If you want a guarantee that a chair will be available to you upon arrival, rent one in advance from an outside company (see page 31).

Wheelchairs are available for rent at each of the theme parks, as are Electric Convenience Vehicles (ECVs). At the Magic Kingdom, the rental area is under the train station; at Epcot, rentals are available inside the entrance plaza on the left, at the shop to the right of the ticket booths, and at International Gateway; at Disney's Hollywood Studios, rentals are handled at Oscar's Super Service, just inside; at Animal Kingdom, the site is Garden Gate Gifts, near the entrance. They may be rented at Downtown Disney Marketplace Guest Relations, too.

Wheelchair rentals cost $10 for a single day, and about $8 per day if a "Length of Stay" pass is purchased. Guests planning to park-hop may get a replacement at the second park at no extra charge (save your receipt). ECVs can be rented at the parks for $45 (plus a

Know Before You Go

- If you want to see a dinner show—especially the Hoop-Dee-Doo Musical Revue—reserve a table when you book your hotel. Reservations are taken up to 180 days ahead; call 407-939-3463.

- Arrange for reservations at WDW restaurants (up to 180 days in advance) by calling 407-939-3463 (WDW-DINE). Refer to page 185 for details.

- Reservations for bass fishing excursions must be made 24 hours to 180 days in advance; call 407-WDW-PLAY or 407-WDW-BASS.

- Call 407-824-4321 or visit www.disneyworld.com to confirm park hours in effect during your visit, and use the schedules provided in this chapter.

- If you're a golfer, reserve tee times as far in advance as possible. Reservations may be made 90 days ahead if you're staying at either a WDW resort, the Swan, Dolphin, or a resort on Hotel Plaza Boulevard, and 60 days ahead if you're not, to secure your preferred time(s) and venue(s). Call 407-WDW-GOLF (939-4653). Also see "Sports" in Diversions.

- Note that tennis lessons may be booked up to 180 days in advance. Call 407-621-1991.

- A few days before you leave home, make a quick round of calls to confirm all arrangements and reservations.

- You must dial the area code for all local calls.

$20 refundable deposit) per park per day. Equipment may not be taken out of the theme park from which it is rented.

Due to the limited number of ECVs, they usually sell out soon after the parks open. To avoid disappointment and to have the freedom to use your scooter or wheelchair everywhere, consider renting from ScootAround (888-441-7575), which provides standard and electric wheelchairs as well as scooters; pickup and delivery is available to all hotels in the Walt Disney World area. Wheelchair Getaways (800-642-2042) and Rainbow Wheels of Florida (800-910-8267) both rent wheelchair-accessible vans and offer pickup and delivery for most hotels in the area.

Certain spots along most parade routes and at nighttime show areas are marked for guests using wheelchairs. Such areas are filled on a first-come, first-served basis. See park maps for locations.

A limited number of courtesy wheelchairs is available in theme park disability parking areas. Guests with limited mobility may use them to travel between their vehicle and the wheelchair rental area only. For guests with visual disabilities, the theme parks offer Braille guides, stationary Braille maps, and audio descriptions designed to accentuate enjoyment of each park. A $100 refundable deposit is required for use of a tape recorder.

Pay phones equipped with Text Typewriters (TTYs) are available throughout the Disney World Resort. For more information, call 407-824-4321.

Assistive Listening devices are available (with a $10 refundable deposit) at City Hall in the Magic Kingdom, and at Guest Relations in Epcot, the Studios, and Animal Kingdom. Handheld captioning and video captioning systems are available at select attractions. American Sign Language interpretation may be available for some live shows; call 407-824-4321 (voice) or 407-827-5141 (TTY).

Also, Reflective Captioning Devices that project dialogue onto a panel placed in front of guests are available for use in some theater shows. Inquire at Guest Relations.

disneyworld.com

Log onto *www.disneyworld.com* to receive an interactive preview or update of WDW's offerings.

Among its more valuable features: ticket sales, customized resort recommendations, a reservations desk, maps, details about special events, and park hours during your stay.

Older Travelers

Walt Disney World is a friendly and welcoming place, but its sheer enormity and energy level, and its mere heat, particularly during the summer, have the potential to overwhelm.

While knowing what to expect is half the battle, planning accordingly is just as important.

Important Numbers

AMC Theatres: 407-298-4488

Behind-the-Scenes Tours:
407-WDW-TOUR (939-8687)

Central Reservations:
407-W-DISNEY (934-7639)

Dining Reservations:
407-WDW-DINE (939-3463)

Disney's Wide World of Sports Complex:
407-939-1500

Dr. P. Phillips Hospital:
407-351-8500

Florida Hospital Celebration Health: 407-303-4000

Golf Reservations/Lessons:
407-WDW-GOLF (939-4653)

Recreation:
407-WDW-PLAY (939-7529)

Theme Park Lost and Found:
407-824-4245

Walt Disney Travel Company: 407-828-8101

Walt Disney World Information: 407-824-4321

Weather: 407-824-4104

The keys to an enjoyable, relaxed visit apply to everyone. Our suggestions:

• Plan your visit for one of the less crowded times of year. That will make for shorter, less harried days. In the parks, eat early or late to avoid mealtime crowds.

• Florida residents can net discounts year-round. Call 407-824-4321 for details. Also, some off-property hotels offer discounts to AARP members.

• Take frequent rest stops (for the best locales in each park, see the "Quiet Escapes" lists in the margins of the *Theme Parks* chapter). Know that if you are overcome at any point, each park has a first-aid station with a friendly and certified staff.

• Don't underestimate the distances to be covered at Epcot and Animal Kingdom. These parks are huge, and visitors often log a few miles in a full day of touring. Some older travelers who enjoy walking around the other parks choose to rent a wheelchair or Electric Convenience Vehicle at these two (they're available at the park entrances).

• No matter how you're getting around, take it slowly. Broken into small increments with plenty of air-conditioned and shaded breaks, it's not as tiring. The

FriendShip launches that cross World Showcase Lagoon in Epcot provide a nice break for weary feet.

• Not all of Downtown Disney's venues are inundated with exuberant twentysomethings. Stop at Raglan Road for an authentic dose of the Emerald Isle, and if you're a Cirque du Soleil fan, catch La Nouba. Don't miss the four-star tribute to Tinseltown's heyday that is Disney's Hollywood Studios. The Art Deco architecture, retro restaurants, and Technicolor tributes to Tinseltown make for a day of nostalgic amusement.

Single Travelers

While Walt Disney World may not exactly be the last word for singles, the fact is, unattached guests and independent travelers can have an absolute blast here.

Some ideas:

• Downtown Disney typically attracts lots of locals on weekends. The restaurants and lounges at Downtown Disney West Side, particularly the concert hall at House of Blues, also attract a fun-loving crowd.

• Consider having a meal (lunch or dinner) at Germany's Biergarten restaurant at Epcot, where smaller parties are seated together, creating a social setting.

• At all four of Walt Disney World's 18-hole golf courses, company is a given; players are assigned to a foursome when tee times are allotted.

• Some of the World's more compelling restaurants have an area with counter seating, which helps take the sting out of dining solo. These noteworthy spots include Flying Fish Cafe, Narcoossee's, Cítricos, Fulton's

For Woofers & Meowers

No pets other than service animals are permitted in the parks. However, Best Friends Pet Care—a full-service pet "resort"—is scheduled to open on Bonnett Creek Parkway in Walt Disney World in 2010. The unique facility will provide a full range of hospitality services, including dog and cat boarding, day care, and grooming services. Pets may be treated to such amenities as nature walks, special culinary treats, and bedtime stories. Think furry friends day camp. For rates, hours, and info, call 407-824-6568. Pets must have proof of vaccinations. Until Best Friends opens, pets stay at one of several on-property kennels. For kennel info, call 407-W-DISNEY.

Crab House, Portobello, Wolfgang Puck Cafe (the sushi bar), and California Grill.

• The casual atmosphere at the BoardWalk makes it a fun place to people-watch, and the eateries, shops, and clubs provide interesting diversions. The Jellyrolls piano bar never fails to entertain.

• Another favorite, and a great destination for sports fans, is ESPN Club. The environment is conducive to frenzied rooting for your home team, as well as calmer discussions about the intricacies of the game with fellow fans.

Rainy-Day Advice

The sun will come out tomorrow (or maybe in a few hours). In the meantime, here are some great ways to pass the time:

• See a movie with all the comforts in the 24-screen AMC Theatres at Downtown Disney.

• Sink into a sofa in the lobby of the Grand Floridian and listen to the graceful music. Or curl up by the fireplace at Wilderness Lodge.

• Pick up a rain poncho (about $7) and head for Epcot, which has more places to escape rain than any other park.

• Experience the high-tech interactive arcade games at Downtown Disney's DisneyQuest.

• Get a massage. Disney spas offer myriad treatments that can be blissful excuses to stay dry.

• Take afternoon tea at the Grand Floridian's Garden View Lounge.

Couples

There is a place for lovebirds at Walt Disney World. Actually, there are many spots in the World perfectly suited to those with romantic intentions.

The Magic Kingdom's carousel-and-castle combo invokes enchantment in true fairy-tale tradition. Epcot's World Showcase has the aura of a whirlwind tour (and inspiration for a future trip?), with countries as exotic and far-reaching as Japan and Morocco. Disney's Hollywood Studios recaptures an era of starry-eyed elegance. And what could be more enjoyable than sharing a safari through Africa at Animal Kingdom?

By day, there is romance in the theme parks for couples who are already inclined to hold hands; by night, the parks sparkle with an intensity that inspires sudden mushiness in those who never considered themselves the type, and that's before the fireworks.

As Disney's themed resorts go about transporting guests to various times and places, they make quite a few passes through settings straight out of everyone's fantasy textbook.

From the endearing Victorian charms of the Grand Floridian to the exotic island getaway that is the Polynesian, it's safe to say that Disney definitely has romantic notions (if not in the form of heart-shaped tubs).

You won't find a more inspiring backdrop than that at the wondrously rustic Wilderness Lodge, marked by geysers, waterfalls, steamy hot springs, and the grandest stone fireplace you've ever seen.

At the nostalgic BoardWalk resort, unique surrey bikes are available for romantic rides along the waterfront. You can pedal all the way to Epcot's

International Gateway. And a romantic stroll around Crescent Lake is an undoubtedly lovely way to cap off the day.

For those too love-struck to think about taking pictures themselves, there's the Romance Photographic Session. For about $300, a photographer follows you and your sweetheart around the park of your choice (for one hour), clicking away. For more information, call 407-827-5099.

Couples with bigger things in mind, like perhaps tying or re-tying the knot, might consider "I do"–ing it here. Each year, more than 2,000 couples exchange their vows here.

Why this place? For some couples it's a matter of mutual Disney admiration; for others it's a convenient answer to the dilemma posed by the bride being from one area of the world and the groom from quite another. (Why not make a vacation of it for everyone?) Stick around for a while, and you've got an instant honeymoon!

While no one yet has likened Mickey Mouse to Eros, newly-weds have beaten such a path to Mickey's doorstep over the years that Disney World rates as one of the most popular honeymoon destinations in the country.

WEDDINGS: In these parts, the sky truly is the limit. Weddings for up to 18 guests start at about $4,500; for larger affairs, figure $12,000 minimum during the week, $15,000 on Fridays, Saturdays, and Sundays (price varies based on season). Coordinators work with couples from three months to a year in advance to create a wedding tailored to their needs—from elegant affairs without a hint of Disneyana to the sort in which the bride arrives in Cinderella's coach and Goofy "crashes" the reception. These wedding gurus can handle any detail and a litany of unimaginables.

Nuptials in the theme parks (which range from $7,500 in Epcot to $55,000-plus in the Magic Kingdom) take place before park opening and allow couples to take their vows in front of Cinderella Castle in the Magic Kingdom or in an English courtyard in Epcot's World Showcase, among other places.

For an extra $3,500 (or much more), a free-spending couple gets pixie dust and a personal fireworks show.

Then there's the Wedding Pavilion, a structure reminiscent of a Victorian summerhouse, which sits on a landscaped island between the Grand Floridian and Polynesian resorts. Surrounded by roses, palm trees, and beaches, the pavilion seats 250 and offers a prime view of Cinderella Castle, which is framed in a window

Religious Services

Protestant services are held on Sundays at 8:30 and 11 A.M. at Community Presbyterian Church at 511 Celebration Ave., Celebration, Florida (for schedule, call 407-566-1633), and 10:30 A.M. at River of Life Presbyterian at 8323 West Sand Lake Rd. (407-351-4333). Catholic masses are held at Mary, Queen of the Universe Shrine at 8300 Vineland Ave. Call for mass times (407-239-6600).

Jewish visitors may attend Conservative services at Temple Ohalei Rivka at 11200 S. Apopka Vineland Rd. (407-239-5444), or Reform services at the Congregation of Reform Judaism at 928 Malone Dr. (407-645-0444). Muslim services are at Jama Masjid at 11543 Ruby Lake Rd. (407-238-2700).

behind the altar. Picture Point—a trellised archway set among the pavilion's gardens, with the castle in the background—is also available for intimate ceremonies.

For couples in the planning stages, the on-site wedding salon—known as Franck's Bridal Studio—is like a three-dimensional bridal magazine.

Ceremonies can be held at many WDW resorts. The garden gazebo at the Yacht Club, Sunset Point at the Polynesian, Sea Breeze Point at BoardWalk, Sunrise Terrace at Wilderness Lodge, and the Grand Floridian's *Grand I* yacht are all popular spots for weddings or vow renewals.

Wedding options vary depending upon the type of ceremony and reception and can offer couples discounted tickets, as well as special resort rates for guests attending the wedding. For more information about Disney's Fairy Tale Weddings, call 407-566-7633 or visit *www.disneyweddings.com/birnbaum*.

HONEYMOONS: Some Disney resorts have designated suites for just-marrieds—ask about them when booking. Magic Your Way vacation packages may be tailored to meet your honeymoon needs. Be sure to mention the celebration of a honeymoon when you book your resort package or dining reservations. For information, call 407-566-7633; *www.disney honeymoons/birnbaum.com*.

Future honeymooners should also visit *www.disneyhoney moonregistry.com/birnbaum*.

The Most Romantic Places in the World

RESORTS
Animal Kingdom Lodge

Grand Floridian

Polynesian

Port Orleans Riverside and French Quarter

Wilderness Lodge

Yacht and Beach Club

RESTAURANTS
Artist Point

Bistro de Paris

California Grill

Cítricos

Le Cellier Steakhouse

Narcoosee's

Victoria & Albert's

LOUNGES
Belle Vue Lounge at BoardWalk

Lounge in Il Mulino New York Trattoria

Victoria Falls at Animal Kingdom Lodge

THEME PARK SPOT
All of Epcot's World Showcase

At Walt Disney World, there's a hotel to suit every taste, budget, and mood.

Checking In

Like a photograph whose mood changes depending upon the frame in which it is displayed, a Walt Disney World vacation is colored by the context in which it is experienced. Guests have quite a variety of frames—rather, resorts—from which to choose, and each yields a unique perspective on the World.

Some hotels imbue the mousedom with surprising elegance; others render it especially whimsical, homey, or romantic. Looking for grand seaside digs or a home base straight out of New Orleans? They're here. Something Polynesian? No problem. From campsites to villas, economy-priced rooms to suites, there are accommodations in Cinderella's neighborhood to suit most every taste and billfold.

If you're the sort who favors a gilded frame for your vacation, you'll find the chandelier quotient you're seeking—and a rich Victorian aura—at Disney's turreted Grand Floridian Resort & Spa.

If rustic romance is more your style, your ultimate roost is the Wilderness Lodge, which patterns its grandeur after National Park Service lodges of the early 1900s.

To stretch your vacation dollar, do try the All-Star and Pop Century resorts. Starting at about $80–$90 a night and augmented by three-story cultural icons, they're the brightest dwellings you'll ever call home.

If you're not sure what you want, that's fine, too. We've covered all of the Disney-owned-and-operated resorts and their favored siblings, the Swan and Dolphin, plus the Disney Cruise Line.

When it comes to the resorts that line Hotel Plaza Boulevard (seven properties that are within Disney's borders but independently managed), we've included our top three choices for adults.

So think about what's important to you in a Walt Disney World resort. Then read on for all the information you'll need to choose the perfect frame.

WALT DISNEY WORLD RESORTS

As an example of the meticulous theming that is a hallmark of the Disney resorts, consider Port Orleans French Quarter, a moderately priced resort designed to evoke the Big Easy's most famous neighborhood. As you check in, you might catch the aroma of fresh beignets wafting over from the resort's food court, decorated as a Mardi Gras warehouse. The lobby has French horns for light fixtures and restrooms with such great jazz coming over the speakers they could almost impose a cover charge.

In addition to compelling theming, Disney's resorts are often marked by staffs trained to bend over backward to ensure guests' happiness, and well-kept, comfortably furnished accommodations comparable in size to those found outside Walt Disney World borders. There are also many practical advantages to staying on-property. Chief among these benefits are convenience and easy access to Disney services.

The Last Word On . . .

Reservations
Book by calling 407-934-7639 or visiting www.disneyworld.com. A deposit (one night's lodging or $200) is required within 10 to 14 days of the time a reservation is made. The deposit will be refunded only if a reservation is canceled at least five days before the scheduled arrival. Packages must be paid in full and cancellations must be made at least 45 days ahead.

Checking In
Check-in time is 3 P.M., except at BoardWalk Villas, Disney's Old Key West, Beach Club Villas, Saratoga Springs Resort & Spa, Animal Kingdom Lodge Villas, and The Villas at Wilderness Lodge, where guests register after 4 P.M., and Fort Wilderness campsites, where it's 1 P.M. Check-out time for all these properties is 11 A.M.

Other privileges enjoyed by WDW resort guests include use of WDW transportation; guaranteed admission (with ticket) to the theme parks (including the "Extra Magic Hours"—see page 15); discounted golf fees; and the option to reserve tee times on Disney golf courses up to 90 days prior to their check-in date. At all WDW resorts, except the Swan and Dolphin and resorts on Hotel Plaza Boulevard, amenities also include Disney's Magical Express service (see page 21), package delivery, and the ability to charge meals, merchandise, and recreation fees to one's room.

This resort listing is organized according to price tiers—Deluxe, Moderate, and Value. Disney no longer uses the term "Home Away from Home" to describe accommodations. It was replaced by "Disney Deluxe Villa Resorts."

These categories are consistent with Disney's rating system for its resorts (explained on page 42). But consider location as well as price, especially if you'll be spending a lot of time touring a particular theme park. The "Vital Statistics" section of each entry will help you place the resorts on the World map. You'll notice that certain hotels are earmarked as "sister resorts." These

are adjacent properties that feature complementary designs and shared facilities. With the exception of Port Orleans Riverside and Port Orleans French Quarter, whose greater separation and distinct identities we feel merit individual attention, sister resorts' descriptions are combined.

We've packed in as much detail as possible about the offerings at each resort; to learn more about restaurants and lounges, see our recommendations in the *Dining & Entertainment* chapter. For details about Disney transportation, consult *Planning Ahead*. For more on recreational opportunities at the resorts, turn to the the *Diversions* chapter. For updated resort rates, call 407-W-DIS-NEY (939-7639).

Amenities Checklist

While there are significant differences in the amenities offered at Disney's Value and Deluxe properties, certain conveniences are provided at all WDW resorts. Namely: voice mail, TVs with the Disney Channel and ESPN, clock radios, in-room safes, guest laundry facilities, dry-cleaning service, an ATM, and either room service or more limited food delivery options.

Deluxe
Animal Kingdom Lodge & Villas

The zebras, ostriches, and Thomson's gazelles out back are neither mascots, nor exotic props, nor escapees from the nearby Animal Kingdom theme park. They and their hoofed and feathered comrades—about 200 animals in all, mostly African expats—live on the resort's carefully plotted pasturelands, giving round-the-clock credence to its claims as Florida's only African wildlife reserve lodge. Of course, this ambitious theme is not carried entirely by the storks and giraffes whose habitat comes within thirty feet of guests' domain. Hardly. The lodge's hut foyer opens to an immense thatched-ceiling lobby with the tantalizing depth of a lion's yawn. Here, pupils swell as the eyes dart from the suspension bridge to the huge mud fireplace, from the gushing approximation of Victoria Falls to the blur of African masks and artifacts and

Mickey Ranks the Resorts

Disney's ranking system for its resorts provides a convenient framework for considering Walt Disney World lodging options. Categories reflect not only the price of a room, but the style of the accommodation and the level of service. The hotels fall into Deluxe, Moderate, and Value classifications. Fort Wilderness Cabins (villa-type lodgings) are considered "moderate," while Disney's Camping category is occupied by the Fort Wilderness campsites.

For the sake of clarity and comparison, we have used these same categories in this chapter, with a few exceptions for Fort Wilderness and other properties with two types of accommodations. In general, here's what to expect in our categories:

- Deluxe properties (the most expensive resort category) are defined by their larger, practically appointed rooms, several restaurants, and such amenities as 24-hour room service. This category generally includes Disney Vacation Club properties.

- Fort Wilderness Camping covers campsites, but not Wilderness Cabins (which fall into the "moderate" resort category).

- Moderate properties (in the middle-ranges, price-wise) feature comfortably sized rooms, full-service restaurants as well as food courts, and bellhop luggage service.

- Value properties (the least expensive resort category) offer fewer frills and smaller yet adequate quarters. Meals are provided at food courts. Recreation options at these resorts are limited.

the chandeliers made of Masai shields. Oh, yes, and the four-story welcome-to-the-savanna window, which is sure to make momentary bumper cars of slack-jawed new arrivals.

Romance and adventure cling to every richly appointed inch of the semicircular lodge, which serves as a five-story animal-observation platform, from its viewing parlors to its restaurants and its expansive swimming pool. Although with 972 rooms (plus 458 villas) the resort is bigger than its African counterparts, it hides the fact well: Built into the landscape, its front drive leads to the third-floor lobby. (Traditionally, such buildings protect against predators.) Nine out of ten guestroom balconies overlook the savanna.

As for the Villas, the first of them, located in Jambo house, opened in 2007. The newest phase, Kidani Village, has hosted guests in its studios, and thatched-roof, timber homes (one- and two-bedroom and grand villas) since 2009. Also included in the village, a large, zero-depth entry pool, fitness center, the Johari Treasures shop, a table-service restaurant called Sanaa, the Maji pool bar, plus two clay tennis and basketball courts, shuffleboard, a barbecue pavilion, and more. For information on this member of the Disney Vacation Club family, call 800-800-9100 or visit *www.disneyvacationclub.com.*

Animal Kingdom Lodge Tips

- Recreational activities are a bit limited due to the presence of animals. Guests may indulge in pursuits such as boat or bike rentals at neighboring Disney resorts.
- Willing to forgo wildlife-watching from your balcony? Rooms *sans* animal views are much cheaper.
- This 33-acre tropical savanna is inhabited by 100 grazing animals and 130 birds—the safari begins as soon as you enter the resort.
- The Wanyama Safari offers a unique look at Animal Kingdom Lodge. This program (groups are limited to 12 guests at a time) offers a private tour of the resort followed by dinner at Jiko. There is a charge and guests must be staying at A.K. Lodge. Call 407-939-3463 for details or reservations.

BIG DRAWS: Luxury laced with an undeniable spirit of adventure and romance. Balconies serve as box seats for animal viewing.

WORTH NOTING: Accommodations at this resort are comparable to those at most deluxe hotels in the World; both the deluxe rooms and the smaller standard guestrooms typically include two queen-size beds. Deluxe rooms have a child's daybed. Ask and you may receive a king-size bed or the polar opposite: bunk beds. Within each room's sandy-colored walls is a unique amalgam of African art pieces, traditionally patterned textiles, and dark-wood furniture hand-

Seasonal Rates for 2010

Rates and dates quoted here were correct at press time, but are subject (and likely) to change during the coming year. Note that within each category there are dates where "holiday" or "weekend" rates apply. Call 407-W-DISNEY (934-7639) for updates.

- Value rates apply from about January 3 to February 11, August 15 to September 30, and November 28 to December 16 for all Value and Moderate resorts; January 1 to February 11 and August 15 to November 18 for the Fort Wilderness Campsites; and January 1 to February 11, July 18 to September 30, and November 28 to December 16 for other Walt Disney World properties (except Swan and Dolphin).

- Regular rates apply from about April 11 to June 3 and October 1 to November 27 for all Value and Moderate resorts; April 11 to August 14 for Fort Wilderness Campsites; and April 11 to July 17 and October 1 to November 27 for other WDW properties (except Swan and Dolphin).

- Peak rates apply from about February 12 to April 10 for all WDW resorts (except Swan and Dolphin).

- Pre-holiday rates apply from about November 19 to December 16 at Fort Wilderness Campsites.

- Holiday higher-than-peak rates apply from about December 17 to December 31 for all WDW resorts except the Swan and Dolphin.

- Summer rates apply from about June 4 to August 14 for Value and Moderate resorts.

- Weekend (Friday and Saturday) rates apply from January 1 to November 21 and December 17 to December 31 for all Value and Moderate Resorts; February 2 to July 17 and December 17 to December 31 for Deluxe Resorts and Fort Wilderness Cabins; and year-round at all Fort Wilderness Campsites.

- For details on Swan and Dolphin seasonal rates, call 800-227-1500.

crafted in Zimbabwe and South Africa. Most rooms have private balconies; animals and their habitats are visible from 90 percent of the rooms. Lest guests lose their sense of place while reading in bed, there are (purely decorative) mosquito nets in many rooms. Hotel rooms have a hair dryer, iron, mini fridge, and weekday newspaper delivery. Club-level rooms with animal views are available. While Kidani Village and the top two floors of Jambo house are part of the Disney Vacation Club, they are available to everyone when not booked by DVC members.

The primary form of recreation here is spying on the impalas, Thomson's gazelles, giraffes, and flamingos from every possible vantage point all day and night. In addition to the floor-to-ceiling window in the lobby, a rock outcropping one story down from the lobby allows views of the animals, and indoor viewing areas line the halls of the U-shaped resort. The pool, sundeck, and two whirlpools have great animal-viewing potential (due to a strategically placed watering hole). The pool area is surrounded by restaurants. Zahanati Fitness Center rounds out the resort's recreation options.

Where to eat: Boma—Flavors of Africa (buffet featuring items prepared on a wood-burning grill in an African market setting); Jiko—The Cooking Place (comfort food meets multiculturally influenced cuisine); Sanaa (Indian and East African-inspired eatery); and The Mara (on-the-go grazing).

Where to drink: Victoria Falls (mezzanine lounge with African drums as tables); Cape Town Lounge and Wine Bar (near Jiko); Maji Pool Bar; and Uzima Springs Pool Bar.

VITAL STATISTICS: Animal Kingdom Lodge enjoys enviable proximity to the Animal Kingdom and Blizzard Beach; Disney's Hollywood Studios is also nearby. Animal Kingdom Lodge; 2901 Osceola Parkway; Box 10000; Bay Lake, FL 32830-1000; 407-938-3000; fax 407-938-4799.

Rates: Standard rooms without savanna views run about $240 in value season, $300 regular, and $365 peak; standard rooms with savanna views are $310 value, $380 regular, and $450 peak; club level rooms with savanna views begin at $350 in value season, $415 regular, and $495 peak. Suites start at $760. Villa rates range from about $275 to $2,005.

A $25 per diem charge applies for each extra adult (beyond two) sharing a room.

BoardWalk Inn & Villas

This fetching resort and entertainment complex recaptures an ephemeral period in Eastern-seaboard history. It has all the charm of a shore village awash in sun-bleached pastels. The name comes from the 48-foot-wide boardwalk out back, where you'll find a piano club, a dance hall, and a major-league sports bar, plus a bakery and a brewpub. When hunger calls, you can have a seafood feast or heaping plate of pasta. For dessert, try a caramel apple or hand-dipped ice cream from the sweet shop. Located lakefront opposite the Yacht and Beach Club, Board-Walk completes this seaside community in romantic fashion.

BoardWalk Tips

- Take advantage of the resort's romantic assets—surrey rides and sunset cocktails on the waterfront.
- When checking in, request a room near the lobby—you'll get enough exercise walking in the parks.
- Big games attract a big crowd at the ESPN Club, so get there early.
- At night, catch a bus to the Board-Walk from Downtown Disney.

The BoardWalk Inn (a 371-room hotel) and BoardWalk Villas (383 villas styled in the tradition of family vacation rooms) share a lobby. Filled with antique miniatures of early boardwalk amusement rides, the lobby fronts an inviting porch with rocking chairs. A sweeping staircase leads to the main recreation area as well as to the restaurants, shops, clubs, and live performers of the Board-Walk entertainment district.

BIG DRAWS: Intimate charm, an entertainment zone right out back, and a walkway to Epcot's International Gateway.

WORTH NOTING: Guestrooms at the BoardWalk Inn are comparable in size to those at Disney's other deluxe properties and offer two queen-size beds; some have a child's daybed. Decor includes curtains imprinted with images and inscriptions from old postcards, and French doors that open to private patios or balconies. Two-story suites feature a master-bedroom loft (with king-size bed and adjoining bath with whirlpool tub), a living room with a wet bar, and a private garden enclosed by a white picket fence. Single-story club level rooms are similarly appointed (no gardens, alas).

The BoardWalk Villas is a Disney Vacation Club resort (see page 58 for details); all of its accommodations have either a kitchenette or a full kitchen. Villas, decorated in the eclectic fashion of seaside cottages, feature balconies or patios and carousel-print curtains. Studios offer a queen-size bed and a double sleeper sofa, plus a wet bar with microwave, coffeemaker, and small refrigerator. Larger villas (with one, two, or three bedrooms) have a dining room, kitchen, laundry facilities, whirlpool tub, and VCR/DVD player. They also have a king-size bed in the master bedroom, a spacious living room with a queen sleeper sofa, and a queen-size bed and double sleeper sofa in any extra bedrooms.

Both properties have room service from 6 A.M. to 12 A.M. Amenities include hair dryers, irons (with boards), and—at the Inn—weekday newspaper delivery. A conference center offers business services (for a fee). Guests have exclusive use of the amusement park–themed pool, two other pools, and three whirlpools.

Other recreational options include fishing excursions, tennis, a health-club (massages by appointment),

A Closer Look

Read (yes, read) the curtains, which were created using imprints of vintage postcards. During construction, a carpenter noticed one from 1933, written by his uncle to his aunt before they were married. They still live at the address on the postcard.

jogging, and croquet. Bicycles and pedal-driven surrey bikes may be rented; Community Hall rents books and videos.

Where to eat: Big River Grille & Brewing Works (microbrews, pub food); BoardWalk Bakery (baked goods, sandwiches); ESPN Club (all-American sports bar, ballpark menu); Kouzzina by Cat Cora (Mediterranean fare); and Seashore Sweets (saltwater taffy and ice cream).

Where to drink: Atlantic Dance (a ballroom/nightclub with a deejay and music videos from the

Resort Primer

- Reservationists cannot guarantee a room location or view, so arrive early to request the best selection.
- Rooms on the upper floors afford the most privacy.
- Connecting or adjoining rooms and king-size beds can usually be requested but are not assured.
- Club-level rooms, in addition to extra service, generally include continental breakfast and afternoon snacks.

1980s and '90s); the Belle Vue Lounge (cocktails and cognac flights); Jellyrolls (dueling pianos); ESPN Club; and Leaping Horse Libations (poolside refreshments).

VITAL STATISTICS: BoardWalk guests have enviable access to Epcot, Disney's Hollywood Studios, and Fantasia Gardens Miniature Golf complex. BoardWalk; 2101 N. Epcot Resorts Blvd.; Box 10000; Lake Buena Vista, FL 32830-1000; 407-939-5100; fax 407-939-5150.

Contemporary Tips

- Rooms in the resort's garden building generally do not yield notable views, which is why the rates are lower than in the tower.

- The bathrooms have virtually no shelf or counter space. Consider this more of a warning than a tip.

- The bedding here is exceptionally luxurious for a WDW resort. No need to pack pillows if you're staying here.

- The marina is full of choices for sailors, from zippy little motorboats to pontoon boats.

- With the completion of Bay Lake Tower (in late 2009), the Contemporary resort officially joins the Disney Vacation Club family! (See page 58 for DVC details.)

- There is a convenient walking path to the Magic Kingdom. It's about a 5- to 7-minute walk.

Rates: At the Inn, standard rooms start at about $340 in value season, $390 regular, and $470 peak; club-level rooms begin at $470 value, $535 regular, and $610 peak; and suites begin at $645. A $25 per diem charge applies for each extra adult (beyond two) sharing a room. At the Villas, studios start at $340 value, $390 regular, and $470 peak; one-bedroom villas begin at $465 value, $525 regular, and $610 peak; two-bedroom villas start at $650 value, $845 regular, and $1,065 peak; and three-bedroom villas start at $1,600.

Contemporary & Bay Lake Tower

First impressions might suggest that the enormous A-frame tower of this legendary resort is simply a 15-story concrete tent that's been pitched here, a stone's throw from Cinderella Castle, for the benefit of the monorail trains regularly passing through it. And the exterior is certainly defined by a 1970s futuristic vision—as is that of the new Bay Lake Tower (a Disney Vacation Club property). But there's more to the resort— namely, the reverie that plays out in its bold decor and stunning views: from the sleek lobby to the guestroom decor; three table-service eateries, including The

Wave; and views of the Magic Kingdom or Bay Lake (the higher, the better).

BIG DRAWS: Location. Monorail service. Ideally suited for water sport enthusiasts. And the California Grill never disappoints.

WORTH NOTING: Many of the guestrooms here are larger than at any other Disney World hotel; most feature two queen-size beds plus a daybed (a king-size bed may be requested). Amenities at the 655-room resort include 24-hour room service, flat-screen TV, DVD player, and high-speed Internet service (for a fee). Club-level services are available to guests on the 12th and 14th floors.

Bay Lake Tower is a new 15-story addition to the Disney Vacation Club family. Its crescent shape hugs a lakeside pool, with room views that include undeveloped stretches of Bay Lake, as well as the Magic Kingdom. Studios sleep up to four and have kitchenettes, a flat-panel TV, queen-size bed, and double sleeper sofa. Sleeping up to five, the one-bedroom villas offer full kitchens, flat-panel TV, two bathrooms, king-size bed in the bedroom, and queen-size sleeper sofa and sleeper chair in the living room. Two-bedroom villas sleep up to nine, and the two-story grand villa sleeps as many as 12.

The Contemporary could be considered something of a recreational hub. It boasts a large pool area (with a free-form pool, an unguarded pool, and two whirlpools), a boat-rental marina, a parasailing program, sand volleyball court, a jogging trail, and a health club (massages by appointment). Waterskiing and fishing excursions may be arranged. One bonus of note: a walking path to the Magic Kingdom. A true time-saver—especially at Kingdom closing time when the line for the monorail can be daunting.

Where to eat: California Grill (West Coast cuisine and a 15th-floor Magic Kingdom vista; in fact, the view from the observation deck is open to restaurant guests only); Chef Mickey's (breakfast and dinner character buffets); The Wave (an excellent restaurant on the first floor); and the snack bar on the fourth floor.

Where to drink: The Wave (pretty lounge with a stellar wine list and full bar); Contemporary Grounds (coffee bar); Outer Rim (comfy alcove overlooking Bay Lake); and Sand Bar (poolside refreshments). DVC members staying at Bay Lake Tower have access to a lounge called Top of the World.

VITAL STATISTICS: The Contemporary resort, which has the Magic Kingdom virtually in its front yard and Bay Lake out back, is the only hotel with a walkway—and one of three on the monorail line—to that park. Monorail links extend the resort's neighborhood to the Polynesian and the Grand Floridian, and provide convenient commutes to Epcot. Contemporary; 4600 N. World Dr.; Box 10000; Lake Buena Vista, FL 32830-1000; 407-824-1000; fax 407-824-3539.

Rates: Standard guestrooms start at about $285 in value season, $330 regular, and $365 peak; tower rooms begin at $400 value, $455 regular, and $525 peak; suites start at $930. A $25 daily charge applies for each extra adult (beyond two) sharing a room.

Grand Floridian Resort & Spa

This romantic slice of Victorian confectionery, near the Magic

Kingdom, recalls the opulent hotels that beckoned high society at the turn of the 20th century.

The Grand Floridian's central building and five guest buildings—white structures laced with verandas and turrets and topped with gabled roofs of red shingle—sprawl over acres of Seven Seas Lagoon shorefront. Every glance embraces towering palms, stunning lake views, or rose gardens.

The resort's magnificent lobby—Victoriana *in excelsis*—features immense chandeliers, stained-glass skylights, and live piano and orchestra music that might inspire a little dancing. Guestrooms have old-fashioned armoires, marble-topped sinks, and decidedly modern TVs.

BIG DRAWS: The height of Disney luxury with a view of Cinderella Castle. Great for honeymoons or an escape to a kinder, gentler era. And the monorail stops here, too.

WORTH NOTING: Standard accommodations at this 867-room resort are a bit larger than those at most deluxe hotels in the World and include two queen-size beds plus a daybed; many rooms have terraces. Amenities include hair dryers, toiletries, robes, minibars, coffeemakers,

high-speed Internet service (for a fee), 24-hour room service, and nightly turndown. Club-level rooms and suites are on the upper floors of the main building and in the Sugarloaf building.

The resort offers some of the best restaurants on-property. Afternoon tea is served in the Garden View lounge. The Electrical Water Pageant (ask at the resort's front desk for information) and the Magic Kingdom fireworks can be seen from many lagoon-view rooms.

Grand Floridian Tips

- For a striking panorama, request a room with a view of the Seven Seas Lagoon.
- You can watch the fireworks over Cinderella Castle from the beach with little or no company.
- Consider a honeymoon room for your second honeymoon.
- Indulge in a treatment (or two) at the spa after a long day in the parks.
- Book a special dinner at Victoria & Albert's 90 days in advance.
- Note that the resort is surprisingly popular with families, despite its posh surroundings.
- For pre-dinner drinks, opt for Cítricos lounge, the lounge at Narcoossee's, or Mizner's Lounge.
- Ask at Lobby Concierge about sailing the Seven Seas on a private yacht (see page 176).

A convention center offers access to business services (for a fee). Boats may be rented, and fishing excursions may be arranged. Volleyball equipment may be borrowed for free. Clay tennis courts are available for $10 per hour, per person. Professional lessons are available; call 407-621-1991. The Grand Floridian Spa & Health Club is among WDW's most complete fitness facilities. The two pools and a whirlpool are open 24 hours, with quiet hours in effect at night.

Where to eat: Cítricos (Florida cuisine that celebrates the flavors of southern Europe); Gasparilla Grill & Games (24-hour light fare); Grand Floridian Cafe (breakfast, lunch, and dinner);

 Narcoossee's (seafood served waterside); 1900 Park Fare (breakfast and dinner

Made-to-Order Surprises

Flowers, custom gift baskets, and champagne can be delivered to any WDW resort (and some off-property hotels) by calling 407-827-3505 before or during your visit.

For an additional fee, Disney personal shoppers will further scour the World to track down favorite character merchandise and other special-request items.

character buffets); and Victoria & Albert's (seven-course dinners).

Where to drink: Cítricos lounge (wines and citrus martinis); Garden View (afternoon tea); Mizner's (classic cocktails); Narcoossee's (wines and spirits); and the Grand Floridian Pool Bar (poolside refreshments).

VITAL STATISTICS: The Grand Floridian's prime Seven Seas Lagoon locale allows for fast access to the Magic Kingdom. Proximity to the Palm and Magnolia links pleases golfers. The monorail stretches the hotel's neighborhood beyond the adjacent Polynesian resort to include the Contemporary resort and provides for easy commutes to Epcot. Grand Floridian; 4401 Floridian Way; Box 10000; Lake Buena Vista, FL 32830-1000; 407-824-3000; fax 407-824-3186.

Rates: Standard rooms start at about $410 in value season, $465 regular, and $495 peak; club-level rooms begin at $530 value, $615 regular, and $730 peak; and suites start at $1,080. A $25 per diem charge applies to each extra adult (beyond two) sharing a room.

Polynesian

This resort echoes the romance and beauty of the South Pacific

with enchanting realism. Polynesian music is piped throughout the lushly landscaped grounds, which boast white-sand beaches with hammocks, torches that burn nightly, and sufficient flowers to perfume the air.

Sprawled amid tropical gardens are 11 two- and three-story village longhouses, all named for Pacific islands, where 847 newly refurbished guestrooms are located. But the Polynesian's centerpiece and primary mood-setter is unquestionably the Great Ceremonial House, which (in addition to the usual front desk, shops, and restaurants) contains a two-story-high garden that all but consumes the atrium lobby.

BIG DRAWS: A breathtaking, you-are-there South Seas ambience

makes the Polynesian exceptionally romantic and helps to explain the resort's busy wedding calendar. And the convenience of monorail service is a definite plus.

WORTH NOTING: Many of the standard rooms, comparable in size to those at the Contemporary, feature two queen-size beds plus a daybed. Those in Tokelau, Tahiti, and Rapa Nui are slightly larger. All rooms have hair dryers, flat-screen TVs, coffeemakers, irons (with boards), mini fridges, and high-speed Internet access (for a fee). All third-floor rooms (and

Polynesian Tips

- For a taste of tropical tradition, catch the Torch Lighting Ceremony. It takes place on nights when the luau dinner show is performed.
- Tahiti is a good choice for its relative seclusion and Magic Kingdom views (request a lagoonside room).
- For a better view, hit the Seven Seas Lagoon on a private specialty cruise. See page 176 for details.
- Tucked down below Sunset Point, in front of Tahiti, is a beach that many guests don't realize is there.
- Couples can celebrate a special occasion with a moonlit dinner on the beach. Call Room Service for more information.
- The Grand Floridian Spa & Health Club is a short walk away.

second-floor rooms in the Tonga, Tokelau, Tahiti, and Rapa Nui buildings) have balconies. Room service is offered until midnight. A club-level lounge with a choice view of the Magic Kingdom is a comfy retreat for guests in Hawaii and all-suite Tonga, the resort's most luxurious digs.

In addition to the impressive volcano-themed pool, there is a second, unguarded pool. Near Tokelau, a grassy knoll known as Sunset Point is a pleasant spot to watch the sun call it a day. The resort boasts great vantage points for Magic Kingdom fireworks and the Electrical Water Pageant. (For information, ask at the front desk.) Boats may be rented, fishing excursions may be arranged, and a 1¼-mile trail invites jogging around the tropical grounds.

Where to eat: Capt. Cook's (24-hour grazing); Kona Cafe (Asian-influenced casual fare and adjoining coffee bar); the Spirit of Aloha dinner show; and 'Ohana (character breakfast and family-style Pacific Rim dinners featuring grilled meats).

Where to drink: Barefoot Pool Bar (poolside refreshments) and Tambu Lounge (tropical drinks).

VITAL STATISTICS: The Polynesian is located on the shore of Seven Seas Lagoon, directly opposite the Magic Kingdom, and offers fast access via monorail to the park. The monorail also links the resort with the Grand Floridian and Contemporary and provides for easy commutes to Epcot. Golfers appreciate having both the Palm and Magnolia courses nearby. Polynesian; 1600 Seven Seas Dr.; Box 10000; Lake Buena Vista, FL 32830-1000; 407-824-2000; fax 407-824-3174.

Rates: Standard rooms start at about $365 in value season, $425 regular, and $495 peak; club-level rooms begin at $505 value, $570 regular, and $675 peak; suites start at $845. A $25 per diem charge applies to each extra adult (beyond two) in a room.

Swan & Dolphin

While they occupy choice real estate within the borders of Disney property, these hotels are

---

Special Room Requests

All WDW resorts offer rooms equipped for guests with disabilities. Smoking rooms are not an option. For more information, inquire with Central Reservations (407-934-7639). For more specifics related to travelers with disabilities, see the "Customized Tips" section of the *Planning Ahead* chapter.

not owned or operated by Disney and attract a lot of business travelers. The motto for these resorts might be "expect the unexpected." Certainly, noted architect Michael Graves designed these postmodern bookends with entertainment in mind. At the Dolphin, a 27-story triangular tower is flanked by buildings that are topped by two 56-foot-tall dolphin statues and covered with a mural of banana leaves. It's more of the same playful luxury next door at the Swan, which carves its own distinctive silhouette with 47-foot namesake statues perched atop its 12-story central building and facades accented with turquoise waves. The Swan has 756 rooms, about half as many as the Dolphin.

BIG DRAWS: Luxury in a light-hearted wrapper. Exceptional facilities. Top-notch service. And you can walk to Epcot, Board-Walk, and, if you're ambitious, Disney's Hollywood Studios.

WORTH NOTING: The Swan and the Dolphin (operated by Westin and Sheraton) are the only two WDW hotels whose value season extends through the summer months. Guests staying at either hotel have access to all recreational activities

and may charge any meals and activities enjoyed at the sister hotel to their room tab. Such charging privileges do not extend beyond the two hotels. Disney's Magical Express program isn't extended to guests here, either.

Rooms at the Swan and Dolphin are comparable to those at Disney's other deluxe resorts. Whereas standard rooms at the Dolphin feature two double beds, queen-size beds are the rule at the Swan (king-size beds are available at

Swan & Dolphin Tips

- Request a corner room with a king-size bed at the Dolphin, and if it's available, you'll get two balconies for the price of one.

- Both hotels have large convention centers. If you're visiting for pleasure, ask if there will be major business action before you book.

- Four tennis courts at the Swan are lighted at night.

- These resorts have been known to run amazing special promotions (with steeply discounted prices) during Walt Disney World's busiest seasons.

- The Dolphin is home to a lovely pampering palace: the Mandara Spa. Visit *www.swandolphin.com* for details.

- The Swan and Dolphin hotels are participants in the Starwood Preferred Guest Program. Are you? For information, visit *www. starwoodpreferredguest.com*.

both). Room amenities at both hotels include stocked mini-bars and 24-hour room service (among the best at Walt Disney World), plus high-speed Internet (for a fee) service, coffeemakers, hair dryers, and irons with boards.

Both hotels boast luxurious presidential suites. In addition to a beach with a volleyball net and boat rentals, the resorts have enviable lap pools, a grotto pool with waterfalls, a kiddie pool, several whirlpools, and a spa.

Where to eat: At the Swan: Garden Grove (park setting), and Il Mulino (Italian bistro). At the Dolphin: The Fountain (burgers and salads); Fresh (Mediter-ranean); Shula's (steak); Todd English's bluezoo (coastal cui-sine); and Picabu (24-hour, self-serve cafeteria with round-the-clock convenience store).

Where to drink: At the Swan: Kimonos (sushi and karaoke bar); Lobby Court Lounge (coffee and cocktails); and Splash Terrace (poolside). At the Dolphin: Cabana Bar & Grill (poolside); Il Mulino Lounge; Shula's Lounge; Todd English's bluezoo bar; and a lobby lounge.

VITAL STATISTICS: The Swan and Dolphin resorts offer easy access to Epcot, Disney's Hollywood Studios, and BoardWalk. Located side by side on the shore of Crescent Lake, a short walk from Epcot's World Showcase, the hotels are flanked by BoardWalk on one side and the Yacht and Beach Club on the other. Walt Disney World Swan; 1200 Epcot Resorts Blvd.; Lake Buena Vista, FL 32830-1000; 407-934-3000; fax 407-934-4499. Walt Disney World Dolphin; 1500 Epcot Resorts Blvd.; Lake Buena Vista, FL 32830-1000; 407-934-4000; fax 407-934-4099.

Rates: At press time, rates at Swan and Dolphin standard rooms began at about $159 in value season and $179 peak. Suite prices started at about $429. A $25 per diem charge applies for each extra adult (beyond two) sharing a room. Up to four people may stay in one room. For more infor-mation or to make reservations, call 800-227-1500 or visit *www.swandolphin.com*.

Wilderness Lodge & Villas

Rustic romance infuses every detail of this resort, patterned after the grand National Park Service lodges of the early 1900s. Hidden away on an isolated shore of Bay Lake, Wilderness Lodge is surrounded by pine forests that provide a drumroll of sorts along

the winding road leading to the timbered hotel.

The soaring atrium lobby kindles the spirit of the American West with an imposing pair of totem poles, tepee chandeliers, a bubbling hot spring, and an 82-foot-tall fireplace whose layered stones actually replicate the Grand Canyon's strata. And the natural landscape is supplemented by a roaring waterfall, a swimming area surrounded by boulders, wildflowers, and even a gushing geyser. The guestrooms at the Lodge are located in two wings that extend back from the lobby to the lakefront, forming a U-shaped frame around an inner courtyard. The adjacent Villas at Wilderness Lodge are styled after the railroad hotels of the late 1800s. They extend the resort's neighborhood with 136 villas. The units are further distinguished by a red-shingled roof and a five-story central atrium. The Lodge and Villas share a lobby, and a covered walkway connects the resort buildings. There's also a club-level floor at the Lodge.

BIG DRAWS: Luxury. Undeniable romance. The bottom line: a truly extraordinary setting at a considerable value to guests.

WORTH NOTING: While all 728 Wilderness Lodge guestrooms have balconies or patios, quarters

Wilderness Lodge Tips

- Tours offer a closer look at the resort's architecture or restaurants.

- Courtyard and lakeview rooms are romantic, with waterfalls gushing and brooks babbling. Woods views provide maximum quiet.

- The Lodge's junior suites are a good value, given their spaciousness. Honeymooners should request room 7084 for its fireworks views and whirlpool tub.

- Some rooms at the lodge come with a queen-size bed and a bunk bed instead of two queens. Be sure to make your preference known.

- The bad news? The Wilderness Lodge is not on the monorail loop. The good? It's less expensive because of it!

here are slightly more compact than those at Disney's other deluxe resorts, and feature two queen-size beds. Quilted bedspreads, buffalo lamps, and armoires etched with mountain scenes maintain the theme.

The Villas at Wilderness Lodge are a Disney Vacation Club resort (see box below); accommodations are equipped with a kitchenette or a full kitchen. Studios and larger villas with one or two rooms have balconies (or patios). Guests staying at the villas enjoy access to the Lodge next door and vice versa.

At the Lodge and Villas, room service is available for breakfast and dinner. All rooms come equipped with coffeemakers, mini refrigerators (unstocked), hair dryers, and high-speed Internet service (for a fee).

Fire Rock Geyser spouts 180-foot water plumes at the top of every hour from 7 A.M. until 10 P.M. An unguarded pool, whirlpool spa, and Sturdy Branches health club are in the villa section. Both resorts share a beach (sunbathing only) on the lake. Guided fishing excursions can be arranged. Boats and bikes may be rented, and there is a path for biking, jogging, and walking that leads to the Fort Wilderness resort.

Where to eat: Artist Point (Pacific Northwest cuisine); Roaring Fork (light fare and snacks); and Whispering Canyon Cafe (high-spirited—and high-decibeled—family-style dining).

Where to drink: Territory Lounge (rustic motif) and Trout Pass (small poolside bar).

Join the Club?

Frequent visitors who consider Disney a second home might want to join Disney Vacation Club. For a one-time purchase price and annual dues, members may stay at Bay Lake Tower at Contemporary, Kidani Village at Animal Kingdom Lodge, Old Key West, BoardWalk Villas, The Villas at Wilderness Lodge, Beach Club Villas, Saratoga Springs Resort & Spa (which offers traditional and "treehouse" villas), or choose from 500 other vacation experiences, including Disney's Hilton Head Island Resort and Disney's Vero Beach Resort (see page 78). They can also opt for the Disney Cruise Line or another Disney resort. DVC members enjoy special discounts, too. For additional information, visit www.disneyvacationclub.com or call 800-800-9100. (Non-members may also book Disney Vacation Club accommodations by the night—based, of course, on availability.) Note that new properties may be joining the "club" soon. Check the aforementioned Web site for details.

VITAL STATISTICS: Wilderness Lodge and Villas; 901 Timberline Dr.; Box 10000; Lake Buena Vista, FL 32830-1000; 407-824-3200; fax 407-824-3232.

Rates: At the Lodge, standard guestrooms begin at about $240 in value season, $300 regular, and $365 peak; suites start at $850. Honeymoon rooms (with whirlpool tub) start at $440. A $25 per diem charge applies for each extra adult (beyond two) sharing a room (at the Lodge only). At the Villas, studios start at $330 value, $375 regular, and $455 peak; one-bedroom villas begin at $450 value, $515 regular, and $630 peak; two-bedroom villas start at $660 value, $845 regular, and $1,010 peak.

Yacht & Beach Club and Beach Club Villas

This setting conjures such a heady vision of turn-of-the-century Nantucket and Martha's Vineyard, you'd swear you smelled salt in the air. Surely, architect Robert A. M. Stern's evocation of the grand old seaside hotels has the gulls fooled. The resort stretches along a picturesque shoreline complete with a swimming lagoon, lighthouse, and marina.

As the five-story gray clapboard structure of the Yacht Club gives way to the sky-blue Beach Club (they're connected), the interior motif shifts from seriously nautical to seashore whimsical. The Yacht Club has a rich, exclusive feel to it—there's a stunning

Yacht & Beach Club Tips

- The stunning views belong strictly to those with lakeside rooms.
- At both resorts, it's a long walk to the lobby from the outermost reaches of guest wings.
- At the Beach Club, all rooms have patios or balconies.
- Balconies at the Yacht Club are generally bigger than those at the Beach Club.
- The resorts are just a short walk from Epcot's back door, aka International Gateway.

globe anchoring the lobby, and polished brass abounds. Next door at the Beach Club, beach umbrellas act as pillars, and clambakes occur nightly. The Beach Club Villas are inspired by Cape May seaside homes designed in the early 20th century.

BIG DRAWS: Compelling theming. Exceptional swimming area. Some of the World's best restaurants. Close access to Epcot and Disney's Hollywood Studios.

WORTH NOTING: There are 621 guestrooms at the Yacht Club and 583 rooms at the Beach Club. Room size is comparable to those at Disney's other deluxe resorts. As a rule, they feature two queen-size beds and a day-bed (king-size beds are avail-

able). At the Yacht Club, rooms maintain the nautical theme. Most rooms have good-size balconies. At the Beach Club, rooms keep the seashore motif.

Amenities at both resorts include an iron and board, a hair dryer, coffeemakers, mini refrigerators, high-speed Internet service (for a fee), and 24-hour room service. Yacht and Beach Club both offer club-level rooms. The five-story Beach Club Villas is a Disney Vacation Club resort. Accommodations have either a kitchenette or a kitchen. The 208 units, which include both studios and one- and two-bedroom villas, feature wooden porches and pastel colors.

A three-acre mini water park called Stormalong Bay earns the Yacht and Beach Club bragging rights for the World's best resort swimming area; the sprawling, sandy-bottomed pool, open only to hotel guests, includes sections with jets, swirling currents, and a slide (traditional whirlpools also stand by). Each resort also has a smaller pool and whirlpool.

The Ship Shape health club is among the most extensive fitness centers at a Walt Disney World property. Boat rentals and a tennis court are available, fishing excursions can be arranged, and there's a volleyball court (equipment is available).

Where to eat: At the Beach Club: Cape May Cafe (character breakfasts and clambake buffet dinners). At the Yacht Club: Captain's Grille (á la carte breakfast, lunch, and dinner) and Yachtsman Steakhouse (dinner). Shared by both hotels is the Beach Club Marketplace (combination eatery/retail shop) and Beaches & Cream (small, classic soda fountain).

Where to drink: At the Beach Club: Martha's Vineyard (cloud nine for wine lovers). At the Yacht Club: Ale and Compass (cozy lobby nook) and Crew's Cup (well-heeled beer emporium). For poolside refreshments and snacks, there's Hurricane Hanna's Grill.

VITAL STATISTICS: The Yacht and Beach Club enjoy close proximity to Epcot, Disney's Hollywood Studios, BoardWalk, and the Fantasia Gardens Miniature Golf complex. Located side by side on a shore of Crescent Lake that offers a footpath to Epcot's International Gateway entrance, these sister resorts are joined lakeside by the BoardWalk, Swan, and Dolphin. Yacht Club; 1700 Epcot Resorts Blvd.; Box 10000; Lake Buena Vista, FL 32830-1000; 407-934-7000; fax 407-934-3480. Beach Club; 1800 Epcot Resorts Blvd.; Box 10000; Lake Buena Vista, FL 32830-1000; 407-934-8000; fax 407-934-3850.

Rates: Standard rooms at the Yacht and Beach Club begin at about $340 in value season, $390 regular, and $470 peak; club-level rooms at the Yacht Club start at $470 value, $535 regular, and $610 peak; Yacht Club suites start at $1,335 and Beach Club suites start at $600. A $25 per diem charge applies to each extra adult (beyond two) sharing a room. At the Villas, studios start at $340 value, $390 regular, and $470 peak; one-bedroom villas begin at $465 value, $525 regular, and $610 peak; two-bedroom villas start at $650 value, $845 regular, and $1,065 peak.

Disney Vacation Club Resorts
Disney's Old Key West Resort

Pastel-hued clapboard guest-houses with tin roofs and white picket fences set the cheerful tone of this Key West-erly retreat. Here, Disney luxury dovetails with a laid-back atmosphere to create the look and feel of a friendly resort community.

A sprawling village, it is bounded by the wooded fairways of the Lake Buena Vista golf links, and anchored at its center by a lighthouse that overlooks the main pool area, which moonlights as a sauna. A waterway called the Trumbo Canal flows from the heart of the resort, eventually uniting with Village Lake. Accommodations equipped with kitchens may set this resort apart, but what gives the place charm is its warmth.

BIG DRAWS: Spacious accommodations, ideal for long stays. Homey environs. Value for groups. Convenience of kitchens. Well located for golfers.

Old Key West Tips

- For a waterfront setting that's removed from the main recreation area, book a villa near the Turtle Shack. Buildings 43 and 44 are good, given their water views and proximity to the pool, snack bar, tennis court, and bus stop.

- All accommodations but the studios feature whirlpool bathtubs.

- One-bedroom villas yield more than twice the space of a studio for a relatively small jump in cost.

WORTH NOTING: This resort was the first Disney Vacation Club property. It features studio accommodations and one-, two-, and three-bedroom villas. The villas have a distinctly Key West feel, and are decorated in light woods with ceiling fans and color schemes of sea-foam green and mauve.

Each studio has a large bedroom with two queen-size beds; a kitchenette with a microwave, coffeemaker, DVD player, and refrigerator; high-speed Internet access (for a fee). Larger villas also have a dining room, kitchen, laundry facilities, and whirlpool bathtub. They feature a king-size bed in the master bedroom, two queen-size beds in each extra bedroom, and a living room with queen-size sofa bed. All accommodations have balconies or porches.

Boats and bicycles are available for rent. Fishing excursions can be arranged. The three tennis courts tend to be relatively quiet and accessible. The main swimming area supplements three smaller pools. There is a fitness center. Conch Flats Community Hall has table tennis, board games, and DVD rentals.

Where to eat: Good's Food to Go (meals and snacks on the go) and Olivia's Cafe (casual all-day dining with Key West flourishes). Grills and picnic tables are available. Conch Flats General Store stocks a small selection of grocery items.

Where to drink: Gurgling Suitcase (tiny pub) and Turtle Shack (poolside drinks and snacks).

VITAL STATISTICS: Well located for golfers. It also has easy access to Downtown Disney and good proximity to Epcot and Disney's Hollywood Studios. Disney's Old Key West Resort; 1510 N. Cove Rd.; Box 10000; Lake Buena Vista, FL 32830-1000; 407-827-7700; fax 407-827-7710.

Rates: Studios start at about $295 in value season, $330 regular, and $390 peak; one-bedroom villas are $400 value, $455 regular, and $525 peak; two-bedrooms are $555 value, $665 regular, and $805 peak; and three-bedrooms start at $1,230 value, $1,370 regular, and $1,550 peak.

Saratoga Springs Resort & Spa

Long for the relaxation of a lakeside retreat—complete with fragrant gardens, bubbling fountains, and a spectacular spa? Look no further. This resort has all of the above, plus colorful Victorian architecture, rolling hills, a lakeside boardwalk and 60 Treehouse Villas for those who want a serious getaway. The property aims to recapture the rejuvenating ambience of Saratoga Springs, New York, circa the late 1800s. Saratoga Springs Resort & Spa is a Disney Vacation Club resort. (See page 58 for details.)

BIG DRAWS: Relaxing environs. Great spa. Golf on-site. Fishing excursions. A stone's throw from Downtown Disney.

WORTH NOTING: There is a total of 1,320 guest units—studios, one- and two-bedroom villas, and grand villas—spread over 15 resort buildings and 60 treehouse villas. Each studio has a queen-size bed and double sleeper sofa, plus a kitchenette with a microwave, coffeemaker, and fridge. Larger villas sleep four to twelve, and all have a dining area, kitchen, laundry room, master bath with whirlpool tub, and a DVD player. They include a king-size bed in the master bedroom, living room with queen-size sofa bed, and either two queen beds or a queen bed and a double sleeper sofa in any other bedrooms.

The resort's treehouse villas, elevated 10 feet off the ground on pedestals and beams designed to blend into the forest, offer lovely views of the natural surroundings. They all have full kitchens, flat-panel TVs, three bedrooms, two bathrooms, and sleep up to nine guests.

Recreational diversions include golf, swimming pools, whirlpools, trails for walking or jogging, tennis, bike rentals, and more.

Where to eat: Artist's Palette offers snacks, sandwiches, and made-to-order entrées. There is a small selection of grocery items available, too. Turf Club has sandwiches, burgers, salmon, and more for lunch and dinner.

Where to drink: Guests may imbibe at the Turf Club (cozy lounge) and at On the Rocks (poolside bar), Backstretch Bar (pool bar), or at Downtown Disney (a boat or bus ride away).

Fort Wilderness Tips

- Bikes and electric carts are, sudden rains aside, the preferred means for getting around.

- A car is the quickest way to get to other parts of the World from here.

- Views of Magic Kingdom fireworks and the Electrical Water Pageant are readily available.

- Tent campers should request loop 1500 or 2000 for quiet; RV campers will find greater privacy on loops 1600 through 1900 (pets welcome).

VITAL STATISTICS: Downtown Disney Marketplace makes for an entertaining next-door neighbor. Breezy environs evoke a true sense of community (a calming one at that). And the spa is superb. 1960 Broadway St.; Box 10000; Lake Buena Vista, FL; 407-827-1100; fax 407-827-4444.

Rates: Studios start at about $295 in value season, $330 regular, and $390 peak; one-bedroom villas are $400 value, $455 regular, and $525 peak; two-bedrooms are $555 value, $665 regular, and $805 peak; and three-bedrooms start at $555 value, $665 regular, and $805 peak.

Fort Wilderness Resort

No fewer than 750 acres of woodland combine with WDW's largest lake to provide the foundation for Fort Wilderness, a retreat that relies on the outdoors for atmosphere.

Cabins (included among Disney's "moderate" resorts) and campsites are arranged on 28 loops, linked by thoroughfares. While some of the 784 campsites are designated for tents, most are devoted to RV camping, while hundreds of spots sport furnished Wilderness Cabins. (They're favored by folks who prefer to be a little less close to nature.) Golf carts may be rented for $49 per

day. Pets are welcome at designated campsites ($5 per day).

BIG DRAWS: Natural setting. Value. And recreation galore.

WORTH NOTING: Most loops have at least one air-conditioned comfort station equipped with restrooms, phones, showers, laundry facilities, and an ice machine. Campsite lengths range from 25 to 65 feet. All sites have a charcoal grill, picnic table, a 20/350-amp electrical outlet, cable TV, and high-speed Internet (for a fee). All RV sites have sanitary-disposal connections.

Wilderness Cabins, which were recently refurbished and are classified by Disney as a "moderate" resort, are separated from other campsites and feature rustic decor and a deck with picnic table; the amenities include a hair dryer and an iron. Each cabin is air-conditioned and offers daily housekeeping service, as well as a fully equipped kitchen, living room with flat-screen TV and DVD, high-speed Internet access (for a fee), and full bathroom. Recreational options include swimming, boating, tennis, and biking. Guided fishing trips may be arranged (407-WDW-BASS).

Horse-drawn wagon rides ($8; no reservations necessary; 45 minutes long) and 25-minute, horse-drawn carriage rides ($45; call 407-939-7529) take guests on a scenic trip between Fort Wilderness and Disney's Wilderness Lodge. The Hoop-Dee-Doo Musical Revue dinner show is presented nightly.

Where to eat: Many guests cook their own meals (a small selection of food is sold at Meadow Trading Post and Settlement Trading Post), but there's also Trail's End restaurant (buffet-style dining). Grocery stores are located just minutes from Walt Disney World. Ask for directions when you check in.

Where to drink: Crockett's Tavern (cocktails; inside Trail's End).

VITAL STATISTICS: Fort Wilderness occupies Bay Lake's southern shore. Its nearest theme park neighbor is the Magic Kingdom, and it borders the Osprey Ridge golf course. The area is served by the WDW bus transportation system. Bus stops are strategically located and plentiful. Fort Wilderness; 4510 N. Fort Wilderness Trail; Box 10000; Lake Buena Vista, FL 32830-1000; 407-824-2900; fax 407-824-3508.

Rates: Preferred sites with full hookups, including water, electricity, sewer, and cable TV, start at about $59 in value season, $80 regular, and $92 peak; Tent/Pop-up sites with electricity hook-ups only are $44 value, $63 regular, and $73 peak. Also available are Premium Campsites. They have the same amenities, but can accommodate "big rigs." Rates for premium sites start at $74 in value season, $95 regular, and $107 peak.

There is a limit of ten people per campsite, and a $2 per diem charge applies to each extra adult (beyond two) sharing a site. Rates for Wilderness Cabins are $270 value, $325 regular, and $360 peak. Maximum occupancy is six, and there is no longer a per diem charge for extra adults (beyond two). Note that the least expensive campsite category—Tent/Pop-up Sites—cannot accommodate RVs of any kind.

Caribbean Beach Tips

- Aruba is a good choice for seclusion and for proximity to Old Port Royale (they're linked by a bridge).

- For honeymoon-style isolation, request a room in Trinidad South. Located just off the main loop, its buildings and beach are especially removed.

- Martinique tends to be the liveliest village.

- The 1.4-mile promenade circling Barefoot Bay is ideal for biking and jogging. Bikes and boats may be rented.

- Families flock here, so plan on encountering plenty of children.

Moderate
Caribbean Beach

In this colorful evocation of the Caribbean, the spirit of the islands is captured by a lake ringed by beaches and villages representing Barbados, Martinique, Trinidad, Jamaica, and Aruba.

Each village is marked by clusters of two-story guest buildings that transport you to the Caribbean with cool pastel facades, white railings, and vivid metallic roofs. Old Port Royale, which houses eateries and shops, takes its cues from an island market.

BIG DRAWS: Excellent value. Cheery environs with a decidedly Caribbean feel. The pirate-themed rooms are a hit with would-be buccaneers.

WORTH NOTING: The resort has 2,112 rooms (400 have a pirate theme). Slightly larger than those at Disney's other moderate resorts, they feature two double beds (king-size beds are available) and soft-hued decor. Amenities include an in-room coffeemaker (with coffee), a mini fridge, and high-speed Internet access (for a fee). Room service, which ventures a tad beyond pizza, is offered from 4 P.M. until midnight.

Villages are sprawled around the resort's Barefoot Bay in a way that can make travel between some guest areas cumbersome despite footbridges and "local" buses.

The resort's whirlpool is nestled into its bustling themed pool. Each village offers its own beach, pool, and courtyards.

Where to eat: Shutters at Old Port Royale (American fare) and a food court with six counter-service options.

Where to drink: Banana Cabana (poolside refreshments).

VITAL STATISTICS: Caribbean Beach is off on its own but well situated for pursuits other than the Magic Kingdom, with Epcot, Disney's Hollywood Studios, and Blizzard Beach close at hand, on one side, and Typhoon Lagoon and Downtown Disney nearby, on the other. Caribbean Beach; 900 Cayman Way; Box 10000; Lake Buena Vista, FL 32830-1000; 407-934-3400; fax 407-934-1940.

Rates: Rooms begin at about $149 in value season, $170 in regular season, $185 in "summer" season, and $195 during peak times. A $15 per diem charge applies for each extra adult (beyond two) in a room.

Coronado Springs

The architecture of this sprawling resort gives its nod to Mexico

Coronado Springs Tips

- There is a 10-percent gratuity automatically added to all purchases made at the Pepper Market food court when you dine on the premises. The charge is waived for take-out.

- January, May, September, and October are popular convention months. Most groups are housed in the Casitas area, near the convention facilities, and a separate check-in area is provided.

- The Ranchos are nearest the pool area; the Casitas are closer to the main building, convention center, and health club; and the Cabanas are convenient to both.

- There's a lot of ground to cover between the central building and some guestrooms. If you want a room near the hub, be sure to make your preference known when you make the reservation.

and the American Southwest, with brightly tinted buildings accented by tile roofs, soaring columns, and arched entryways. Three clusters of regionally themed guest buildings rim the 15-acre Lago Dorado lagoon. The terra-cotta Casitas occupy a citylike landscape that segues into rural surroundings. Here, pueblo-style Ranchos invite guests to dwell among cacti adjacent to a dry stream bed. In the resort's third section, the scenery shifts once more, with rocky beaches, hammocks, and Cabanas filling the horizon. Rooms in each area are similarly appointed, with yellow, scarlet, or deep-blue accents.

Walkways around the lagoon lead from guestroom areas to the main recreation zone (dominated by a five-story Mayan pyramid) and the central building that holds the resort's temporal treasures: an intricately tiled rotunda lobby, two eateries, a lounge, and a gift shop.

BIG DRAWS: A standout among the moderates for its health club, suites, and business hotel facilities.

WORTH NOTING: Guestrooms at this 1,921-room resort are smaller than those at Disney's deluxe hotels. Most of the 46 suites are in the Casitas area. Decor reveals Mexican and Southwestern influences, and reflects the style of each guest area. Standard rooms feature two double beds (some king-size beds are available). Amenities include a coffeemaker, mini fridge, hair dryer, iron, high-speed Internet or Wi-Fi (for a fee), and limited room service.

In addition to a themed pool—which has a whirlpool and a sand volleyball court on the side—there is a pool in each guest area. La Vida health club and the Casa de Belleza salon are in the Casitas area. Bikes and boats may be rented at the marina. The nearly mile-long path around the lake, known as the Esplanade, is good for biking and jogging. A convention center offers business services.

Where to eat: Maya Grill (steak and seafood); Cafe Rix (lounge with tapas-style appetizers); and the Pepper Market (food court).

Where to drink: Rix Lounge (modern lounge); Laguna bar (outside the lobby); and Siestas Cantina (pool bar).

VITAL STATISTICS: Located near Animal Kingdom and Blizzard Beach. Coronado Springs; 1000 W. Buena Vista Dr.; Box 10000; Lake Buena Vista, FL 32830-1000; 407-939-1000; fax 407-939-3837.

Rates: Rooms begin at about $154 in value season, $175 regular, $190 "summer," and $200 peak; suites start at $350. A $15 per diem charge applies for each extra adult (beyond two) in a room.

Port Orleans Riverside

Southern hospitality takes two forms at this 2,048-room resort: pillared mansions with groomed lawns and *Gone with the Wind* elegance and, upriver, rustic homes with tin roofs and bayou charm. Rooms in the three-story Magnolia Bend mansions and the two-story Alligator Bayou lodges are similarly appointed.

The man-made Sassagoula River curls around the resort's main recreation area like a moat. Bridges link guest lodgings with this area and the steamship-style building that houses eateries, a gift shop, and check-in facilities.

BIG DRAWS: Excellent value. An exceedingly lovely natural setting.

WORTH NOTING: Rooms here are smaller than those at Disney's deluxe hotels, but pleasantly inviting. Each features two double beds (some king-size beds and trundle beds are available). This is a sprawling resort with twice as many rooms as its

Port Orleans Riverside Tips

- The Sassagoula River Cruise is a pleasant outing and a convenient means of transportation to Downtown Disney.
- For optimal atmosphere and minimal walking, request a room in Magnolia Bend's Oak Manor, or lodge number 18 or 27 in the resort's Alligator Bayou section.
- Mansion rooms exude honeymoon-style elegance and seclusion.
- Elevators are available in the resort's Magnolia Bend section only.
- The resort offers horse-drawn carriage rides.

French Quarter counterpart; some accommodations are quite a bit removed from the central building or the nearest bus stop. Amenities include coffeemakers, hair dryers, mini fridges, and high-speed Internet access (for a fee).

Room service delivers pizza from 4 P.M. to midnight. Bikes and boats may be rented. The resort's pathways are well suited for joggers, and a carriage path leads to Port Orleans French Quarter. Five more pools (open 24 hours, provided swimmers stay quiet) are sprinkled around the Bayou and Mansion guest areas. There is a whirlpool near the main pool.

Fishing excursions are offered. Call 407-WDW-BASS for information and to make reservations. Guests may use the pool at Port Orleans French Quarter in addition to the one here. Carriage rides allow for a romantic 25-minute tour of the resort area ($45; call 407-WDW-PLAY for reservations).

Where to eat: Boatwright's Dining Hall (casual restaurant specializing in Southern cuisine) and Riverside Mill (food court).

Where to drink: River Roost (fireplace and occasional entertainment) and Muddy Rivers (poolside refreshments).

Port Orleans French Quarter Tips

- A convenient, though tiny, water shuttle ferries resort guests to and from Downtown Disney.

- This is too pretty a place to wake up to a view of the parking lot, so consider reserving a room overlooking the gardens or splurge on riverscape digs. Note that pool views can spoil the ambience.

- Experience the area's romantic atmosphere via a bike ride along the river.

- Don't miss the fresh beignets (a true taste of the Big Easy), whose aroma regularly wafts through the festive food court.

VITAL STATISTICS: Port Orleans Riverside, located on a bank of the Sassagoula River, is within walking distance of Port Orleans French Quarter. Epcot and the Studios are close by, as are two of WDW's 18-hole golf courses. Port Orleans Riverside; 1251 Riverside Dr.; Box 10000; Lake Buena Vista, FL 32830-1000; 407-934-6000; fax 407-934-5777.

Rates: Rooms begin at about $149 in value season, $170 regular, $185 "summer," and $195 peak. A $15 per diem charge applies for each extra adult (beyond two) in a room.

Port Orleans French Quarter

New Orleans's historic French Quarter is evoked in this resort's prim row house–style buildings, which are wrapped in ornate wrought-iron railings and set amid romantic gardens and tree-lined blocks. Old-fashioned lampposts add to the ambience, as do street signs such as *Rue D'Baga* and *Café Au Lait Way*.

The resort is entered via Port Orleans Square, an atrium with adjoining buildings that house the front desk, gift shop, and arcade on one side, and a lounge and food court on the other.

Rooms are located in seven three-story buildings, which are set on either side of the central thoroughfare that begins just beyond Port Orleans Square. The whole enclave is set alongside a

stand-in Mississippi known as the Sassagoula River. The Sassagoula River Cruise, which transports guests to Port Orleans Riverside and Downtown Disney, is a pleasant and convenient way to travel.

BIG DRAWS: A good bang for the buck. The charming environs

rank among Disney World's most memorable. It's the least sprawling of the moderate resorts.

WORTH NOTING: The homey rooms are a bit smaller than those at Disney's more expensive hotels but are comfortable. Each of the 1,008 rooms features two double beds; some king-size beds are available. Amenities include coffeemaker, hair dryer, mini fridge, and high-speed Internet access (for a fee).

A Dixieland band occasionally entertains in the courtyard; a street artist may be available for portraits. A carriage path—ideal for jogging, strolling, and biking —wends along the river to nearby Port Orleans Riverside.

Bikes and boats may be rented from Riverside Levee at Port Orleans Riverside. In addition to the swimming pool and whirlpool here, French Quarter guests may use Riverside's pool; they can also take advantage of its fishing hole. Guided fishing trips depart from the resort daily (reservations are required; 407-WDW-BASS).

Where to eat: Boatwright's Dining Hall (Port Orleans Riverside) and Sassagoula Floatworks & Food Factory (food court with Mardi Gras ambience).

Where to drink: Mardi Grogs (pool bar) and Scat Cat's Club (for specialty drinks).

VITAL STATISTICS: Port Orleans French Quarter enjoys special access to Downtown Disney Marketplace via water taxi, which also links it with Port Orleans Riverside. It's close to Epcot, Disney's Hollywood Studios, and two 18-hole golf courses as well. Port Orleans French Quarter; 2201 Orleans Dr.; Box 10000; Lake Buena Vista, FL 32830-1000; 407-934-5000; fax 407-934-5353.

Rates: Rooms begin at about $149 in value season, $170 regular, $185 "summer," and $195 peak. A $15 per diem charge applies for each extra adult (beyond two) sharing a room.

Value
All-Star Movies,
All-Star Music, and
All-Star Sports Resorts

Bright in a manner normally reserved for toy packaging, these sprawling, fun-loving resorts exist at the intersection of entertainment architecture and pop art. Picture a landscape in which three-story football helmets, cowboy boots, and Dalmatians are the norm, and you have an idea of the oversize sense of whimsy that governs the All-Star resorts.

Each All-Star property has its own central check-in building, complete with food court, and its own pair of signature swimming pools. Each features ten guest buildings that are divided into five (movies, music, or sports) themes and thematically correct rooms.

Sports fans enjoy All-Star Sports resort's homages to basketball, baseball, football, tennis, and surfing. The All-Star Music resort makes exaggerated overtures to calypso, jazz, Broadway, rock, and country music. All-Star Movies reprises *101 Dalmatians*, *The Mighty Ducks*, *Fantasia*, *The Love Bug*, and *Toy Story*.

BIG DRAW: All the advantages of staying on WDW turf at a fraction of the cost of its other resorts.

WORTH NOTING: Requests for specific motifs cannot be guaranteed, but are likely to be met, considering the resorts' large capacity (384 rooms per theme, five themes per resort).

The rooms, which are among the smallest of those at any Disney resort, are perfectly adequate, if

All-Star Resorts Tips

- These resorts attract families with small children in droves. All-Star Music tends to host large groups of young guests (think school bands, cheerleaders, etc.).

- For more quiet, request a third-floor room in a building far from the food court or main pool.

- Reservations are required for luggage assistance upon check-out; call the night before.

- All-Star guests can rent boats at any of the other WDW resorts.

- Unless you plan to drive every-where, request a room near the lobby (i.e., bus stop).

lacking in drawer space. All rooms have hair dryers and high-speed Internet access (for a fee). Rooms with king-size beds are available on request, as are mini refrigerators ($10 per day for the fridge). There are also 215 "Family Suites." Featuring two bathrooms and sleeping up to six, each suite includes a kitchenette with a microwave, coffeemaker, fridge, and sink.

On-site recreation is limited to two swimming pools at each resort. Pizza delivery is available until midnight.

Where to eat: Each hotel has a vast, themed food court: All-Star Sports (End Zone); All-Star Music (Intermission); All-Star Movies (World Premiere).

Where to drink: At All-Star Sports: Team Spirits pool bar. At All-Star Music: Singing Spirits pool bar. At All-Star Movies: Silver Screen Spirits pool bar.

VITAL STATISTICS: The All-Star resorts are close to Animal Kingdom and Blizzard Beach; Epcot and the Studios are also nearby. All-Star Movies; 1991 W. Buena Vista Dr.; Box 10000; Lake Buena Vista, FL 32830-1000; 407-939-7000; fax 407-939-7111. All-Star Music; 1801 W. Buena Vista Dr.; Box 10000; Lake Buena Vista, FL 32830-1000; 407-939-6000; fax 407-939-7222. All-Star Sports; 1701 W. Buena Vista Dr.; Box 10000; Lake Buena Vista, FL 32830-1000; 407-939-5000; fax 507-939-7333.

Rates: Rooms begin at about $82 in value season, $105 regular, $119 "summer," and $125 peak. A $10 per diem charge applies to each extra adult (beyond two) sharing a room. Family suites start at $190.

Pop Century Resort

Open up a 20th-century time capsule and throw in a yo-yo, bowling pin, Rubik's Cube, cell phone, and other icons of the century's toys, fads, dance crazes, and classic and kooky catchphrases, and then turn it into a place for travelers to stay. That's

Pop Century, one of the newest additions to Disney's family of value-priced resorts. Pop Century is made distinctive by an intentionally kitschy decorative style and larger-than-life icons found throughout the landscape.

BIG DRAW: Pop Century provides a true Disney resort experience at a fraction of the cost of most resorts.

WORTH NOTING: The ten buildings in the 2,880-room Classic Years each have themes based on a different decade from the 1950s through the 1990s. Rooms (which are smaller than those at other Disney resorts) are available with two double- or one king-size bed. All rooms have hair dryers and high-speed Internet access (for a fee). Mini fridges may be requested ($10 per day).

Three pools to choose from. Pizza delivery is available.

Where to eat: Everything Pop food court. It has counter-service stations, plus a "grab and go" area.

Where to drink: Petals pool bar (beside the Hippy Dippy pool). It serves drinks and fast food.

VITAL STATISTICS: The resort is near ESPN Wide World of Sports complex. Pop Century; 1050 Century Dr.; Box 10000; Lake Buena

---

Pop Century Resort Tips

- Pop Century resort boasts a whopping 2,880 guestrooms, which could make reserving a room at the last minute a bit easier than at smaller resorts.

- Want to be near a pool? Request a room in the 1950s, 1960s, or 1980s lodge buildings; they're adjacent to the Bowling Pin, Hippy Dippy Pool, and Computer pools, respectively. Keep in mind that all three pools are equally bustling.

- This colorful resort is very popular with families. Buildings and areas by the Computer pool have a slightly less frantic atmosphere.

Vista, FL 32830-1000; 407-938-4000; fax 407-938-4040.

Rates: Rooms start at about $82 in value season, $105 regular, $119 "summer," and $125 peak. A $10 daily charge applies to each adult (beyond two) sharing a room.

Disney Cruise Line

The Disney Cruise Line fleet features two 2,700-passenger ships, each casually elegant and designed to recapture the majesty of early ocean liners. They're equipped to satisfy even the most savvy of cruisers, with a mix of traditional diversions and Disney touches. Recreation areas are designed to lure families and adults *sans* kids to different parts of the ship. Each ship has a pool, restaurant, and nighttime entertainment "district" earmarked for adults only.

Lest anyone forget who owns these vessels, Disney characters crop up from stem to stern. A statue of Mickey as helmsman greets arriving guests on the *Disney Magic*, and Goofy hangs over the stern. Characters are also on hand to mix, mingle, and otherwise assist the captain.

By day, fun in the sun alternates with lunch, indoor distractions, and catnaps. When the sun goes down, the focus shifts to dining and party spots.

Cruise Line land-sea vacations pair a stay at a Walt Disney World resort with a voyage on a Disney ship. At Port Canaveral, guests embark on a three- or four-night cruise to the Bahamas. (Seven-night Caribbean cruises with Eastern and Western itineraries take place aboard the *Disney Magic*.) En route to Castaway Cay, Disney's private isle, the *Wonder* makes a stop at Nassau. It's also possible to experience special 10- and 11-night itineraries.

BIG DRAWS: The ultimate surf-and-turf experience, Disney style. Private island rendezvous.

Disney Cruise Line Tips

- Room keys can be used to charge drinks, merchandise, and salon services, as well as gratuities for servers and cabin crew.
- Palo, the adults-only dining room, is the only restaurant that requires reservations. Book it as soon as you're onboard or at *www.disneycruise.com*.
- Unlike a visit to World Showcase, you really do leave the country on a Disney Cruise Line vacation. Pack a passport.
- Two new ships—with new destinations—are soon to join the Disney Cruise Line fleet. For details, visit *www.disneycruise.com*, or call 800-910-3659.

Land Ho!

Each Disney Cruise Line voyage that departs from Port Canaveral includes a day at Castaway Cay, Disney's charted yet private isle. With all the perks of a tropical paradise, an afternoon at Castaway Cay is sure to cure even the most severe cases of Gilligan envy. Disney has maintained the island's natural beauty while accommodating a variety of activities, including volleyball, snorkeling, biking, and boating. The 1,000-acre Bahamian island features a mile-long stretch of secluded sand reserved for adult sun worshippers, as well as those seeking private open-air massages in cabanas overlooking the ocean. There's also a lunch buffet, bar, and more for Bahama mamas and papas to explore.

WORTH NOTING: Each room has a safe, TV, small cooling box, hair dryer, and telephone with "land line" (check rates before dialing). Facilities include three pools, a sports deck, and the Vista Spa & Salon. The ship boasts adult-oriented enrichment programs, deck parties, and two theaters (showing first-run films and musical stage shows).

Where to eat: On the *Disney Magic*, Animator's Palate (room undergoes a spectral metamorphosis), Parrot Cay (casual Caribbean), Lumière's (continental, casually elegant), and Palo (Italian fare, reserved for adults). Topsider Buffet is a casual daytime spot. On the *Disney Wonder*, Triton's replaces Lumière's, and Beach Blanket Buffet replaces Topsider.

Where to drink: Both ships are home to the Promenade Lounge (a lively bar), Diversions (sports bar), and Cove Cafe (adults-only coffee/cocktail lounge). Exclu-sive to the *Disney Magic* are Rockin' Bar D (band and deejay) and Sessions (an intimate piano bar). The *Disney Wonder* has Wave-Bands (deejays) and The Cadillac Lounge (elegant cocktail spot). Both ships have pool bars.

VITAL STATISTICS: Shipboard accommodations are about 25 percent roomier than cabins on most other ships. Most have a queen-size bed or two twin-size beds and a convertible sofa or pull-down bed. A majority are outside staterooms with a bath and a half; almost half have verandas.

Rates: Twelve stateroom categories correspond to comparable rooms at WDW resorts. Inside and ocean-view staterooms yield Moderate resorts; veranda staterooms net Deluxe resorts.

Basic land-and-sea packages generally include Walt Disney World resort accommodations, a stateroom, and shipboard meals and recreation.

Packages including park admission, airfare, and more may be available. Call 800-910-3659, or visit *www.disneycruise.com*.

Resorts on Hotel Plaza Boulevard

These resorts occupy a unique position among non-Disney resorts because they, along with four other hotels (Best Western Lake Buena Vista, Holiday Inn at Walt Disney World, Doubletree Guest Suites, and Regal Sun), are within the boundaries of Walt Disney World.

Guests have easy access to Disney golf courses and reservations at select restaurants and dinner shows.

All the hotels have Disney gift shops, as well as ESPN, and a Walt Disney World information channel. They also sell park (and, usually, other) tickets, and provide free bus service to all theme parks, water parks, and Downtown Disney (allow extra time for bus travel). *Note that the Hilton is the only resort on Hotel Plaza Boulevard that participates in the theme park "Extra Magic Hours" program (for details, see page 15).*

Rooms can be booked through the individual hotels or through

Hilton Tips

- Rooms with the best views overlook the pools or the fountain at the hotel's entrance.
- For easy access to the pool, request a ground-floor room.

WDW Central Reservations (407-934-7639).

Hilton

Set on 23 well-groomed acres, the 814-room Hilton has an air of laid-back gentility.

BIG DRAWS: Located across the road from the Downtown Disney Marketplace. Pool areas with adult appeal. Free transportation to all Disney golf courses.

WORTH NOTING: All guestrooms have minibars; some suites have balconies. There's a health club, two swimming pools, and a whirlpool, plus in-room dining.

Where to eat: Andiamo Italian Bistro & Grille; Benihana Steakhouse and Sushi (Japanese); Covington Mill (breakfast and lunch in a cheery, casual setting); and Mainstreet Market (deli, ice cream counter, and well-stocked country store).

Where to drink: Rum Largo Poolside Bar & Cafe (tropical drinks); John T's (sports bar); and Mugs (coffee and ice cream).

VITAL STATISTICS: Conveniently located just across the road from the Downtown Disney Marketplace. Hilton; 1751 Hotel Plaza Blvd.; Lake Buena Vista, FL 32830; 407-827-4000 or 800-782-4414; fax 407-827-3890; *www.hiltonorlandoresort.com.*

Rates: Rooms are $99 to $1,500, and suites are $149 to $659, depending on the season.

Royal Plaza

Royal Plaza is a sophisticated hotel with a definite appeal for adults. Besides an outstanding pool area, there are four lighted tennis courts on the resort grounds.

BIG DRAWS: Nice pool area with large whirlpool; adult ambience.

WORTH NOTING: The 394 rooms, including 23 suites, are divided between a 17-story tower and two-story wings. Each room has a sitting area, desk, hair dryer,

Royal Plaza Tips

• There are separate gamerooms for adults and for kids, and no one under 16 is allowed in the large fitness room.

• Some baths feature oversize tubs and separate glass-enclosed showers.

coffeemaker, iron, and safe. Many rooms come with oversize Roman tubs, and some have whirlpools.

Where to eat: Giraffe Café; Marketessen (for snacks).

Where to drink: Giraffe Lounge and SIPS (poolside bar).

VITAL STATISTICS: Located about a half mile from the Downtown Disney Marketplace. Royal Plaza; 1905 Hotel Plaza Blvd.; Lake Buena Vista, FL 32830; 407-828-2828 or 800-248-7890; *www.royalplaza.com.*

A Great Beach Add-on

A stay at Disney's Vero Beach Resort—an oceanfront Disney Vacation Club property just two hours away from Walt Disney World by car—combines nicely with a WDW vacation. The resort's homey comforts are similar to those at Disney's Old Key West Resort (see pages 61–63).

Among its assets are pristine beaches and proximity to manatee retreats and dive trips. A tropical tangle separates the resort and beach. Packages combining a Vero Beach trip with a WDW visit are available. For more information, call 407-939-7540.

Rates: Guestrooms are $99 to $229 for up to five guests; suites range from $129 to $459.

Buena Vista Palace Hotel & Spa

The largest of the resorts along Hotel Plaza Blvd., the Buena Vista Palace Hotel & Spa is a cluster of towers. The grounds are lushly landscaped, with shaded walkways. Inside, the decor is elegant. The reception area offers several cozy sitting nooks, and the Island Suite building has secluded courtyards. Many of the 1,014 rooms and suites have a private patio or balcony with a view of Spaceship Earth.

BIG DRAWS: A European-style spa (see page 180); popular night-spots; and many recreational options. Close proximity to the Downtown Disney Marketplace.

WORTH NOTING: All guestrooms have ceiling fans, two phones (one bedside, one on the desk), voice mail, and 24-hour room service. One- and two-bedroom

Buena Vista Palace Tip

Try the Castaway Grill and Shipwreck Bar for a snack or frosty beverage as you take time to relax on Recreation Island.

suites are available. There's a fitness center, a luxurious spa, a sand volleyball court, three pools, lighted tennis court, and two lakeside gazebos.

Where to eat: The Outback Restaurant (specializing in fresh seafood and Black Angus beef; not part of the chain bearing the same name); Watercress Cafe (baked goods and deli items).

Where to drink: The Lobby Lounge, the Kook Sports Bar, and the Castaway Grill and Shipwreck Bar.

VITAL STATISTICS: Across from the Downtown Disney Marketplace. Buena Vista Palace; 1900 Buena Vista Dr.; Lake Buena Vista, FL 32830; 407-827-2727 or 866-379-6516; fax 407-827-6034; *www.buenavistapalace.com*.

Rates: Room rates start at $229; rates for suites start at $329.

Spectacular fireworks come with the territory at Walt Disney World.

Theme Parks: The Big Four

To experience Walt Disney World's quartet of major theme parks without children is tantamount to celebrating a major holiday without the complication of traffic or in-laws. It's positively liberating.

Let the theme parks runneth over with strollers and too-tired toddlers. As adults free to roam the Magic Kingdom, Epcot, Disney's Hollywood Studios, and Animal Kingdom on our own terms, we need not be concerned with such things. We are a minority (read: non-school-age individuals under no obligation whatsoever to facilitate the entertainment of any maturity-challenged person within 40 or so square miles) in one of those rare settings in which the minority holds all the advantages.

If we sometimes feel a bit conspicuous touring the theme parks as unaccompanied adults, it's because we're flaunting the inherent freedom. We're taking advantage of the fact that we're among friends who readily agree that a shaded bench, a nap in a hammock, or a soak in the whirlpool back at the resort would really hit the spot right now. We are free to buzz through the Magic Kingdom at a clip no character-conscious family could maintain, or meander through Epcot's World Showcase pavilions at what might be called an escargot's pace. All the while we're taking advantage of time-saving techniques like Disney's Fastpass, which allows walk-on access to several popular attractions in all four theme parks.

With a dizzying array of attractions to choose from, the task of mapping out an itinerary is a critical one. Fight the urge to see and do everything, and craft a manageable list of must-sees. You're on vacation. It's a time to relax and have fun.

You may want to devote day one to the Magic Kingdom to get that long-anticipated dose of classic Disney magic. Then, with Cinderella's castle a delightful memory, you'll appreciate a day at Epcot on its own merits. Follow Epcot with a day at Disney's Hollywood Studios. (Enchantment is a great chaser for enlightenment.)

If you're raring to go on safari or be chased by a dinosaur, spend your fourth day exploring Animal Kingdom. (This is also the order in which the parks opened: Magic Kingdom, 1971; Epcot, 1982 [see below]; Disney's Hollywood Studios, 1989; and Animal Kingdom, 1998.)

MAGIC KINGDOM

As once-upon-a-timish and happily-ever-afteresque a place as exists, the Magic Kingdom is proof that you can judge a park by its largest icon (in this case, Cinderella Castle). While it is the most character-intensive and certainly the strongest kid magnet of all the parks, flying elephants couldn't keep us away.

What puts the Magic Kingdom on the adult map? For starters, it's manageable. Most of the essentials here are easily traversed in a day. High on the list of imperatives are three members of Disney's own mountain range—Space Mountain, Splash

Mountain, and Big Thunder Mountain Railroad—a thrilling trio of rides. (Space Mountain underwent a major refurbishment in 2009.)

What it lacks in fine cuisine and opportunities to imbibe, it makes up for in magic. Disney has made a real art of coaxing folks into a state of wonderment that seldom occurs in adulthood, and this park represents that art taken to its highest level. It's a rare adult who doesn't fall under the spell of the Magic Kingdom's ballroom of waltzing apparitions, or its convincing den of leering pirates. For nostalgic whimsy, there are kiddie rides such as Peter Pan's Flight that don't aspire to recapture the magic of childhood so much as to momentarily revive it.

The nighttime parade is also bound to reacquaint you with your inner child. This spectacle of fiber-optic delight showcases 600,000 miniature bulbs that light in wildly changing patterns and move in perfect concert with sound effects and a musical score. This illuminating processional is presented on select nights throughout the year.

Of course, wall-to-wall kids can get on anyone's nerves after a while, so some strategies are in order. First, master the art of noticing little ones only when they are being cute. To keep the "magic barometer" from falling, take advantage of less crowded evening hours, and weave in and out of major traffic zones. (Fantasyland and Mickey's Toontown Fair are generally the most congested areas.)

Seek refuge in the shade and in such havens as The Hall of Presidents; for a bigger break, indulge in a leisurely lunch at one of the resorts that are accessible via monorail.

Save Time in Line

Want to waltz onto an attraction without waiting in a long line? By using Disney's Fastpass system—complimentary to guests holding all valid ticket media—at selected attractions in all four theme parks, you can do just that. How does it work? Slip your admission ticket into the machine. It will spit out your ticket along with a timed voucher. Come back at any point within the voucher's time frame and you'll bypass the long wait (aka "the standby line"). Consult the Touring Priorities on page 87 for a roster of Fastpass attractions, and check each park's guidemap for a current list of attractions that feature this service.

GETTING ORIENTED: Go through the turnstiles, pass an area with rental lockers, and you're in Town Square, the cul-de-sac at the foot of Main Street. From here look straight out to the park's most recognizable landmark, Cinderella Castle. It's at the opposite end of Main Street, behind an area known as the Hub, or Central Plaza. On the left before the Hub is the main **Tip Board**, an information board listing current waiting times for the park's most popular attractions. It's helpful to think of the layout of the Magic Kingdom as a tree. Main Street, U.S.A., is the trunk; the other six themed areas—Adventureland, Fantasyland, Frontierland, Liberty Square, Mickey's Toontown Fair, and Tomorrowland—dangle at the ends of the tree's gnarled boughs (actually bridges). The

first bridge on your left leads to Adventureland; the second bridge to Liberty Square and Frontierland; the pathway straight ahead passes through Cinderella Castle on its way to the heart of Fantasyland; another bridge passes to the right of the castle to enter Fantasyland nearest Mickey's Toontown Fair and Tomorrowland; and the bridge on your immediate right leads directly to Tomorrowland. The lands are also linked via a broad footpath that winds its way behind the castle.

A Walking Tour

Let's begin our tour in **Town Square**, which is important as the location of **City Hall**, where a person can make all manner of inquiries and arrangements (no, you can't get married here). Even if you don't need to pick up a guidemap, make reservations for a restaurant, exchange foreign currency, or check the Lost and Found, stop by to play Q & A with the informed folks behind the counter. Note that the local ATMs are here and near the lockers at the park entrance.

The archway we walked under to get here is the foundation of the **Walt Disney World Railroad** depot. A 1928 steam engine that

---

Magic Kingdom Hours

The Magic Kingdom is usually open from about 9 A.M. to 8 P.M. or later. Park hours are extended during holiday periods and summer, abbreviated during slower times.

Call 407-824-4321 or log onto *www.disneyworld.com* for details. One-day park admission is about $75, plus tax, for adults. Prices are likely to change.

once carted sugarcane across the Yucatán now hauls freight (largely first-time visitors, train buffs, and homesick commuters) on a 20-minute loop around the Magic Kingdom. It's a fine way to get to Frontierland and Mickey's Toontown Fair if you don't want to walk. Onward.

Main Street, U.S.A.

Main Street is notable as the tidy strip of storefronts where adults gawk at, then feel compelled to photograph, Cinderella Castle. There's no shame in it; but don't be so distracted that you overlook the street's early 1900s charm. Amusements here are decidedly low-key. For grooming as entertainment, there's the Harmony Barber Shop (tucked in between the Emporium and the Car Barn), where the Dapper

Dans sometimes accompany a haircut. Definitely check out their sweet four-part harmonies. Main Street stays open a half hour after the rest of the park has closed, although the shops (see "Shopping" in the *Diversions* chapter) tend to be less crowded in early afternoon.

Tomorrowland

Futuristic in a way that would likely go right over Buck Rogers's head, Tomorrowland is a city of the future that never was. In fact, take a spin on the Tomorrowland Transit Authority and you can get an upclose look at the "retro metro" society.

Tomorrowland news flash: After being shuttered and refurbished for much of 2009, **Space Mountain**, the beloved ride that's been on the top of most must-do lists for more than three decades, is back in business for 2010. The spiffed-up attraction features a rocket-ride through a space-age sheath of darkness,

shooting stars, and flashing lights. It's a fast and furious ride with special effects—an absolute must for the adventurous, and an unforgettable adventure for the suddenly courageous. Space Mountain is also a turbulent ride, so passengers must be in good health and free from heart conditions, back and neck problems, and other physical limitations (such as pregnancy), as the posted signs warn. If you've just eaten, wait awhile. If you decide you would rather survey the land going a mere seven miles per hour, the **Tomorrowland Transit Authority** offers a preview of Buzz Lightyear's Space Ranger Spin and other sites on a track that's strictly horizontal. The train is boarded in the heart of Tomorrowland near **Astro Orbiter** (an elevated ride with rockets that's for kids but good fun for adults; it seems to go faster the lower you fly in your Buck Rogers-mobile).

Next door, in the spot that used to house an attraction featuring a fearsome alien, is **Stitch's Great Escape!** Like its predecessor, this attraction also involves an AWOL alien—but this time, he's really more of a menace than a threat and merely impolite, as opposed to angry. The alien in question is none other than Experiment 626, aka Stitch, from the Disney film *Lilo & Stitch*.

In this "prequel" to the movie, the rambunctious critter is being transported to the Prisoner Processing Center at Galactic Federation Headquarters. Audience members are enlisted to guard him while he awaits his sentence. No offense, but theme park guests make lousy guards, as Experiment 626 escapes several dozen times a day. During his little bouts of giddy freedom, he is known to wreak havoc on audience members. Don't be surprised if he messes your meticulously coiffed do or hocks an alien loogie on your head. And to think, you *paid* for this. . . .

Across the way is **Monsters, Inc. Laugh Floor**, an attraction based on the feature *Monsters, Inc.* The interactive, digitally animated experience is light on clever quips, heavy on slap-schtick. (Grown-ups value it most as a way to escape the Tomorrowland crowds or the searing Florida heat.) Next door you'll find the Day-Glo adventure zone known as **Buzz Lightyear's Space Ranger Spin** (yes, grown-ups love it). Here, *Toy Story*'s Mr. Infinity and Beyond solicits your assistance in cuffing the universe's most insidious battery hoarder. The 4½-minute journey is part video game, part shooting gallery, thanks to your spaceship's spin-control joystick and laser guns. (How else to combat the likes of Rock'em Sock'em Robot?)

At **Walt Disney's Carousel of Progress**, the stage stays put and you rotate around it during the 20-minute show. The attraction is a warm and fuzzy portrayal of how electricity has altered—and ostensibly improved—our lives.

Heading north toward Fantasyland, you pass Space Mountain and come upon the rather low-octane **Tomorrowland Speedway**.

Mickey's Toontown Fair

This tiny blip between Tomorrowland and Fantasyland is a land geared toward the very young. When you visit the area, you'll find an old-fashioned county fair.

The cuteness is in the details (Mickey's ear-bearing crops, Minnie as the local craft queen). Don't miss your chance to tour the country homes of Mickey and Minnie. At **Mickey's**

Touring Priorities

DON'T MISS	DON'T OVERLOOK	DON'T KNOCK YOURSELF OUT
Splash Mountain*	Walt Disney World Railroad	The Barnstormer
Big Thunder Mountain Railroad*	Liberty Belle Riverboat	The Enchanted Tiki Room— Under New Management
The Haunted Mansion	Mickey's Toontown Fair	Swiss Family Treehouse
Pirates of the Caribbean	Mad Tea Party	Snow White's Scary Adventures
Buzz Lightyear's Space Ranger Spin*	Tomorrowland Transit Authority	Dumbo the Flying Elephant
It's a Small World	Tomorrowland Speedway	Stitch's Great Escape!*
Peter Pan's Flight*	Carousel of Progress	Tom Sawyer Island
The Many Adventures of Winnie the Pooh*	Astro Orbiter	The Magic Carpets of Aladdin
Mickey's PhilharMagic*	Cinderella's Golden Carrousel	Monsters, Inc. Laugh Floor
Jungle Cruise*	*Fastpass attraction as of press time.	Country Bear Jamboree
Space Mountain		
The Hall of Presidents		

Country House, take a peek in the kitchen, but watch out—he's in the process of remodeling. Attractions are primarily for kids, but it's still fun to wander. For a one-stop character meeting, the **Toontown Hall of Fame** can't be beat. Wanna meet the big cheese himself? Mickey greets guests in the Judge's Tent behind his cottage. And if you're looking to take some baby steps before venturing on to Space Mountain, **The Barnstormer at Goofy's Wiseacre Farm** may be just your speed.

Fantasyland

The optimum way to take in this cheery land is to visit just before and during the daily 3 o'clock parade or in the evening when the parks are open late. Because there is nothing adult about Fantasyland—whimsy is the name of the game.

That said, certain attractions are so artfully executed that they transcend the kiddie genre. Of these, the spruced up **It's a Small World**—a 10-minute boat ride through the happiest, busiest, and most diversely populated dollhouse on the planet—is surely the most elaborate. Much more subtle is **Peter Pan's Flight**, an alluring sprinkle of

pixie dust in which you can—and do—fly for three minutes above absolutely delightful scenes of Captain Hook and nighttime London in a pirate ship built for two.

Fantasyland's newest attraction, **Mickey's PhilharMagic**, brings many of your favorite characters to in-your-face life in a 3-D musical show starring Mickey and Donald, plus such other Disney favorites as Ariel (of *Little Mermaid* fame), Aladdin and Jasmine (from *Aladdin*), and Simba (direct from *The Lion King*)—all coming your way from a towering 150-foot-wide screen.

Then there are the purely nostalgic attractions, worth your time only if you're hankering to relive a certain story or amusement ride from your past.

Have a thing for carousels in general or **Cinderella's Golden Carrousel** in particular? Go for it. Think you'd get a huge kick out of squeezing your group into an oversize teacup and spinning yourselves silly? Get to the **Mad Tea Party**. And don't skip **Dumbo the Flying Elephant** if you'll regret it later. But at the same time, don't expect to be wowed by the straightforward kiddie attraction known as **Snow White's Scary Adventures**. Although it has more happy moments than it did in the old days, the twisting journey still feels like a trip through a witch-filled fun house. **The Many Adventures of Winnie the Pooh**, however, is a sweetly tempting honey jar of a journey through the Hundred Acre Wood.

Whatever you do, don't miss the mosaic murals beneath the open archway of **Cinderella Castle**. No less than a million well-placed pieces of Italian glass tell the tale—ugly step-sisters, glass slipper, and all.

Liberty Square

Tucked between Fantasyland and Frontierland, this small area tends to be relatively peaceful. Brick and clapboard buildings carry the theme—Colonial America—as does the Liberty Tree, a 130-something oak tree hung with 13 lanterns to recall the original Colonies.

Though Liberty Square has just a few attractions, it still takes more than an hour to see them all. **The Hall of Presidents** merits attention not just as a well-delivered 20-minute dose of patri-otism in which Abraham Lincoln, George Washington, and Barack Obama speak (that's really Mr. Obama's voice you'll hear), but as a chance to observe all chief executives of our country in action. The convincing presiden-tial performance begins as the curtain rises on the impeccably dressed group of Audio-Anima-tronics figures. The pace is slow, but just right for an air-condi-tioned theater with comfy seats. Don't be intimidated if there is a big line—this is one *big* theater.

The Liberty Belle Riverboat —a large, romantic, paddle wheel–driven, Liberty Square–based steamboat that makes 17-minute loops around Tom Sawyer Island —is a pleasant distraction, espe-cially on a steamy afternoon. Don't ask what **The Haunted Mansion** is doing in Liberty Square. Just note that it is a not-to-be-missed experience overrun with clever special effects and ghoulish delights (your typical ballroom of waltzing ghosts, door knockers that knock by themselves, and spirited grave-yards). On your way in, be sure to stop and read the epitaphs. They're killer funny.

Frontierland

This land conjures the Old West, with a little country charm thrown in for good measure. Although there's more to Frontierland than mountains, it is most notable as the home to two of the Magic Kingdom's most addictive thrills—Splash Mountain and Big Thunder Mountain Railroad.

(Relatively) Quiet Escapes

- Rose garden on the right as you face Cinderella Castle
- Cinderella Wishing Well, near the castle
- Walt Disney World Railroad
- Harmony Barber Shop
- Shaded tables behind the shops in Liberty Square
- *Liberty Belle* Riverboat
- Rocking chairs on the front porches of Frontierland and Liberty Square shops
- Tomorrowland Transit Authority
- Tables by Aunt Polly's on Tom Sawyer Island
- Anywhere but Fantasyland and Toontown

The first thing to know about **Splash Mountain** is that it's okay to feel anxious just watching the log boats plunge down this ride's big drop—you're looking at one of the steepest flumes in the world (although it appears to be a straight drop, it's actually 52 feet down at a 45-degree angle). Even so, this water-bound ride themed to Disney's *Song of the South* is tamer than it looks from the ground. Steep plunge aside, there are just three smaller dips during the 11-minute trip.

If you're like us, the first time around you'll be way too nervous about when "it" is going to happen to fully appreciate the delightful humor, appealing characters, and uplifting "Zip-A-Dee-Doo-Dah" ambience. But coax yourself into riding once and you'll be hooked. If you prefer to get splashed, not drenched, sit in the back and on the left of the log. Onlookers should note that a water cannon takes aim at the observation bridge without warning. A note on timing: Both Splash Mountain and Big Thunder Mountain Railroad tend to draw big crowds all day; your best bet is to shoot for early morning or evening.

Think of **Big Thunder Mountain Railroad** as a

thrilling ride on the mild side. As roller coasters go, this one's exciting as much for the surrounding scenery your runaway mine train races past—bats, goats, a flooded mining town—as for the ride itself. Big Thunder Mountain Railroad is not nearly so fast or turbulent as Space Mountain, and nothing in its four-minute series of reverberating swoops and jerky turns comes close to Splash Mountain's intimidating plunge. For a bigger thrill, ride it after dark, when you can't clearly see what lies ahead, even from the first car. For the wildest of rides, request a seat near the back.

But Frontierland's appeal extends beyond its two high-profile attractions. The **Country Bear Jamboree**, a 16-minute musical variety show put on by 20 or so hopelessly corny Audio-Animatronics bears, is the perfect attraction to hit when you're feeling a little punchy. **Tom Sawyer Island**, just a raft ride away, provides a nice break from the more structured parts of the park.

Adventureland

Adventureland has been transformed into the marketplace of *Aladdin*'s Agrabah. One part is **The Magic Carpets of Aladdin**, a Dumbo-style ride on which riders pilot mystical flying carpets. Among this land's other attractions are the immensely popular Pirates of the Caribbean and Jungle Cruise, best visited during the early morning and evening.

The Enchanted Tiki Room— Under New Management is worthy of a traffic-stopping whistle. The nine-minute affair

91

still showcases Disney's earliest Audio-Animatronic figures, but adds plucky company to the chirping, chattering birds of yore. *Aladdin*'s Iago and *The Lion King*'s Zazu push the limits of caged-bird choreography. Remember **Pirates of the Caribbean** as an elaborate, engaging boat ride in which you watch pirates raid a Caribbean village. A classic attraction, it provides plenty of leering, jeering examples of how wonderfully, almost frighteningly realistic Disney's Audio-Animatronics can be. Note that the ten-minute Pirates of the Caribbean ride includes a small dip and some loud cannon blasts. And, fans of the Pirates feature films, rejoice: Captains Sparrow and Barbossa have joined this Kingdom's band of swashbuckling marauders.

The **Jungle Cruise**, another classic, transports passengers on a steamy, ten-minute boat trip through the Nile Valley and the Amazon rainforest. Although the flora is quite beautiful, the lines for this ride can be prohibitively long—use Fastpass if it's offered. Finally, if you feel up to climbing some serious stairs, **Swiss Family Treehouse** is a replica of the Swiss Family Robinson's ingenious perch that's worth the effort, even though the tree itself is a product of the prop department's imagination.

Entertainment

The raucous Move It! Shake It! Celebrate It! street party takes place several times daily. It features five gift-wrapped floats and Disney characters in a party mood. Get ready to do the conga!

The character-laden floats in the Celebrate a Dream Come True parade take over Main Street daily at 3 P.M. The Dapper Dans often pop up on Main Street to serenade guests with four-part harmonies.

When the park is open late, the fireworks show, Wishes, is presented on select nights. The dazzling SpectroMagic light parade wends its luminous way down Main Street on special nights, too.

If there are two performances of the parade, the later one is often less crowded. Check a park guidemap and Times Guide for the route and show schedules.

EPCOT

Think of Epcot as an extraordinary balancing act. This park is huge—about three times the size of the Magic Kingdom—and it performs two rather ambitious feats simultaneously. While the part of Epcot known as Future World offers a multifaceted look at what lies ahead for humankind, its alter ego, World Showcase, transports guests (at least in spirit) to many different countries. This division of labor works well, and it certainly keeps things interesting here. While the more serious-minded Future World is striving to spark the imagina-

Epcot Hours

Epcot's hours are staggered: Future World opens at about 9 A.M. and closes at 7 P.M.; World Showcase comes to life around 11 A.M. and closes at 9 P.M. Hours may be extended during holidays.

Visit www.disneyworld.com or call 407-824-4321 for details. One-day park admission is about $75, plus tax, for adults. Prices are likely to change.

tion, illuminate the technological future, and heighten environmental awareness, lively World Showcase is serving forth Oktoberfest, traditional English pub grub, and panoramic views of France, China, and Canada.

As Future World is ushering visitors into an ultramodern hydroponic greenhouse, World Showcase is escorting others along a calm river deep in the heart of Mexico and over a stormy Norwegian sea. Together, the two entities stimulate guests to discover new things about people, places, and, indeed, their own curiosity.

If Epcot boasts a tremendous following among legal voters, it's because it has more of the things adults appreciate: live entertainment; quiet gardens; beer, wine, and frozen drinks; tasteful shops and galleries; international cuisine; sophisticated restaurants;

and specialty coffees—and that's just the supplementary stuff. Epcot also woos the older crowd by making Mickey a little more scarce and by splicing enrichment of one form or another into the greater part of its amusements. It appeals to adults on a purely aesthetic level as well: World Showcase, wrapped around a vast lagoon, has a commanding natural and architectural beauty that changes with each border crossing. And Future World more than holds its own with the massive, gleaming silver geosphere of Spaceship Earth. Not surprisingly, we've met a number of Walt Disney World regulars who spend their entire vacations here at Epcot.

Epcot has its die-hard Future World fans and its World Showcase fanatics, but most visitors list favorite pavilions on both sides of the lagoon. Ongoing renovations and additions to Epcot make this especially true today. Disney Imagineers have made smart changes in

Entertainment

Epcot's entertainment slate is ever-changing. So pick up a Times Guide at Guest Relations (or elsewhere in the park) and check it often.

In Future World, acrobats and a trash-can percussive unit dressed in custodial wear are popular head-turners.

The Innoventions Fountain erupts into a computer-choreographed water ballet every 15 minutes.

In addition, each World Showcase pavilion has performers, any of whom could be appearing at some point during your visit. Among the possibilities: a rock 'n' roll band in Canada, a mop-top band paying tribute to the British Invasion in the United Kingdom, belly dancers in Morocco, drummers in Japan, oompah musicians in Germany, and acrobats in China.

The American Adventure features an outstanding a cappella group known as the Voices of Liberty and stage shows at America Gardens Theatre.

Epcot's IllumiNations: Reflections of Earth all but sets fire to the senses in its dramatic, hypnotic simulation of our planet's evolution. This nightly finale starts off with a bang and ends on an even more explosive note. Stand anywhere along the promenade and prepare to be moved.

Keep in mind that the lineup of entertainment is ever-changing and may be altogether different when you visit Epcot.

Epcot's entertainment mix that have lightened up Future World, livened up World Showcase, and, in the process, earned the theme park a fresh crop of admirers— both young and old.

We'll describe the attractions later so that we can first present "The Official Six Things We Bet You Didn't Know You Could Do at Epcot" list: (1) You can get some terrific gardening tips. (2) You can experience the British Invasion. Or at least think you did, when you hear the band playing Beatles tunes. (3) You can watch a butterfly open its wings for the first time. If you want, you can nibble on a freshly picked spearmint sprig while that beautiful orange-barred sulphur butterfly decides when to flee the hatching box. (4) You can send a picture of your "future self" anywhere in the world via e-mail. (5) You can get an impromptu belly dancing lesson from an obliging Moroccan dancer. (6) You can come snout to schnoz with a dolphin.

An important thing to know about Epcot is that it is no small undertaking. Even the choosiest visitor will need two full days to cover the park at a comfortable pace. Since Future World and World Showcase keep different

Hot Tips

- Not a morning person? Head to crowd-free World Showcase (opening around 11 A.M.) while everyone else is in Future World.

- Soarin' and Test Track are wildly popular. Get a Fastpass for your favorite first thing in the morning.

- Epcot is bigger than it seems, so allow yourself plenty of time to get from place to place—especially if you've already got reservations for a meal at a World Showcase restaurant.

hours, strategically-minded guests will do well to follow our lead. In the name of efficiency, here's what we say: Take in a few key Future World pavilions during the hours before World Showcase opens. Explore World Showcase during the early afternoon, when Future World is most congested. Return to Future World to explore a few more pavilions during the relatively uncongested hours of late afternoon and early evening. Finally, revisit World Showcase during pleasant evening hours to experience the beauty of the park at twilight, as well as IllumiNations.

GETTING ORIENTED: It's helpful to think of Epcot as the park with the hourglass figure. In this conception, the gleaming silver ball of Spaceship Earth is the head and northernmost point; the other Future World pavilions, arranged on either side of Spaceship Earth, form the outline of Epcot's "upper body"; and the promenade of World Showcase pavilions connects to Future World at Epcot's "waist" and, tracing the lines of a long, full skirt, wraps around World Showcase Lagoon. The American Adventure pavilion, located due south of Spaceship Earth along the bottom hem of the World Showcase skirt, effectively serves as the foot of Epcot.

Visitors should come prepared to do a great deal of walking, as the World Showcase Promenade itself is 1.2 miles around. Avid walkers and the health-conscious will be interested to know that a person typically covers more than two miles in one full day of touring Epcot. Don't be dismayed, though; the park is equipped with plenty of resting spots (see the box on page 108 for tips to the whereabouts of said nooks), as well as a key foot-saving alternative. Water taxis link Showcase Plaza at the foot of Future World with Germany and Morocco, located at the farthest corners of World Showcase. Some seniors who choose to tour the smaller theme parks on foot rent a wheelchair or a self-driven Electric

Convenience Vehicle (ECV) here at Epcot.

A Walking Tour

Our tour begins at the main entrance. This is where you take care of logistics while the gleaming ball of Spaceship Earth offers a 16-million-pound hint as to the precise direction of Future World. Epcot's monorail station is right outside the gates here, as is an ATM (located on the far left just before you enter the park). On the right side of the entranceway, also outside the gates, you can exchange currency, make a phone call, and pick up any cumbersome purchases you arranged to have forwarded here during your visit.

Note: If you need to use any of these services mid-visit, hold on to your admission ticket upon exiting so that you may re-enter the park. Lost and Found is in the Guest Relations lobby at Innoventions East. As you close in on the big ball, remember that there are still more services in its shadows. If you need a storage locker, pass around Spaceship Earth's right side. Otherwise, keep left. This course will lead you past the stroller and wheelchair rentals.

If you haven't made dining plans, stop by Guest Relations

near Spaceship Earth to make restaurant reservations or hold your horses until you get to the eatery of your choice. Otherwise, focus on Innoventions Plaza, where you'll find one of three **Tip Boards**, listing wait times for popular attractions.

Future World

You know you're in Future World when you see a thunderous fountain that acts like it owns the place, something resembling a remarkably oversize golf ball that would require a club bigger than the Empire State Building, kaleidoscopic fiber-optic pat-

terns in the walkway, gardens that could pass for modern art, and freewheeling water fountains that do swan dives and geyser imitations.

This land is awash in the sort of grand music that might trumpet the credits of an Academy Award–winning film. And it wears its sleek architecture and futuristic landscaping like a power suit.

The themed pavilions that make up Future World document humanity's progress in this world and offer visions of our technological fate. Such major concerns as transportation safety and

Touring Priorities

DON'T MISS

Soarin'*
Test Track*
Universe of Energy
Spaceship Earth
The Seas with Nemo & Friends
France**
The American Adventure**
Canada**
IllumiNations (nightly fireworks show)
Mission: SPACE*
(The "less intense," non-spinning version)

DON'T OVERLOOK

China**
Italy
Japan
Living with the Land*
Honey, I Shrunk the Audience*
Mexico
Morocco
Germany
United Kingdom
Circle of Life
Maelstrom*
Norway

DON'T KNOCK YOURSELF OUT

Gran Fiesta Tour in Mexico
Innoventions
Journey Into Imagination with Figment

* Fastpass attraction as of press time

** Pay close attention to performance schedules.

alternative energy sources serve as springboards for the attractions, which make stimulating experiences of topics that can make boring conversation.

If you haven't paid a visit here lately, you'll notice that an ongoing tweaking spree has invigorated Future World. In fact, Test Track, Mission: SPACE, and the extremely popular Soarin' attraction put Epcot in a novel spot—atop the thrill seeker's list.

A reminder: This park tour is designed to provide a sense of place, not an itinerary.

Spaceship Earth

This 180-foot-tall "geosphere" sticks out like a wayward planet come to roost. You may be interested to learn that the silver exterior comes from layers of anodized aluminum and polyethylene, and is composed of 11,324 triangular panels, not all of equal size or shape (although it takes a keen eye to discern any differences). Or maybe you would rather hear the story of how the gleaming exterior funnels every raindrop that hits it into World Showcase Lagoon.

The new-and-improved **Spaceship Earth** ride (it was "refreshed" in 2007) inside the geosphere winds (very slowly) past exquisitely detailed three-dimensional scenes, tracing the evolution of human communication using Audio-Animatronics figures that here, in their element, seem more natural than many sitcom actors. In about 14 minutes you've gone from Cro-Magnon to outer space and back again. The point? To explore how humans continue to re-create the future. If you've been here before, do revisit your old friend Spaceship Earth. You'll be happily surprised by the enhanced journey.

The finale provides a forward-looking finish for Spaceship Earth. The new "Project Tomorrow" post-show area is worth checking out, too. This popular attraction—your worst bet first thing in the morning—is least crowded during the hours just prior to park closing.

Innoventions

Think of the latest incarnation of Innoventions as a trip down future lane. Disney's showcase of technological goodies is certainly worth exploring. Housed in two sprawling buildings (known as East and West), Innoventions is a bright labyrinth of activity that many guests find difficult to pass through quickly. Well-marked, hands-on exhibits ensure that you won't miss a single innovation, er, make that innovention.

The Seas with Nemo & Friends

Formally known as The Living Seas, this pavilion has been taken over by a curious clownfish named Nemo and his cohorts from the film *Finding Nemo*. In addition to an attraction featuring the aforementioned undersea residents, you'll encounter a richly stocked coral reef environment (pop.: 2,000) that even a scuba diver would find extraordinary. (Don't be surprised if you see one!) During the toasty summer months, it's particularly refreshing to ogle The Seas' *pièce de résistance*, a 5.7-million-gallon tank in which a simulated Caribbean Sea and man-made reef support a glorious array of life, including sharks, dolphins, and sea turtles.

While **The Seas with Nemo & Friends** attraction was crafted with youngsters in mind, its charm isn't lost on the more mature fans of the fin-challenged fish. So climb aboard a "clam-mobile" and enjoy the quest to find Nemo (yep, he's wandered off again). Afterward, you can linger all you like in front of enormous eight-inch-thick windows to the undersea world. In addition to colorful sea life (including real-life versions of Finding Nemo characters), you can actually interact with Crush, that wacky, animated turtle. The short but enormously popular "Turtle Talk with Crush" has to be seen to be believed.

Of course, no seafaring adventure is complete without the opportunity to shout, "Land ho!" so it's only right that The Land is the next pavilion.

The Land

This popular plot explores themes related to food and farming while planting seeds of environmental consciousness. Underneath this pavilion's dramatic skylighted roof, you'll find a well-balanced slate of attractions, a bountiful food court, and a lazy Susan of a restaurant, the Garden Grill, which rotates very slowly past several of the ecosystems featured in the pavilion's boat ride. All things considered, The Land merits two green thumbs-up as the purveyor of one of Future World's strongest line-ups.

The **Living with the Land** boat ride is an informative 13½-minute journey that escorts you through a stormy prairie, a windswept desert, and a South American rainforest en route to

experimental greenhouses and an area given over to fish farming. The dripping, squawking rain-forest is so realistic, you'd need to chomp on a faux fern to convince yourself it's all plastic. The narration is an interesting commentary on the history and future of agriculture. The greenhouses show futuristic technology at work on real crops (many of which are served right here at Epcot), with NASA experiments and cucumbers in desert training among the high-lights. This popular attraction is best visited in the morning or during the hours just prior to park closing. *The Circle of Life* is an environmental fable featur-ing Timon and Pumbaa, the wisenheimer meerkat-warthog duo from *The Lion King*, as developers, and Simba as the environmentally sensitive lion. The 20-minute film includes stunning nature footage.

If you, like many humans, have ever had that happy dream in which you can fly—this is your chance to live it while actually *awake*. **Soarin'**, which came east after making its debut at Disney's California Adventure park, has quickly become one of the most beloved attractions in Walt Disney World history. It invites guests to swoop and soar above the clouds, while taking in vari-ous scenes of the California countryside. To achieve the effect, guests sit in special seat belts-mandatory, hang-glider–type vehicles and are suspended 45 feet in the air, above a giant IMAX projection dome. It appeals to guests of all ages. We love it.

If heights aren't your thing, consider sitting this one out. Other than that, it's exceptionally smooth sailing, er, flying— unless you're highly susceptible to motion sickness. You may want to stash loose-fitting shoes

A Healthy Crop

If you're eating your vegetables (and fruits) at the Garden Grill, Coral Reef, or Sunshine Seasons, odds are good that you're shar-ing in The Land pavilion's bounty. Some 30 tons of produce are harvested each year from The Land's greenhouses. Talk about fresh local ingredients!

in the basket beneath your seat—just in case.

Imagination!

While you'd think that glass buildings would leave very little to the imagination, the glass pyramids that house the Imagination pavilion have quite the opposite effect. If necessity is truly the mother of invention, then this is where she resides, playing with minds as if they were Play-Doh. Fronted by foun-

tains that seem to have agendas of their own, this pavilion is one of Epcot's more whimsical.

Ever curious about what it feels like to be an inventor with those little lightbulbs always appearing above your head, you enter the **Journey Into Imagination with Figment** attraction and discover that you have stumbled upon an open house hosted by the Imagination Institute.

This attraction features the antics of a character named Figment. The little purple dragon is here to teach you a few secrets about capturing the imagination. In doing so, he treats you to a tour of various labs at the Institute. It's all meant to trigger an appreciation for imagination.

Afterward, stop by **Image-Works**, an interactive area meant to stimulate sensory skills. *Note that ImageWorks and Journey Into Imagination may not be operating in all of 2010.*

Future World Unplugged

For a close-up look at Future World, check out:

- **Epcot Seas Aqua Tour:** Non-scuba divers can use snorkel equipment at The Seas with Nemo & Friends in this 2½-hour tour (about $140) of the Disney version of the deep. Call 407-WDW-TOUR (939-8687).

- **DiveQuest:** This 3-hour program (about $175) invites certified scuba divers to a dive in The Seas' aquarium. For information, call 407-WDW-TOUR (939-8687).

- **Dolphins in Depth:** A bit more (about $175) buys you a 3-hour introduction to dolphin research and conservation, 30 minutes in the water with the dolphins at The Seas, and a videotape to prove it. Call 407-WDW-TOUR (939-8687) for details and reservations.

Truth be told, the attraction at the Imagination! pavilion that earns kudos from Epcot die-hards is **Honey, I Shrunk the Audience**. If you have time to visit many attractions at Epcot, this 3-D experience movie should be on your list. The 25-minute film (which was a tad blurry on our last visit) is so riddled with effects that the audience is consistently reduced to a squirming, giggling mass. The experience is not rough, but the effects are heightened with a bit of suspense, so we'll say no more. Crowds are smallest early in the morning and late in the evening. If you're spooked by snakes or mice, sit this one out.

Test Track

Behind this pavilion's steely doors lies the fastest ride at Walt Disney World. In this super-charged introduction to the world of automobile testing, the ride's computer-controlled vehicles barrel up steep hills, zip down straightaways, squeak around heavily banked hairpin turns, and slam on the brakes. Test Track is much more than a thrilling ride: It's a realistic run-through of tests performed on real cars at real facilities, known as proving grounds.

As you walk through the plant, you see everything from the all-important seat-squirming test to the crucial trials endured by air bags,

tires, and the human interface clan (our courageous crash-prone counterparts) to ensure our safety. Then you hop into a six-person vehicle, fasten your seat belt, and—making note that you've got a video display, but no steering wheel or brake pedal—prepare for an exciting five-minute road trip. As the sporty open-top cars traverse the nearly one-mile track, you experience a rough-and-tumble suspension workout, become seriously indebted to antilock brakes, narrowly avoid a crash, and whiz outside and around the pavilion at speeds up to 65 miles per hour. Incredible insight into cars is a given; you'll also gain respect for the complex systems contained therein. On the way out, be sure to stop and check out the smarty-pants car demo and the "Inside Track," which features gear for car buffs.

Test Track is an altogether different experience by day and by night (you can guess which is more intense). If it's raining, we suggest you turn your face to the sky and ask yourself this question: Would I enjoy zooming down a highway in a convertible with the top down right about now?

For the least intimidating crowds, grab a Fastpass (early in the day) or jump on the single riders line

(the latter moves faster than the standby line). While Test Track may keep longer hours than other Future World attractions, the cars head to the garage when IllumiNations begins.

Note: Since this is something of a rough attraction, riders must be free from heart conditions, back and neck problems, and other physical limitations.

Mission: SPACE

Three . . . two . . . one . . . liftoff! Words you only expect to hear from flight control at Cape Canaveral are now part of the ever-expanding lexicon at Walt Disney World. Mission: SPACE is one of Epcot's most popular and engaging attractions. Its bold mission? To train guests to be astronauts.

The training process begins with guests strapping themselves into 4-person simulator pods. In lieu of an actual blastoff, guests are shot into orbit via a motion simulator—not unlike the ones real astronauts use. Former NASA advisers and astronauts worked with Disney Imagineers to lend more than a bit of authenticity to this thrill ride.

Think you have the right stuff to enjoy the original, highly intense version of this ride? Ask yourself: Do I have a heart condition? Have

I *ever* experienced motion sickness? Does moving in a circle make me queasy? Am I pregnant? Claustrophobic? Do I have *any* health issues whatsoever? If the answer to any of the above is yes or maybe, sit this one out. And consider this: Mission: SPACE is the first theme park attraction in history to provide motion-sickness bags. Still, most who don't get sick seem to enjoy it.

The good news? Epcot also provides a much gentler version of the ride for those who have health issues or simply would rather not take the risk. The experience is a bit different on this "Mission: SPACE-lite," but at least it gives everyone a chance to ride without turning green. We thoroughly enjoy the "less intense," non-spinning mission to Mars. Note that both versions have height and health restrictions. The ride-vehicle capsules are so realistically snug that claustrophobes are advised to take a pass on this one.

Universe of Energy

Behind its mirrored facade lies a pavilion on a serious power trip (it draws some of its electricity from photovoltaic cells mounted on the roof). Universe of Energy has always been notable for its lifelike dinosaurs, some of Walt Disney World's largest Audio-Animatronics animals. But the show here also boasts some familiar faces and fetches a few nominations for Best Comedy in an Epcot Pavilion. Unfortunately, it tends to be open only during peak times of year.

The Energy pavilion is given over entirely to a 45-minute presentation that explores the origins of fossil fuels and muses about alternative energy sources. **Ellen's Energy Adventure** is powered by Ellen's sudden yen for knowledge about such things when she lands on her favorite game show.

Bill Nye, the Science Guy, offers to educate a befuddled Ellen, and just happens to have some rather extensive visual aids handy. As Bill lectures Ellen, arresting visuals are shown on a series of huge screens. (Keep your eyes peeled for a cameo by a caveman you'd swear was a famous sitcom actor.)

When Bill insists they travel back 220 million years to seek greater knowledge, the seating area rotates and splits into six vehicles that then move into the clammy air of the primeval world. Here, you encounter erupting volcanoes, an eerie fog, and prehistoric creatures locked in combat, rearing up suddenly from a tide pool and gazing down at you like vultures. You also come upon an Audio-Animatronics Ellen, desperately attempting to reason with a creepy, snakelike dinosaur. She makes it out of the forest and happily hits the big time, if only in her dreams.

A large group is let into the theater every 17 minutes, so don't let a crowd scare you. If the line extends beyond the marquee, try again later.

Leave Future World by walking through Innoventions Plaza. As you head to World Showcase, be sure to look to each side. On the right, you'll pass an ATM near a spontaneously erupting fountain delivering a merciless soaking (mostly to children). Down on the left, you'll spot what appears to be an ancient pyramid. Welcome to the flip side of Future World!

World Showcase

Think of World Showcase as a handful of gourmet jelly beans, the sort so flavorful, they make your taste buds believe you're actually putting away strawberry cheesecake, champagne punch, and chocolate pudding. You know they're just jelly beans, of course, but you pretend, fully savoring the essence of that piña colada.

In the same way, World Showcase cajoles your senses into accepting its international pavilions at face value, enveloping you in such delectable representations of Germany, Japan, Mexico, and more, that you are content to play along.

This parade of nations, a cultural thoroughfare wrapped around a lagoon the size of several football fields, is marked by dramatic mood swings. The atmosphere changes markedly with each border crossing, going from positively romantic to utterly serene, toe-tappingly upbeat, patriotic, festive, wistfully Old World, or cheerfully relaxed in a matter of yards.

Of course, the World Showcase pavilions are not simply outstanding mood pieces but occasions to get uniquely acquainted with the people, history, and beauty of the world's nations. Each pavilion has a strong, unmistakable sense of place that announces itself with painstakingly re-created landmarks and faithful landscaping that ensures bougainvillea in Mexico and lotus blossoms in China. Each contributes culinary specialties from the apple-tart-to-ice-cream smorgasbord that makes World Showcase one of the hottest meal tickets in Walt Disney World.

To transport yourself totally, try to supplement the smattering of attractions—panoramic films, theater and dinner shows, boat rides, and the nightly not-to-be-missed fireworks extravaganza—with the legions of less structured pursuits.

Start by trying to catch at least one street performance per country. So frequent it's practically ongoing (check your Epcot Times Guide for schedule), this feast of live entertainment encompasses everything from mariachi bands to acrobats and belly dancing, and it makes a great accompaniment to a mobile wine-tasting. Take time, too, to chitchat with the "locals" in each village (nearly all of whom claim the represented country as their homeland).

To personalize your journey even more, make a mission of snacking, drinking, shopping, gallery-hopping, or even bench-warming your way around the World. For adults, these relaxing activities are the very essence of a visit to World Showcase.

Structurally, World Showcase is perhaps the most user-friendly area of Walt Disney World's theme parks. You may get tired walking along the 1.2-mile promenade that leads past all pavilions as it encircles the lagoon, but you won't lose your sense of direction. While locations of countries here don't

(Relatively) Quiet Escapes

Parts of Epcot boast an energy that interrupts the calm you might crave; here are some of our favorite quiet spots.

- The romantic piazza within the Italy pavilion
- Stave Church Gallery in Norway
- Benches near the reflecting pools in China
- Lagoonside benches near the gondola in Italy
- The shops in France
- Bijutsu-kan Gallery and hillside gardens in Japan
- Tucked-away garden with benches in France
- Gardens at rear of United Kingdom pavilion and Rose & Crown Pub
- Waterfall and mountain setting in Canada

correspond at all to their placement on the planet, the landscape offers a wealth of Eiffel Tower–like clues that *almost* preclude the use of a map. Because World Showcase focuses less on attractions (six of the 11 pavilions have no attractions, per se), it requires less strategic maneuvering.

If World Showcase came with instructions, the handy booklet might say:

- Touring is a clockwise or counterclockwise proposition best begun on an empty stomach.
- Shops are optimally saved for the afternoon, when the throngs from Future World have descended, lengthening lines for movies, rides, and shows.
- The movies at Canada, France, and China are often better appreciated when spaced out over two days.
- IllumiNations is the biggest entertainment draw in all of Epcot. The nightly spectacle of fireworks, lasers, and music is visible from most any point around World Showcase.

Moving along, this Epcot tour describes pavilions in the order they're encountered when entering World Showcase from Future World and walking counterclockwise around the lagoon.

Canada

In a marked departure from the real world, a refreshment stand poised a good 50 yards before the border makes it possible to arrive in Canada with a cup of Moosehead in hand. This pavilion is the site of an outstanding, recently updated, panoramic film, an "underground" steak house, interesting shops, and the coolest spot in World Showcase.

International Gateway

Think of this second entrance as Epcot's back door. The turnstiles here provide a direct "in" to World Showcase, depositing guests between the France and United Kingdom pavilions. Because the International Gateway is connected via walkway to the Yacht and Beach Club, BoardWalk, Swan, and Dolphin resorts, guests at these lodgings have exceptional access to Epcot. (Water launches also make the trip.) Note that:

- Parking at the aforementioned resorts is reserved for guests staying in them. Day guests must park in the Epcot parking lot.

- Wheelchairs are available for rent at this entrance.

- Nothing in World Showcase opens until about 11 A.M., so guests arriving earlier must walk to Future World.

- You can make a quick exit from here after IllumiNations.

It covers an impressive amount of territory in its bid to capture the distinctive beauty and cultural diversity of the Western Hemisphere's largest nation. An artful ode to the Indians of Canada's Northwest (towering totem poles and a trading post) leads to an architectural tribute to French Canada (the Hôtel du Canada here is a hybrid of Ottawa's Château Laurier and Quebec's Château Frontenac).

From here, follow the sounds of rushing water to find the cooling sprays of a mini Niagara Falls that's tucked neatly into the face of a Canadian Rocky and may be blessed with a rainbow. A feature film, a visual anthem of sorts, *O Canada!* is shown in all its Circle-Vision 360 glory within the mountain itself.

The recently updated 14-minute standing-room-only movie places you in the middle of most things Canadian, including a hard-hitting hockey game, enormous reindeer herds, and the Royal Canadian Mounted Police.

As you leave, check out the bountiful greenery inspired by the famous Butchart Gardens, in Victoria, British Columbia—while not as cool as the falls, they're still a great place to claim a bench, especially when the ever-so-engaging Off Kilter troupe of Celtic rock musicians is performing.

United Kingdom

This cheery neighborhood, which reveals its cultural identity via the bright red phone booths dotting its cobblestoned streets, is a fine place for a bit of shopping or a pint of ale. What's less obvious: the herb garden tucked behind the thatched-roof cottage (note the spearmint plants); the butterfly hatchery on the hill; and the courtyard at the rear of the pavilion, where you'll find a traditional English hedge maze.

Tired of Walking?

The *FriendShip* water taxis link Showcase Plaza at the foot of Future World with Germany and Morocco, across the lagoon at the farthest corners of World Showcase. It's convenient—but keep in mind that it may be quicker to walk.

You may even catch a decidedly Beatles-esque rock group that performs in the garden. A table at the Rose & Crown Pub is the best perspective from which to view this pavilion, because the Tudor, Georgian, and Victorian structures seem all the more real from the window of a friendly pub.

Architectural enlightenment is a great excuse to dally in the fine shops. You can cover 300 years of building styles just by walking from the slate floor of The Tea Caddy straight through to the carpeted room with the Waterford crystal chandelier, which signals your arrival at the Neoclassical period and the shop known as The Queen's Table.

France

A footbridge from the United Kingdom leads across a picturesque canal to one of the most romantic areas of World Showcase. Petite streets and Eiffel Tower aside, you're looking at Paris during the *Belle Epoque* ("beautiful age") of the late 19th century.

The one-time Parisian institution Les Halles is re-created here, as is a one-tenth-scale Eiffel Tower that would be infinitely more evocative were it not so obviously perched atop a

For the Lovebirds. . .

Epcot's World Showcase has some romantic spots, namely:

- The lovely courtyard at the rear of the United Kingdom
- Italy's piazza and gondola landing
- Every inch of France

building. Luxurious boutiques, sidewalk cafes, and, of course, pastries that announce their presence *par avion* are among the big draws here, as is the wine-tasting counter at the nicely stocked La Maison du Vin. Beckoning, too, is one of the most peaceful spots in all of Epcot—a quiet park on the canal side of the pavilion that might have leapt off the canvas of Georges Seurat's *A Sunday Afternoon on the Island of La Grande Jatte*.

But the biggest lure here is the 18-minute film ***Impressions de France***, which puts its five 21-by-27-foot screens to terrific use in a *tour de France* that ranges from Alpine skiing to the foothills of buttery pastries. If you know France, you'll love it; if you aren't familiar with the country, you'll want to be. The superb score, featuring French classical composers, could stand on its own. *Impressions de France* is least congested during the morning and early evening hours.

Morocco

This enchanting area—arguably the most meticulously crafted of all the represented nations—also happens to be one of the loudest World Showcase pavilions. The authenticity has something to do with the fact that nine tons of tile were handmade, hand-cut, and hand-laid by Moroccan artisans into the mosaics seen here. The prayer tower at the entrance takes after the famous Koutoubia Minaret, in Marrakesh. The Bab Boujouloud gate, patterned after one in the city of Fez, leads to the Medina (old part of the city), a tangled array of narrow passageways where baskets, leather goods, and brass items are among the wares for sale.

The Medina also brings you to the entrance of the Marrakesh restaurant, notable for its North African menu, its belly dancers, and the fact that it's one of the only full-service restaurants in World Showcase where you can often get a table without advance reservations. You can also savor Mediterranean-style chicken, beef, and lamb sandwiches, salads, and desserts at the more casual Tangierine Cafe.

Stop at Mo'Rockin' for Arabic rhythms with a contemporary flair. Make a point of checking out the extraordinary tile work and costumes displayed at the Gallery of Arts and History, and be on the lookout for visiting artisans demonstrating their crafts.

It's interesting to note that the gardens are irrigated by an ancient working waterwheel located on the promenade. Morocco is easily toured any time of day. If you'd like a more structured look at the pavilion, sign up for a guided tour at the

Where the Art Is

Exhibits change periodically, but here's an indication of what you can expect to see:

- American Heritage in The American Adventure presents "National Treasures"—featuring the likes of George Washington's chair and Thomas Edison's phonograph.

- Mexico's "Animales Fantasticos" exhibit features traditional wood carvings of Oaxaca.

- Norway's tiny Stave Church Gallery hosts a Viking exhibit.

- Japan's Bijutsu-kan Gallery becomes a toy museum with "The Kitahara Collection of Tin Toys."

- Morocco's Gallery of Arts and History showcases intricate tile work and costumes.

- China's House of Whispering Willows hosts an exhibit called "Tomb Warriors—Guardian Spirits of Ancient China."

Morocco National Tourist Office inside. The complimentary tours last from 20 to 40 minutes and are available at 1, 3, and 5 P.M.

Japan

As quietly inviting as Morocco is vibrantly enticing, Japan is a pavilion of considerable beauty and serenity. Its most prominent landmarks are the red torii gate (a good-luck symbol), which stands close to the lagoon, and the five-tiered pagoda, created in the mold of an eighth-century shrine located in Nara. Each level of the pagoda represents one of the elements that, according to Buddhist teachings, produced everything in the universe (from bottom to top: earth, water, fire, wind, and sky).

The most compelling features of this pavilion are the entertainment (Matsuriza drummers), the elaborate detail of its manicured

gardens, and an art exhibit called "The Kitahara Collection of Tin Toys" at the Bijutsu-kan Gallery.

Japan also claims one of the largest shops in Epcot. Housed inside a structure reminiscent of a section of the Gosho Imperial Palace, which was originally constructed in Kyoto in 794 A.D., the Mitsukoshi department store counts bonsai trees, kimonos, dolls, tea sets, incense, jewelry, and decorative ceremonial swords among its offerings.

All that shopping may spark your appetite. At Teppan Edo, a feast consisting of vegetables, steak, chicken, and seafood is prepared tableside by authentic Japanese chefs.

The American Adventure

The centerpiece of World Showcase is so devoted to Americana, it can bring out the Norman Rockwell in you even when you're cranky. Housed in a Colonial-style manse that combines elements of Independence Hall, the Old State House in Boston, Monticello, and various structures in Colonial Williamsburg, it's dressed for the part.

The 28-minute show inside—an evocative multimedia presentation about American history—is among Disney's best, both for its astonishingly detailed sets and sophisticated Audio-Animatronics figures and for its ability to rouse goose bumps from unsuspecting patriots. Ben Franklin and Mark Twain lead what's been called "a hundred-yard dash capturing the spirit of the country at specific moments in time."

A superb a cappella vocal group, the Voices of Liberty, sometimes entertains in the lobby before the show begins.

The wait for The American Adventure attraction can be long because the show itself is lengthy, so check a park Times Guide or stop by for curtain times and plan accordingly.

This patriotic pavilion also features an All-American fast-food restaurant and the lagoon-side **America Gardens Theatre**, where you just may find some stirring entertainment. An interesting aside: The garden alongside The American Adventure pavilion acknowledges the days before red, white, and blue by showcasing different plants used traditionally by Native Americans for food as well as for medicinal purposes.

Finally, be sure to check out the National Treasures exhibit inside the pavilion. Items change, but expect to see things like original Thomas Edison inventions and an authentic World War II Purple Heart medal.

Italy

This little Italy is defined by an abiding you-are-there ambience and meticulous authenticity that extends from the gondolas tied to striped moorings at the pavilion's very own Venetian island to the homemade spaghetti at its popular restaurant.

Look to the very top of the scaled-down Venetian campanile dominating the romantic piazza here and you'll see an angel covered in gold leaf that was molded into a spitting image of the one atop the bell tower in the real St. Mark's Square in Venice.

The Doge's Palace here is so faithfully rendered that its facade resembles the marbled pattern of the original. Adding to the effect are tall, slender stands of Italian cypress, replicas of Venetian statues, an abundance of potted flowers, and fragrant olive and citrus trees.

This Italy pavilion has no major attractions per se, but between its memorable street performers and the strolling musicians, it has all the entertainment it needs.

Among the various shopping options is a gem of a gourmet food purveyor, called La Bottega Italiana, that also stocks fine Italian wines.

Germany

In a word: *oompah*. Arguably the most festive country in all of World Showcase, Germany is immediately recognizable by its fairy-tale architecture. To the rear of the central cobblestoned square (which is named for Saint George), you'll see an enormous cuckoo clock, complete with Hummel figurines that emerge on the hour. Immediately past this clock lies the Biergarten, the vast restaurant and entertainment hall that—thanks to spirited dinner shows primed with German beer, sausages, and yodelers— serves as the pinnacle of this festive pavilion's entertainment.

Germany also scores with tempting shops and the Wein-keller, which offers wine-tasting

opportunities. Outside, note the miniature 1930s German village, complete with castle, farmhouse, monastery, and even a wee commuter railroad. Germany is easily toured at any time of day.

China

This pavilion is marked by a dramatic half-scale replica of Beijing's Temple of Heaven set behind stands of whistling bamboo and quiet reflecting pools. Traditional Chinese music wafts over the sound system. In addition to its gardens, the pavilion features the House of Whispering Willows, an exhibit of ancient art and artifacts from well-known collections that's always worth a look. Live entertainment here is invariably stirring, especially when it's a demonstration by the local acrobats.

Another reason to visit China

is the Circle-Vision 360 film shown in the Temple of Heaven. Basically, you stand and **Reflections of China** whisks you on a 12-minute, blink-and-you've-missed-the-Great Wall journey that reflects the ways in which China has changed over the past 20 years—with the addition of Hong Kong and Macau. From ancient Mongolia and Beijing's Forbidden City to ultra-modern Shanghai, the film provides fascinating glimpses of China and its people. Pay close attention to the fleeting, mist-enshrouded Huangshan Mountain, if you can; the filming of this amazing view of China was no small endeavor. The film crew and 40 laborers had to haul the 600-pound camera nearly a mile uphill for those three seconds of footage. Note that there are no seats in the theater.

You won't go hungry here—the pavilion is home to a duo of eateries: Nine Dragons and Lotus Blossom Cafe.

Norway

This 11th addition to the World Showcase landscape is immediately intriguing. A curious array of buildings rings the pavilion's cobblestoned square, including a reproduction of a wooden stave church (an endangered species of sorts, with just 28 remaining in Norway) and a replica of the 14th-century Akershus Castle that still stands in Oslo's harbor. Beside a grassy-roofed, thick-logged structure, there's a statue of a Norwegian running champion, living legend Grete Waitz. This Land of the Midnight Sun has added some twists to the World Showcase lineup—among them, the promise of troll encounters and Norwegian handicrafts of the hand-knit sweater variety.

The stave church houses an exhibit about Vikings (don't skip it, if only to see the inside of this teensy church). But Norway scores with **Maelstrom**, a trip in dragon-headed boats through Viking territory that is enjoyable, if not thrilling. A voyage that surprises you with a troll here, a backward plunge there, a sudden waterfall here, a storm there,

Maelstrom doesn't throw big punches; but it keeps you guessing.

The 5-minute trip lets you out at a Norwegian village, then finishes up with a film on the essence of Norway. If you'd like to take an in-depth look at this pavilion or learn more about Norway, stop at the Tourism Information desk at the end of the ride. Free tours are given twice daily.

Mexico

There's no mistaking this pavilion's identity. A wild thicket of tropical foliage leads to a great pyramid. Inside, you wend your way through a brief but engaging cultural exhibit to the main event. What you see next—a thoroughly romantic vision of a quaint Mexican village at dusk— is among the most escapist visions in World Showcase. True to form, there are stands selling colorful

sombreros, baskets, pottery, and piñatas. In the rear of the plaza, note the dimly lit San Angel Inn and, behind it, the river and smoking volcano.

Here, too, you'll find the embarkation point for the **Gran Fiesta Tour Starring The Three Caballeros**, a colorful boat ride through Mexico. It involves the disappearance of one Donald Duck and the quest by José and Panchito to find him in time for the caballeros' big reunion performance in Mexico City. Note that the mariachi band that performs at this imposing pavilion is quite good.

Drinks Around the World

There's Samuel Adams lager at The American Adventure and at least one good imported excuse to bend the ol' elbow in each World Showcase country. Namely: Moosehead and more from carts in Canada; shandies, Guinness, black and tans, Tennent's, and beyond from the Rose & Crown Pub in the United Kingdom; a bottle of Kronenbourg from the Boulangerie Pâtisserie or a glass of wine from La Maison du Vin in France; Kirin beer or sake specialty drinks in Japan; vino from Italy can be sampled (with a pastry, of course) at La Bottega Italiana in Italy; Beck's beer and Kreusch Reisling wine at Germany's Sommerfest; Chinese wine and beer at the Lotus Blossom Cafe; Carlsberg drafts in Norway; and what else but margaritas at a stand near Mexico's Cantina de San Angel.

DISNEY'S HOLLYWOOD STUDIOS

Like an actress just right for the part, Disney's Hollywood Studios is perfectly cast as the vivacious, showbiz-obsessed theme park that is seemingly incapable of keeping a secret. Since its debut, this park has worked to make the transition from sidekick to leading lady, and it has succeeded.

Think of the Studios as the adults' Magic Kingdom: magical, but in a more sophisticated way; marked by a whimsicality far more ageless than that which  pervades the Magic Kingdom. Sure, it has a Beauty and the Beast stage show, and there's a funny 3-D Muppet movie, but these hardly constitute a satellite Fantasyland. At times the Studios even seems to have been scripted for a mature crowd, crafted with a wink of the eye by (and for) grown-ups to elicit knowing laughs and no-holds-barred nostalgia.

GETTING ORIENTED: Disney's Hollywood Studios is smaller than Epcot, but somewhat difficult to navigate since it has no distinctive shape or main artery. You enter the park—and 1940s Tinseltown—via Hollywood Boulevard, a bustling shopping venue. The first major intersection you come to is Sunset Boulevard, an equally starry-eyed venue that branches off to the right of Hollywood Boulevard; this shopping and entertainment strip ends in a cul-de-sac right at the foot of the park's tallest (and spookiest) landmark, the 199-foot Tower of Terror.

Hollywood Boulevard ends where The Great Movie Ride begins—at a convincing replica of Grauman's (formerly Mann's) Chinese Theatre. This ornate building is tucked behind the 12-story Sorcerer Mickey hat, the most centrally located landmark at the Studios; the plaza fronting

Disney's Hollywood Studios Hours

The park is usually open from about 9 A.M. to about sunset; hours are extended during holiday weekends and summer months and abbreviated during slower periods. Some shows don't open until late morning, depending on the season. Call 407-824-4321 for schedules. One-day admission is about $75 (plus tax) for adults. Prices are subject to change.

it is called Hollywood Plaza. If you stand in Hollywood Plaza facing Disney's Chinese Theater, you'll see an archway off to your right; this leads to Pixar Place, an area with a backstage feel, where a backlot tour and an interactive trip with the gang from *Toy Story* are among the attractions. If you make a left off Hollywood Boulevard and proceed past Echo Lake, you are on course for such attractions as Sounds Dangerous Starring Drew Carey, Indiana Jones Epic Stunt Spectacular, and Star Tours. Just past Star Tours lies one more entertainment pocket. Muppet*Vision 3-D is the main draw here, together with realistic reproductions of American city streets. Walk left past the skyscraper end of the street and you're on a track back to Hollywood Plaza and the Chinese Theater.

A Walking Tour

Just inside the gates, you may be too distracted by the bright Art Deco looks of Hollywood Boulevard to notice a building on your left. This is Guest Relations, where you can go for information as well as first aid. Stop here or at Crossroads of the World (the gift stand in the center of the entrance plaza) to pick up a guidemap if you need one. To your immediate right, check out Oscar's Super Service, which has a 1949 Chevrolet tow truck parked out front. This is one of several striking and utterly unscratched classic autos you'll notice along the streets. (We're not sure how they got through the turnstiles.) Oscar's is the spot for lockers and wheelchair rentals; the Lost and Found, along with package pickup, is right next door. There is an ATM just outside the turnstiles here.

Hollywood Boulevard

One look at this main drag and you have a hunch you're not in Central Florida anymore. The strip oozes star quality with a Mae West sort of subtlety. Movie tunes from Hollywood's Golden Age waft through the air. Palm

Hot Tips

- Many guests adore Fantasmic!, a look into the dream world of Mickey Mouse, highlighted by fireworks, lasers, and special effects. This lavish musical is very popular, so plan ahead: If there are two shows, opt for the second, and allow 90 minutes before showtime for good seating (we recommend sitting toward the back for the best view—and the easiest exit). It is presented on select nights.

- There is a walking path that leads from the Studios to the Board-Walk resort area and on to Epcot. (It takes about 20 minutes.)

trees make like Fred and Ginger in the tropical breeze. Streamlined storefronts with neon and chrome Art Deco flourishes line the boulevard like would-be movie sets hoping to get noticed.

Note that the shops along Hollywood Boulevard typically stay open about a half hour after the rest of the park has closed. (Consult the "Shopping" section in the *Diversions* chapter for specifics on our favorite shops; wares generally include a sampling of movie memorabilia and plenty of Disney character merchandise.)

However you get there, it's important to stop at the corner of Hollywood and Sunset boulevards to check the **Tip Board** (it lists current wait times for popular studios' attractions).

Until 1 P.M., this is also the place to make advance reservations for full-service restaurants.

Sunset Boulevard

This Studios block is a broad, colorful avenue every bit as glamorous as Hollywood Boulevard. It has the same high-cheekbone style and its own stock of towering palms, evocative facades, and tempting shops. It also has stage presence, in the form of the 1,500-seat Theater of the Stars amphitheater, where you can see live performances of *Beauty and the Beast*. Sunset Boulevard begins innocently enough, with a friendly farmers' market, and a shop called Once Upon A Time that's in a replica of the Carthay Circle Theatre where *Snow White and the Seven Dwarfs* premiered. But don't let your guard down: the white-knuckle Tower of Terror looms at the end of the road.

Somehow, **Beauty and the Beast—Live on Stage**, a lively

production that was the *raison d'être* behind the Broadway musical, manages to remain oblivious to its eerie neighbor. The show is 30 minutes of rich music, costuming, choreography, and uplifting entertainment. While a canopy keeps the sun's heat at bay, we still aim for an evening performance during the summer. For early birds, note that this show generally opens soon after the park does.

Then there's **The Twilight Zone™ Tower of Terror**, a hair-raising experience. Because few of us have a natural yen to drop several stories (more than once, we might add) down a dark elevator shaft, this one requires some bravery. It helps to know what to expect. And, if you're brave enough to ride more than once, you may experience a whole new sequence of ups and downs!

Basically, "guests" enter the mysteriously abandoned Hollywood Tower Hotel and are invited into a library, where even the cobwebs seem to be circa 1939. Here, Rod Serling appears on a black-and-white television set to brief you (dark, stormy night, Halloween 1939, lightning strikes, guests disappear from hotel elevator) and welcome you to tonight's episode of *The Twilight Zone™*.

When you reach a boarding area—last call for chickening out—and file into an elevator, look at the diagram above the doors and pray you haven't been assigned to the front row. Once you are seated and seat belts are secured, the doors shut and the elevator ascends. You're soon so entranced by astonishing special effects—apparitions that appear in a corridor that vaporizes into a dark, star-filled sky and a gigantic eye straight from the fifth dimension—that dread becomes (almost) secondary. When the

elevator moves over into a second, pitch-black shaft, anything can happen, since Disney's Imagineers deviously transformed this ride from a two-screamer into a five-screamer. The bottom falls out more than once, and not subtly: Multiple plummets are scripted. One thing's for sure: Your cue to strike a great casual pose is when you're at the top of the shaft. You want to look good in the group picture, which is taken as a panorama of the park suddenly gives way to a drop. The plunges are incredibly fast downward pulls with surprisingly smooth landings. It may be a small comfort, perhaps, but the really hairy part is over faster than many vocal cords are able to respond.

A few notes: The jitters tend to stay with you a bit after the 12-minute drama has ended. If you have back or neck problems, a heart condition, or are pregnant, we suggest you pass on this one.

If you've been on the ride before, you're no doubt familiar with the "scary seat." That used to be the lone seat that had a simple lap belt as opposed to a sturdy steel bar as restraint. Well, the good news is: Every seat is now a scary seat! Yep, the lap bars are history.

If you're willing (and able) to continue the thrill fest after your tumultuous stay in The Holly-

Touring Priorities

DON'T MISS	DON'T OVERLOOK	DON'T KNOCK YOURSELF OUT
Tower of Terror*	Voyage of The Little Mermaid*	Honey, I Shrunk the Kids Movie Set Adventure
Toy Story Mania!*	Indiana Jones Epic Stunt Spectacular!*/**	Playhouse Disney—Live on Stage!
Muppet*Vision 3-D		
The Great Movie Ride	Studio Backlot Tour	Sounds Dangerous— Starring Drew Carey
Beauty and the Beast —Live on Stage**	Lights, Motors, Action! Extreme Stunt Show	
Rock 'n' Roller Coaster*	Star Tours*	* Fastpass attraction as of press time. Consult a guidemap for new additions.
Block Party Bash	Walt Disney: One Man's Dream	
Fantasmic!		**Pay close attention to performance schedules.
The American Idol Experience	The Magic of Disney Animation	

wood Tower Hotel, get ready to shake, rattle, and roll on the **Rock 'n' Roller Coaster**. As the first WDW roller coaster to flip you upside down, this dark, indoor, steel construction goes from zero to 60 miles per hour in just under three seconds.

The premise: You've just scored backstage passes and VIP transport to a sold-out Aerosmith concert at the Hollywood Bowl. During your drive through Southern California, you twist and turn to a rockin' sound-track—and feel like you may have stepped inside a runaway music video.·

Pay attention to the warning

signs posted as you enter the ride. If you have back or neck problems, a heart condition, or if you're pregnant, sit this one out. Finally, we urge you *not* to try it on a full stomach. (We made that mistake once. It wasn't pretty.)

Animation Courtyard & Pixar Place

Adjacent to Sunset Boulevard and Hollywood Boulevard is the section of the park that takes you under the sea with a diminutive mermaid and into working television production studios. Passing under an archway located off Hollywood Plaza, you see Animation Courtyard immediately in front of you, with Pixar Place to your left.

(Relatively) Quiet Escapes

- Starring Rolls Cafe
- Tune-In Lounge
- Far corners of the Sunset Ranch Market (between meal rush hours)
- Benches on Sunset Boulevard near Theater of the Stars
- Shaded benches around Echo Lake
- Brownstone stoops in the Streets of America area

Since Disney shut down the working Animation studio, this attraction has dropped a notch in appeal. However, we still consider **The Magic of Disney Animation** a worthwhile detour, if no longer a must-see.

The **Studio Backlot Tour** is a two-pronged gig that begins with an entertaining six-minute demo of how a realistic sea storm or naval battle might be filmed. The second segment, a 30-minute tram ride, starts calmly enough, but sit on the right side to stay dry. You visit the wardrobe area and the lights, camera, and props departments. (The backlot's "Residential Street" of famous facades, which used to be part of the tour, is but a memory.) All of a sudden, there you are,

smack-dab in the middle of a special-effects zone called Catastrophe Canyon, which specializes in nature's wrath: violent downpours, fiery explosions, flash floods, and the like. Things calm down with a visit to a realistic-looking city street. (It's a neighborhood of building facades made mostly of fiberglass and Styrofoam.) Lines here tend to be shorter in the late afternoon (ask the attendant for an ETA, and if it's more than 30 minutes, check back later). The tour exits through the **American Film Institute Showcase**, a revolving display of costumes, props, and partial sets that features interactive elements related to film lore and legends.

At the Lights! Camera! Action! theater, you won't want to miss **Walt Disney: One Man's Dream**, a tribute to the man who really did start it all. A combination artifact-filled walk-through exhibit and retrospective film, the attraction looks at the life and times of Walter Elias Disney as both imagineer and innovator. Its neighbor, the dazzling (and ludicrously popular) **Toy Story Mania!**, is Disney Imagineers' highly ambitious follow-up to the Magic Kingdom's beloved Buzz Lightyear attraction. Here, guests enjoy a similar "Yowsa—I've morphed into a character *inside* a video game!" experience . . . and then some. High-tech digital imagery, "spring-action shooters," and 3-D glasses make for one eye-popping, giddy "midway game" adventure. It's a hit with riders of all ages.

The newest kid on the block—**The American Idol Experience**— hit the scene in 2009. The star of this show? It just might be you. And you might be TV's next American Idol! How? Guests have a chance to win an audition for the real show. So start rehearsing now! But if you'd rather not take on Disney's "Simon," just grab a seat and prepare to vote for your favorite contestant. Note that one need not be familiar with the TV show to get a major kick out of this energetic re-creation.

If you can get near **Voyage of The Little Mermaid**—and at this 15-minute musical adapted from the movie, that's no easy task—give it a go. What makes the show so compelling is the upbeat music, amusing puppetry, the occasion to watch children ogle this real, live mermaid *whose tail is moving*, and the mist-infused feeling that you are underwater. Check the Times

The Mouse Is Spoken For

Walt Disney himself supplied the voice for Mickey Mouse from 1928 to 1946.

Guide for schedule. Seats in the middle to back rows afford the best views.

Only if you're eager to return to your *Romper Room* roots, follow the trail of giddy toddlers to **Playhouse Disney—Live On Stage!** (keeping in mind that there are no seats in the theater, though you are welcome to sit on the floor). If this isn't your speed, it's time to move on to bigger and better things.

Echo Lake Area

Heading back through the archway into Hollywood Plaza, you come upon **The Great Movie Ride**. This drive-through theater of sorts is a classic in its own right and the best ticket we know to a quick video rental decision your next time out. Housed in an artful replica of Grauman's Chinese

Theatre, this impressive 22-minute attraction is bursting with Audio-Animatronics figures that bring motion-picture legends and moments from almost every genre to life. It's "Chim Chim Cher-ee" meets "Here's looking at you, kid," cigarette-puffing Clint Eastwood meets broom-brandishing Wicked Witch of the West, *Alien* meets *Singin' in the Rain,* and then some—be prepared for surprises.

The ride has meticulous detailing and astounding realism. And with a queue that winds by *Wizard of Oz* and *Mary Poppins* props and a screening of famous movie scenes, it provides one of the most entertaining waits in WDW (or anywhere, for that matter).

Heading through Hollywood Plaza toward Echo Lake, the next spot you encounter is the ABC Sound Studio, home of **Sounds Dangerous—Starring Drew Carey**. But you'd better arrive all ears. Expect 12 of the most interesting minutes you have ever spent wearing headphones—in the dark. Easy listening this is not.

Here's the deal: You're attending a sneak preview of a live-action TV show that stars Drew Carey as an undercover detective. Thanks to a camera discreetly tucked into Carey's tie tack, you see everything his tie tack wishes it could see. And, of course, no one whispers, crashes, or so much as whimpers during the determined detective's madcap pursuit of diamond smugglers without word—or major vibrations—getting back to your headphones.

When a bad move by a panic-stricken Carey (open mouth, insert camera) zaps the television picture, you have no choice but to follow the action in the dark. Those clean ears you toted into the theater strain and contort with every twist in the furious plot. Fully enveloped in the audacious realism of 3-D audio, you attempt to sit calmly while your ears carry you into a swarm of 5,000 restless bees.

Listen carefully and marvel at the palpable snip, snip, snip of the barber's scissors. Your head will spin with the wildly screeching tires of Carey's speeding car. And as attuned as you become, you'll likely still be unprepared for the

A Striking Resemblance

- Chinese Theater—Grauman's Chinese Theatre in Hollywood

- Once Upon A Time storefront—Carthay Circle Theatre in Hollywood, where Disney's *Snow White* premiered

- Mickey's of Hollywood storefront—Frederick's of Hollywood

- Muppet*Vision 3-D theater—the theater from *The Muppet Show*

- Hollywood Brown Derby—Brown Derby of Hollywood's heyday

finale (think close encounters with a circus elephant). *Note that this attraction may not be operating in all of 2010.*

If you are a fan of the action-movie genre, it's worth risking life and limb to catch a performance of the **Indiana Jones Epic Stunt Spectacular!** Arrive a good 45 minutes before showtime to snare a seat toward the front of the 2,000-seat amphitheater. The half-hour performance steals its thunder from *Raiders of the Lost Ark* and begins with the selection of a few fearless "extras" (they're put to use during a scene involving a sword fight in Cairo).

Nimble stuntpeople perform one death-defying caper after another, leaping between buildings, dodging snipers and boulders, and eluding fiery explosions. You feel the heat of the flames, you fear for the Harrison Ford look-alike. Tricks of the trade are revealed and you're *still* impressed. The Indiana Jones Epic Stunt Spectacular nearly always plays to capacity audiences, so your best bet for getting a great seat is the first or last show of the day. Seating begins 30 minutes prior to each performance. Keep in mind that a Fastpass does not guarantee a seat.

As exciting as the Indiana Jones Epic Stunt Spectacular is, the attraction just around the corner packs even more punch. At **Star Tours**, you don't sit in an amphitheater; you strap yourself into a flight simulator.

You don't live vicariously through professional stuntpeople; you experience the sensation of

VIP Tour Allure

You may have seen them in the theme parks—those perky people in the plaid vests. They are VIP guides, happily leading guests on customized trips through Walt Disney World.

The VIP program minimizes the hassle factor while maximizing the overall magic component. In addition to the aforementioned guide, tours entitle guests to special seating for many stage shows and parades. VIP transportation is also an option. For pricing information or to make a reservation, call 407-560-4033.

barreling through space at the speed of light for yourself. The premise: Enterprising droids R2-D2 and C-3PO are working for an intergalactic travel agency whose fleet of spacecraft makes regular trips to the Moon of Endor. As luck would have it, you draw a rookie pilot who gives new meaning to "reckless abandon." Soon you're spiraling through space, dodging lasers and giant ice crystals.

Why might one consider passing up Star Tours? It's pretty bumpy. Skip it if you just ate, have a heart condition, experience motion sickness, or are pregnant. The lines are generally shortest in the morning, with shorter waits the rest of the day.

Streets of America

Moving along, you arrive at the Studios' back corner. This is a glimpse at several American cityscapes—with a few alterations, including the Empire State Building's dimensions and the size of the puppet population (correction: *Muppet* population).

The special effects–laden presentation of **Muppet*Vision 3-D** may have been around a while, but it's still fabulously entertaining. Miss it and you've deprived your sense of humor. So head straight for the Muppet theater

and fill up on a 25-minute stream of amusing Muppet antics that push the creative envelope of 3-D movies with such effects as a cannon blast through the screen, some bubble magic, and a floating banana cream pie. (Yes, Muppet fans, the curmudgeons from Jim Henson's *The Muppet Show* are in attendance, in their familiar balcony spot, cynical and crotchety as ever.)

After bonding with the Muppets, stroll along the city street, where you can take in the skyline or sit down on a stoop. A sign in the window of our favorite brownstone cautions NO SOLICITING, but it says nothing about stoop trespassing. So we take a seat, do some people-watching, and simply gaze at the Empire State Building. Disney used a technique called forced perspective to make the four-story version here appear to have

102 floors. If passersby ask for directions, it's good to know that the **Honey, I Shrunk the Kids Movie Set Adventure** playground is behind one of the facades here. And if they want to know where to find Pizza Planet Arcade, tell them it's across from the Muppets.

Ever wonder how Hollywood pulls off high-speed car chases, ominous motorcycle leaps, and other seemingly death-defying displays? Some of your questions should be answered by the "insiders" hosting the **Lights, Motors, Action! Extreme Stunt Show**. It offers a behind-the-scenes peek at the techniques used to pull off some of the most astounding stunts. Inspired by the popular Stunt Show Spectacular in Disneyland Paris, the high-octane show stars specially designed cars, motorcycles, and Jet Skis.

There is ample seating in the stadium, but it's always wise to arrive 20 or more minutes before showtime.

Entertainment

Disney's Tinseltown sticks close to its Hollywood heritage in its live entertainment. Because the marquee is ever changing, it's essential to check a Times Guide. Don't be surprised if you run into budding starlets and gossip columnists along Hollywood Boulevard.

Block Party Bash, a high-energy extravaganza, is a unique twist on the parade concept. Led by *Toy Story*'s Green Army Men and featuring favorite stars from classic Disney•Pixar films, it includes rolling stages (which stop rolling to allow for mini shows within the show), acrobats, trampolines, and audience participation.

Last, but hardly least: Fantasmic!— a 26-minute extravaganza— cranes necks in a lagoon-endowed amphitheater behind Tower of Terror. Shown just after dusk (on select nights), this expression of Mickey's dreams (and nightmares) is filled with dancing fountains, characters, and special effects synchronized to classic Disney tunes. Note that the best seats are actually toward the back of the theater.

DISNEY'S ANIMAL KINGDOM

So strong is this park's sense of purpose that it's as if the animals of the world put their antlers and antennae together and created it themselves—to celebrate their aardvark-to-zebra diversity, remind us of their prehistoric heritage, and rally support for wildlife conservation efforts. Not that Disney's creative hand isn't greatly evident in this park.

Endangered-species breeding programs coexist with blockbuster attractions. Sophisticated Audio-Animatronics dinosaurs share the marquee with more than 1,700 animals (some 250 species), whose habitat needs dictate much of the landscape. (One glimpse at the park and it's no surprise that Animal Kingdom is accredited by the American Zoo and Aquarium Association, an organization that

supports conservation, education, science, and recreation.)

GETTING ORIENTED: Although greenery reigns in these parts, relegating concrete, and indeed most architecture, to garnish status, successful penetration of this particular jungle requires no compasses, scythes, or snakebite kits. The park is set up as a set of themed lands decidedly unlike any you've encountered in your neighborhood.

To see the forest through the trees, look up: Like the icons of its Worldly siblings, Animal Kingdom's Tree of Life serves as an instant beacon for the momentarily disoriented. This massive spectacle also anchors the park's most central land, Discovery Island.

The layout of this park might be compared to the silhouette of a simple daisy. Acting as the stem is the lush expanse of the

Oasis. Discovery Island (the land that serves as the park's hub), encircled by a river, is the flower's center. And extending from the center like petals are bridges leading sharply southeast to the primeval area known as DinoLand U.S.A.; northeast to Asia; northwest to Africa, the park's largest land; and southwest to Camp Minnie-Mickey, a character vacationland.

It's true that Disney's Animal Kingdom is more than double Epcot's size, but thanks to the considerable roaming room designated for animal residents only, it takes no more legwork to circumnavigate this park than to explore Epcot. As anyone who's been to Epcot can attest, this is still a good amount of walking—so follow our efficient touring plan and take advantage of the park's many pleasant resting spots. Seniors who opt to tour the smaller parks on foot may choose to rent a wheelchair at Animal Kingdom—or better yet, given the steep inclines throughout the park, a self-driven Electric Convenience Vehicle (ECV).

A Walking Tour

Our tour begins much like any other intrepid adventure, assuming that intrepid adventurers have inexplicably omitted mention of turnstiles that must be traversed en route from urbane Central Florida to the Great Unknown. No matter. You're about to be enveloped by **The Oasis**, a canopy of nature that serves as

Touring Priorities

DON'T MISS

Expedition Everest*
Finding Nemo—The Musical**
Kilimanjaro Safaris*
Dinosaur*
Maharajah Jungle Trek
It's Tough to be a Bug!*
Festival of the Lion King**
Flights of Wonder
Pangani Forest Exploration Trail

DON'T OVERLOOK

Rafiki's Planet Watch
Discovery Island Trails
The Oasis
Kali River Rapids*

DON'T KNOCK YOURSELF OUT

The Boneyard
TriceraTop Spin
Primeval Whirl*

* Fastpass attraction as of press time. Consult a guidemap for new additions.

** Pay close attention to performance schedules.

Animal Kingdom's inviting foyer. Two paths lead north to Discovery Island and the looming Tree of Life. As you proceed farther into the fragrant tangle of tropical trees and flowers, allow yourself to be distracted by waterfall-laden streams and glimpses of macaws, iguanas, and giant anteaters. Then tell yourself it's all a mirage and move on.

Emerging from the northern reaches of The Oasis entry zone, you arrive at a bridge to Discovery Island and receive your cue to gasp—a panoramic view of Animal Kingdom's central land, the moatlike river, the soaring Tree of Life, and the balance of the park before you.

Discovery Island

Exotic in a neither-here-northere-but-certainly-not-North America sense, Discovery Island is awash in the sort of vivid color paintbrushes dream about imparting. Meticulously carved and painted building facades and smatterings of Balinese folk art add to the eye-catching allure of environs intended to replicate a village in the tropics. Notable as the land that serves as the gateway to all other Animal Kingdom lands, it also happens

to be the park's core dining and shopping zone.

Take a minute to glance at the **Tip Board**, listing showtimes and current waiting times for popular attractions. This board is on the right as you enter Discovery Island. Checking the board to align your schedule with certain showtimes (listed in a park Times Guide) will help you structure your day.

The big draw here is the **Tree of Life**. The man-made tree looms 145 feet over the park as its main icon. Even dung beetles have their place on this arboreal masterpiece, whose 50-foot-wide trunk and windblown limbs contain nose-to-nose carvings of every animal Disney artists could fit. Certainly, Mickey's lineage is represented. The

carvings are a tribute to the richness and diversity of animal life on our planet.

Don't neglect to check out the cockatoos, flamingos, deer, and other wildlife living among the tree's roots along **Discovery Island Trails**.

Before you leave the Tree of Life vicinity, consider the possible advantages of starting small. If you can bear eight minutes of animated insects creeping and crawling into your personal space, see **It's Tough to be a Bug!**, a 3-D special-effects show put on—where else?—inside the tree. It's a decidedly Off-Broadway show, starring Flik (from the film *A Bug's Life*) and a cast of a million bugs whose previous credits include such shows as *Beauty and the Bees* and *My Fair Ladybug*.

You become an honorary bug in an effort to understand their world, but things go awry when several of Flik's buddies don't appreciate a visit from you.

After a demonstration of their talents, you may suddenly cease to be fazed by any creature with fewer than six legs.

Note: Anyone leery of spiders, roaches, and the like is advised to skip the performance, or risk being seriously bugged.

DinoLand U.S.A.

Once you stroll beneath the big brachiosaurus skeleton, you'll enter what appears to be a kitschy park created around a remote paleontological dig site.

This zone features intimate rendezvous with winners (crocodiles), as well as sore losers of the Cretaceous period's Survival of the Meteorproof. The big attraction here is **Dinosaur**, a time-travel trip fraught with asteroids and frightening run-ins with Disney's largest and most realistic Audio-Animatronics figures yet.

A 3½-minute thrill attraction, Dinosaur is inside the Dino Institute, a museum-like building that reveals nothing of the fast, jarring ride ahead. Of course, there's a larger mission that has nothing to do with the desire for an adrenaline rush and everything to do with the selfless intention to save an iguanodon. (Don't worry, we'll explain.) Basically, you have it on good authority that if you shoot 65 million years back in time, there's a chance you can bring back an iguanodon for paleontologists to study. The catch: You must do this seconds before the meteor blast thought to have sealed the dinosaurs' fate and ended the Cretaceous period. So you strap yourself into the vehicle and contemplate what to say to the 16-foot-tall creatures.

And so it is that you find yourself in a race against time, ducking meteors and attempting to blink away encroaching non-vegetarian dinosaurs as your vehicle rages out of control. Just when you think you're in the clear, you'll notice the nostril-flaring carnotaurus hot on your tail. What happens next is for us to know and for you to find out. Skip it if you have dinophobia, are pregnant, suffer from back or neck problems or motion sickness, or have a heart condition.

Don't leave this area without taking in **Finding Nemo—The Musical**. The engaging stage show retells the story of that lovable, wandering clownfish, Nemo, through original songs, dance, and theatrical puppetry. This show is presented several times daily at the enclosed (and air-conditioned!) Theater in the Wild.

Asia

A footbridge that wouldn't look out of place in the Himalayas, were it not filled with strolling theme park guests, leads from Discovery Island to this chip off Earth's largest continent. Your gateway to Asia is the kingdom of Anandapur, where a musical welcome is provided by tiny brass bells that dangle from the eaves of pagodas, dancing in the wind. Speckling the landscape are temples overtaken by gibbons, ruins frequented by tigers, a pavilion leased to fruit bats, and the like.

That mountain range ahead includes a replica of the world's tallest peak—Mount Everest itself. Housed inside this not-so-natural wonder is a thrilling ride known as **Expedition Everest**. Are you free of heart conditions, back problems, and other health issues *and* feeling brave? Climb aboard the train and brace yourself for a breathtaking, high-speed roller coaster experience. It starts out

---

Did You Know . . .

- The carvings on the Tree of Life represent about 325 of the 1.4 million existing species.

- Many of the plastic benches in Animal Kingdom were made from recycled material.

- Disney's Worldwide Wildlife Conservation Fund helps nonprofit organizations protect endangered animals. You can donate by adding a dollar for conservation projects to your shop purchase.

- Most of the animals here were born in other zoological parks. Many are registered in special management and breeding programs called SSPs (Species Survival Plans).

- WDW has eliminated most of its insecticide use, replacing chemicals with millions of predatory insects—many of which are bred at The Land in Epcot.

---

calmly enough—with a peaceful tour of the environs surrounding the majestic mountain. After climbing what feels like an 80-degree slope, well, that's when the real fun begins. But wait. Look up ahead. Are the tracks *broken*?! Uh-oh. You are, among other things, about to hurtle through caverns and canyons (backward no less)—and meet one mighty angry Yeti (aka Abominable Snowman). Hang on!

If you survive the Yeti encounter and are up for more adventure (and a quick shower), head to **Kali River Rapids**. You'll know you're in the right queue if you see a stream of soggy people filing by.

Once your raft shoves off from the boathouse, it parts the waters beneath a fog-shrouded steeple of greenery. Don't be lulled into security, no matter how sweetly the birds chirp. Soon you'll be trading this calm for a smoldering obstacle course lined with freshly shish-kebabbed forest. Yes, just ahead lies a precarious game of limbo, under an abandoned logging truck and a burning tree. The sum total is a jostling five-minute ride that is best left to nonpregnant people *sans* heart conditions and neck or back problems.

Note that cameras and other non-waterproof valuables should

Quiet Escapes

Who says you can't find peace in a jungle? Consider these relatively relaxing spots and seek out others.

- The Oasis in the afternoon
- Discovery Island Trails (especially near the back of the Tree of Life)
- Pangani Forest Exploration Trail
- Tables along the river at Flame Tree Barbecue in Discovery Island (except at lunchtime)
- Rafiki's Planet Watch
- Anywhere but Camp Minnie-Mickey

not be taken on Kali River Rapids. While there is a storage space in the middle of the raft, we suggest entrusting them to a nice, dry locker or nonriding member of your party.

Continue your Far East itinerary with the **Maharajah Jungle Trek**, a tour through the nearest Southeast Asian rainforest in the most primitive of tour vehicles (your own two feet). Led by an unobtrusive, insightful guide (yourself), you do what great explorers in the wilds can't: parade unharmed past roving tigers and Komodo dragons.

Don't be afraid to linger. Even Olympians of these species can't breach Disney's security systems. Chicken out on passing through the darkened bat chamber, and you may never see a *Pteropus*

vampyrus—the closest thing to a Chihuahua with a six-foot wingspan—eating pineapple chunks. But you'll still spot Malaysian tapirs, birds, and acrobatic gibbons galore.

Speaking of chickens, here's another feather for your explorer's cap. The Caravan Stage, which struts out performances of **Flights of Wonder** several times daily, can accommodate 1,000 people and all manner of flappers. Check a Times Guide for the schedule.

Note: This show is more enjoyable than one might expect. It's also a nice opportunity to rest your feet and escape the sun.

Africa

If imitation is the sincerest form of flattery, then Africa has got to be blushing. In creating this largest section of the park, Disney seems to have stopped just shy of moving mountains (Kilimanjaro is conspicuously missing). The artfully reconstructed African savanna and woodland aren't merely stunning to behold. They're designed to satisfy the habitat specifications of each meerkat, zebra, and elephant. Countless trips to the continent, exhaustive planning, and some slick adaptations have enabled Disney to mesh the intimacy of a zoo with the aura of a safari.

Disney's Africa is truly a land of opportunities, among them: treading just a few yards from cavorting gorillas; observing rhinos, gazelles, and hippos en masse; exchanging glances with a passing giraffe; getting up to speed on wildlife protection and conservation efforts; and chasing renegade ivory poachers.

Of course, you wander over and find yourself suddenly surrounded by hippos and elephants. You acclimate to the continent in the atmospheric village of Harambe, patterned after modern coastal communities in East Africa. Harambe is important as the spot for food, drink, and shopping during your stay in Africa. It is also the gateway to some exceptional attractions.

Kilimanjaro Safaris, Disney's variation on the classic African travel adventure, is one to beat a path to. The 20-minute guided trip through a simulated savanna escorts you within boasting distance of many of the world's most beloved animals—so close you'll begin to wonder which of the 30 or so people in your open-air gawkmobile (as we've loosely dubbed the roofed, rugged transportation of choice) has irrepressible animal magnetism. As the vehicle bumps along the dust-caked road, you'll observe animals on the move and watch for elephants, gazelles, rhinos, baboons, and lions. Such animals as giraffes and zebras may draw quite near.

Your guide will fill you in on less familiar species; for a

preview, steal quick glances at the species identification cheat sheet above the seat in front of you. These animals have room to roam and thus better things to do than stare back at you. Of course, as on a real safari, you might not see certain animals on a given trip; they could be sleeping, hiding, or otherwise engaged. So consider riding more than once during your visit.

A good follow-up to the safari is a walking tour that invites lingering and offers a closer look at gorillas and other animals. Also accessible from Harambe, **Pangani Forest Exploration Trail** segues from a research lab to the enchanting environs of a free-flight aviary and an aquarium. Beyond that, you'll come upon a stream dammed with glass—the site of a synchronized swimming demonstration by hippos. Okay,

Animal Kingdom Snacks

For a healthy treat, try the juice blends at the Safari Bar next to Rainforest Cafe or a piece of fresh fruit from a stand in Africa. If you need a sweet treat, head for the fresh-baked cookies or ice cream at Dino Bite Snacks in DinoLand, or the pastries and other goodies at Kusafiri Coffee Shop & Bakery, in Africa. For a cool pick-me-up, try chocolate-covered frozen bananas or Mickey's premium ice cream bars from a vendor, or the frozen lemonade from Harambe Fruit Market. Or go for the gusto and try the ever-popular (and enormous) smoked turkey legs, on Discovery Island.

so maybe it's not synchronized. But the buoyant beasts don't have to wear nose plugs to be amusing in their underwater glory. Even so, we know what you're thinking: "Are we there yet? Where are the gorillas?" Rest assured, the chest-thumpers are close at hand.

There's a bit more to see before you reach the gorilla sanctuary, however, namely, a scenic savanna overlook and an ensemble of Timon's meerkat cousins. (FYI: Don't expect to see any Pumbaas.

Entertainment

Entertaining distractions include African musicians and super-knowledgeable wildlife experts who wander the park with interesting animals. And don't miss Mickey's Jammin' Jungle Parade, featuring off-road-style floats like Rafiki's Adventure Rover and Goofy's Safari Jeep. Check a park Times Guide for current entertainment schedules.

Meerkats and warthogs don't pal around in the real world.)

After you peer into their habitat at close range through floor-to-ceiling glass, walk over a suspension bridge to the gorilla valley, and begin turning your head U.S. Open–style to take in the antics of the family brood and the bachelor brood now flanking you (provided that they're in the mood to be seen). Back in Harambe, you'll find the train depot for the **Wildlife Express to Rafiki's Planet Watch**, a narrated 5½-minute train trip that chugs quietly behind the scenes

of Africa, providing a reverse perspective of Kilimanjaro Safaris, along with insights into the park's inner workings. For those wanting a rest, it offers a leisurely lift (and the only mode of transportation) to and from **Rafiki's Planet Watch**, the attraction that serves as Animal Kingdom's ideological cornerstone. As a center for wildlife preservation efforts and veterinary care, it crystallizes the park's environmental themes and encourages active support of wildlife programs while the safari's still fresh in your mind.

Animal Kingdom Unplugged

If Rafiki's Planet Watch doesn't sate your curiosity, there are two 3-hour tours that will. Backstage Safari, basically Animal Care 101, takes you through such creature facilities as the animal nutrition center and the veterinary hospital and on a special safari ride. The tour is offered at 8:30 A.M. and 1 P.M. on Monday, Wednesday, Thursday, and Friday, and costs $70, plus park admission.

Another tour, Wild by Design, shows how Disney's Animal Kingdom came to be—from architecture to artifacts and a whole lot more. It's offered at 8:30 A.M. on Monday, Wednesday, Thursday, and Friday. The cost is $60, plus park admission. Call 407-939-8687 for details and reservations.

Camp Minnie-Mickey

If you want to commune with animals more accustomed to standing still for pictures, take a trip to Camp Minnie-Mickey.

The not-to-be-missed attraction here is **Festival of the Lion King**, an entertaining 30-minute spectacle of dance, song, and acrobatics by a troupe of talented tribal performers. The theater is huge (and air-conditioned)—and the show is popular. Arrive 30 to 45 minutes before showtime.

Make a splash and dive in to activities beyond the theme parks.

Diversions: Sports, Shopping, and Other Pursuits

You've flown with Peter Pan in the Magic Kingdom, blasted into outer space at Epcot, gotten a backstage peek at Tinseltown at Disney's Hollywood Studios, and bonded with bugs and dinosaurs at Animal Kingdom. Now what?

The World beyond the major theme parks offers a slew of terrific diversions that, interspersed between park visits, help establish perfect symmetry in a well-rounded Walt Disney World vacation. Once you get over the shock of finding such activities here in the first place, you're still pinching yourself because the quality of the experiences is so good. You'll find that even more world-class adventures for adults (thoroughly described on the following pages) exist within the playground that is Walt Disney World.

We're just hinting at the possibilities when we mention golf courses, widely considered among the country's best; tennis courts, health clubs, and the Disney's Wide World of Sports complex—all perfect examples of Disney's ability to dazzle in the most unexpected arenas. On the shopping front, tantalizing stores (including a collection of character-defying options at Downtown Disney) are popping up property-wide. Add the last word in water parks, including a sky-scraping waterslide and a humongous wave pool, and the list is still incomplete. For a full inventory of distractions (the categories: sports, shopping, and other pursuits) so compelling you might wonder why anyone bothers with those theme parks, read on.

Sports
Golf

Walt Disney World's golf—second only to the Mouse in drawing power—is renowned for the challenge, variety, and fairness of its courses. WDW is a familiar name on *GOLF Magazine*'s biennial list of the best golf resorts in the country. *Golf Digest* has tabbed some of the World's par-72 courses as outstanding ("plan your next vacation around it") or very good ("worth getting off the interstate to play").

KNOW BEFORE YOU GO: WDW's peak golfing season extends from January through April. During this period, it is especially important to secure reservations well in advance for play in the morning and early afternoon (though starting times after 2 P.M. are usually available at the last minute). Tee times are particularly difficult to get during the third and fourth weeks of January, when some 30,000 serious golfers descend on the area for the PGA of America's Merchandise Show and during the Children's Miracle Network Classic (early November). During such busy periods, the advance reservations and guaranteed tee times can be absolutely indispensable. Further, guests who opt for the Magic Your Way premium or platinum package may choose golf as an activity and book tee times 120 days in advance. (That's a full month before anyone else can.)

Rates: Greens fees for the 18-hole courses vary according to when you visit (peak versus non-peak seasons), which course you play (Magnolia and Osprey Ridge are more expensive), and your guest status (WDW resort guests get a break). Basically, though, you can count on paying about $40 to $170 per round (depending on your tee time), which includes the required cart. Throughout the year, golfers can save some money by teeing off in the late afternoon, when twilight rates may afford savings of nearly

Course for Celebration

The nearby town of Celebration, Florida, is home to the Celebration Golf Club, a joint venture of father-and-son designers Robert Trent Jones, Sr., and Robert Trent Jones, Jr. The par-72 course is not affiliated with the Walt Disney Company (nor is the town of Celebration); call 407-566-4653 for rates.

50 percent. The biggest savings can be had from May through late September, when rates for all courses drop to about $50 after 10 A.M. At Oak Trail, a 9-hole walking course, play starts at about $38. Play a second round and you get it at half price. Annual Golf Memberships ($50), available to Florida residents only, can provide big savings for play after 10 A.M., and also include use of a cart and a discount on golf lessons given by the PGA teaching staff. The annual golf pass also permits members to bring up to three guests to get the discount.

For up-to-the-minute info, visit *www.disneyworldgolf.com.* The site also offers a virtual tour of each WDW golf course.

Reservations: Golfers who book lodging at any on-property resort may secure tee times up to 90 days in advance (with the exception of those on the Magic Your Way premium or platinum package, who may book 120 days ahead). For everyone else, the window of opportunity is 60 days out. It can be tough to get a last-minute tee time—book as early as possible. Four golfers are assigned to each starting time, so parties may be matched up. To book, call 407-WDW-GOLF (939-4653) or visit *www.disneyworldgolf.com.* Reservations must be made with a credit card. Cancellations must be made 48 hours in advance or you'll be charged in full.

Transportation: Free private transportation (taxi) is provided for all guests staying at a Disney resort. Simply present a "key to the world card" (aka room key) to

Golf Rates

The following greens fees were in effect at press time for the Walt Disney World golf courses. Prices do not include tax and are likely to go up in 2010. Prices fluctuate between Peak and Non-peak seasons. Walt Disney World resort guests get $20 off the Day Visitor Rate.

Day Visitor Rates
(subject to change)

- Osprey Ridge: from $109* to $174

- Magnolia: from $109* to $174

- Palm: from $99* to $154

- Lake Buena Vista: from $99* to $154

- Oak Trail: starts at about $38 (for 9 holes, year-round)

* Summer discounts (late April through late September) mean rates for all courses drop to about $49 to $59 as of 10 A.M.

Twilight rates begin at 3 P.M. during much of the year, starting an hour earlier in certain seasons. Rates range from $39 to $94, depending on tee time and course chosen.

Guest Services, concierge, or valet and receive a voucher to get you to the golf course. When you're done, you can flash said card at the pro shop to get a return voucher. The taxi vouchers include the price of the ride and gratuity. If you are not staying at a participating resort, ask bell services to call a cab to take you to the greens. You'll have to foot the bill, but it shouldn't set you back more than 20 bucks. Single-rider adaptive golf carts and clubhouse accommodations are available for guests with disabilities at all Walt Disney World resort golf courses.

Dress: Proper golf attire is required on all courses. Collared or golf-style collarless shirts only, and if shorts are worn, they must be Bermuda length. Soft spikes only.

Equipment rental: Gear, including FootJoy shoes ($10) and range balls ($7 a bucket), is available for rent at all WDW pro shops. Golf club rentals run $55 plus tax; photo ID required. Prices are subject to change.

INSTRUCTION: Players looking to improve their games can arrange for one-on-one instruction at the Palm and Magnolia with Disney's PGA professionals. The concentration of the 45-minute sessions varies from guest to guest (lessons are customized to all levels of experience). Video analysis may be used; cost is $75 plus tax.

Reservations are required for lessons; call 407-WDW-GOLF (939-4653) or visit *www.disneyworldgolf.com* up to 120 days in advance.

TOURNAMENTS: The Children's Miracle Network Classic, which draws top PGA Tour players every fall, is among the most celebrated events on Disney's sports calendar.

Venues for the tournament are the Palm and Magnolia courses. During the first two days of the competition, the pros play each course once with an amateur player. After 36 holes, the field narrows to the low 70 pros, who compete for a percentage of the tourney's multimillion-dollar purse in the final two rounds, played on the Magnolia. Tickets are available on-site each day of the tournament. At press time, a one-day price for each round was about $20. The weekly badge, good for admission throughout the tournament, costs about $30. Practice rounds (held several days before the tournament) are open to spectators at no cost. Note that pricing and ticket structures are subject to change in 2010.

Those who are willing to pay big dues may play the Classic alongside the pros. Card-carrying members of the Classic Club play with a different competing pro each day for the first two rounds of the tournament. Some memberships include lodging, reduced greens fees on Disney courses for a year, and admission to the theme parks for a week. For details, call 407-824-2250.

Mickey and Mini Golf

Leave it to Disney to create 18-hole miniature-golf courses that eschew the typical tackiness for clever designs, both fanciful and devious. The first round is about $13; it's half price for the second. Hours are 10 A.M. to 11 P.M. Call 407-WDW-PLAY (939-7529) for more on these locations.

- Disney's Fantasia Fairways, one of the two courses at the Fantasia Gardens Miniature Golf complex near the BoardWalk, is ruled by daunting doglegs, water traps, par 3s, and par 4s. Astute players may notice shrunken signature holes from famous links. (Play time: about 1½ hours.)

- At the Gardens, the second course near the BoardWalk, whimsical tees offer odes to *Fantasia*. En route, balls hit chimes and xylophone stairs, and spur waterspouts and fife-playing. (Play time: about an hour.)

- Disney's Winter Summerland, vacation spot to Santa and Christmas elves, offers the best of both seasons. Near Blizzard Beach, surfboards and sand castles speckle the summer-themed course, while igloos and ice sculptures give the wintry course the freeze. (Play time: about an hour per course.)

The Courses

OSPREY RIDGE: Tom Fazio has taken his signature mounding along fairways and around greens to monumental heights here—most dramatically with a name-sake ridge that meanders through the property and elevates some greens as high as 25 feet above the basic grade. The designer counts Osprey Ridge among his best efforts, and the sentiment is echoed in the course's consider-able popularity among experi-enced golfers. The long par-72 layout winds through a remote and thickly forested part of the property near Fort Wilderness; it has a deceptively gentle start, then raises the stakes en route to its three great finishing holes. Along the way, players will con-front the signature par-3 third hole, with its elevated tee, and the fierce 14th, a long par 4 with a carry over water. Osprey Ridge plays to 5,402 yards from the front tees, 6,680 from the middle, and 7,101 from the back.

Facilities include a driving range, a putting green, pro shop, restau-rant, and lounge. Course record: 65 (Daniel Young, 1992).

PALM: This prickly yet pictur-esque course (located just west of the Polynesian resort) is marked by tight, wooded fairways, a wealth of water hazards, and

Slope Scope

The slope ratings for the three par-72 Disney courses from the back tees are: Magnolia, 136; Palm, 138; and Lake Buena Vista, 133. By way of comparison, an average slope rating is around 115. The famously challenging links at Pebble Beach check in at 139; the formidable TPC Stadium course at Ponte Vedra at 135.

elevated greens and tees, which bear Joe Lee's unmistakable signature and make for challenging club selections. The par-72 Palm plays shorter and tighter than its mate, the Magnolia, and measures 5,311 yards from the front tees, 6,461 from the middle, and 7,010 from the back. The palm-dotted venue hosts the Children's Miracle Network Classic, along with a fellow Lee design, the Magnolia course. Of the holes garnering the most locker-room curses (numbers 6, 10, and 18), the sixth, a 412-yard par 4, is the most notorious. There's a lake on the left, woods and swamp on the right, and more water between you and the two-tier green. Although Palm number 6 is the number one handicap hole, number 18 (the number 2 handicap hole) has consistently baffled the pros more than any other Disney hole. The course—whose greens were resurfaced and tee boxes laser-leveled and rebuilt in 2004—opened in 1971 with the Magnolia and the Magic Kingdom itself. Facilities shared by the Palm and the Magnolia include two driving ranges, a putting green, and a pro shop. Walt Disney World Golf Instruction is also based here. Course record: 61 (Mark Lye, 1984).

MAGNOLIA: Like the Palm, the Magnolia opened with the Magic Kingdom in 1971. Its greens were resurfaced, and several of its holes were tweaked in 2005. Course designer Joe Lee realigned teeing areas, recontoured greens, and replaced the original playing surface with a "faster" grass, among other things. The Magnolia features abundant water and sand, but what sets it apart—aside from the 1,500 magnolia trees and a mouse-eared bunker beside the sixth green—is exceptional length, vast greens, and a flaw-exposing layout that requires precision and careful course management. Meandering over 175 acres of wetlands and rolling terrain, the par-72 course measures 5,232

Tee Time

Want to increase your chances of getting a WDW course tee time? Heed this advice:

- Play on Monday or Tuesday.
- Tee off in late afternoon.
- Come in the summer (when special rates are available).

The Ten Most Humbling Holes

Cumulative toughest-playing holes since 1983:

1. Palm No. 18
2. Palm No. 6
3. Palm No. 10
4. Magnolia No. 5
5. Magnolia No. 18
6. Palm No. 4
7. Magnolia No. 17
8. Magnolia No. 15
9. Magnolia No. 1
10. Palm No. 12

right of the green.

It is the Magnolia that has final say in the outcome of the Golf Classic at Walt Disney World Resort, and it takes full advantage with a final hole that rates among the tournament's testiest. Facilities shared by the Magnolia and the Palm are two driving ranges, two putting greens, and a pro shop. Course record: 61 (Payne Stewart, 1990).

OAK TRAIL: This 9-hole, par-36 walking course in a 45-acre corner of the Magnolia is a good venue for beginners, yet it's no cream puff for better players. The 2,913-yard layout unleashes plenty of challenges—including two fine par 5s—and boasts well-maintained greens.

yards from the front tees, 6,642 from the middle set, and 7,516 from the back markers. Among the signature holes is number 17, a long par-4 dogleg left that dares long hitters to bite off the edge of a lake, then avoid water to the

LAKE BUENA VISTA: This Joe Lee design is a Rodney Dangerfield of sorts. One of the shortest of the four 18-hole courses, it features a good amount of water, and its fairways, hemmed in by stands of pine and oak, are Disney golf's tightest. Lake Buena Vista honors its reputation as a friendly course for less experienced golfers. But it is also well equipped to challenge more skilled players. As golf writer Glen Waggoner once put it, Lake Buena Vista may be the weakest link in the Disney chain, but it's still head and shoulders above the Number 2 venue at most other golf resorts in the U.S.

The course's toughest holes—the 11th and the 18th—were at one time counted among the ten most humbling tests in the history of the Classic at Walt Disney World Resort. But perhaps no one has greater respect for the course than Calvin Peete, who, in the 1982 Classic, blitzed the Palm in a record-breaking 66 strokes, only to give it all back—and more—on little ol' Lake Buena Vista.

The course plays to 5,194 yards from the front tees, 6,264 from the middle, and 6,749 from the rearmost markers. Facilities at Lake Buena Vista include a driving range and a practice green. Course record: 61 (Bob Tway, 1989).

Tennis

Even if you can't quite picture Mickey with a midsize racquet in his hand, Walt Disney World can still serve up plenty of tennis action for players of any caliber. There is a total of about 16 courts scattered around the World, including four located at the Dolphin hotel and shared with the Swan. You'll find one hard court at Yacht and Beach Club, two at BoardWalk, two more at Fort Wilderness (watch out for swinging toddlers), two at Saratoga Springs, and a nice, quiet trio at Old Key West.

The Grand Floridian resort's duo of courts boasts clay surfaces. Tennis courts lighted for night play are available at many Disney resorts; this is a big deal, given the daytime heat during much of the year. The fee to play at the Grand Floridian is $10 per person, per hour (all other courts are free). Professional tennis lessons cost $80 per session.

The Grand Floridian Resort and Spa serves as the tennis hub of Walt Disney World. In addition to independent play, it offers group and individual instruction.

Experienced players may also take part in the "Play the Pro" program. For more information, or to book a lesson, call 407-621-1991.

KNOW BEFORE YOU GO: Courts are busiest during June and July, but they are first come, first served (so to speak). February, March, and April also tend to be busy, especially around holidays and spring break. January, October, and November should be considered prime time to play. The courts are generally open from 8 A.M. to 7 P.M., but hours vary seasonally. Equipment rentals are limited in availability.

Dress: It's usually hot, so we recommend cool, loose-fitting tennis whites. As for footwear, opt for flat-bottomed tennis shoes (cross-trainers and running shoes tear up courts).

Fishing

Drop a line, it's promptly answered. That's typical fishing at Walt Disney World. Bay Lake, which adjoins man-made Seven Seas Lagoon, was stocked with 70,000 largemouth bass in the mid-1960s. A restrictive policy allowed the fish to swell in numbers and size.

On these waters you're not just likely to catch fish—you're apt to catch largemouth bass weighing eight pounds or more. And it's not uncommon for a group to catch 15 to 20 fish over a couple of hours, or for a first-timer to reel in half a dozen good-size bass.

The official policy is catch-and-release, and no license is required for fishing on WDW guided excursions. Fishing guides know their territory well, keep close track of where the fish are biting, and serve in whatever capacity guests prefer—from straight chauffeurs to casting coaches and even all-out facilitators.

Reservations for fishing excursions must be made at least 24 hours in advance and may be made up to 180 days ahead. Call 407-WDW-BASS (939-2277); or visit *www.disneyworldfishing.com* for reservations and current pricing information.

Guided Fishing Trips

BAY LAKE & SEVEN SEAS LAGOON: Guided expeditions offering first-rate largemouth bass fishing depart from the Fort Wilderness marina at 7 A.M., 10 A.M., and 1:30 P.M. (hours vary seasonally) for two-hour trips on Bay Lake and Seven Seas Lagoon. Trips are made on Nitro bass boats or pontoon-style boats (which can hold up to five passengers).

The fee per boat runs from $225 to $250 (tack on about $100 more for an extra hour) and includes guide, gear, and beverages. Guests may be picked up at the Contemporary, Fort Wilderness, Grand Floridian, Polynesian, and Wilderness Lodge marinas. Note that excursions as long as four hours are available. Call 407-WDW-BASS (939-2277).

VILLAGE LAKE: Guided two-hour excursions plying Village Lake and adjacent waterways depart in the morning and the afternoon from the Downtown Disney Marketplace marina. On the earliest trips, anglers have the lake and the largemouth bass therein all to themselves (later, rental boats may infringe on prime fishing territory).

The cost for up to five people, including a guide, gear, and

beverages, is $230 to $260 for two hours. Guides will also pick up guests at Port Orleans French Quarter, Port Orleans Riverside, Saratoga Springs, and Old Key West. Call 407-WDW-BASS (939-2277).

CRESCENT LAKE: Daily fishing excursions depart at 7 A.M., 10 A.M., and 1:30 P.M. from the Yacht and Beach Club Bayside Marina or from the BoardWalk dock. Cost is $200 to $235 for two hours (about $100 more for an extra hour) for up to five people, including guide, fishing gear, bait, and refreshments. Trips are made on Nitro bass

Fishing Tips

Although the fishing is good here year-round, it's most pleasant from November through May, when temperatures are cooler. As for strategy, one local recommends going with plastic worms. To stack your odds, he suggests shiners (they're included). Also, top-water baits work well in spring and fall.

boats and pontoon-style boats. The latter can hold up to five passengers. Call 407-WDW-BASS (939-2277).

Fishing on Your Own

Resort guests who prefer to fish solo may do so on the canals of Fort Wilderness—catch-and-release only (no license necessary). Poles may be rented for about $4 per half hour at the Fort Wilderness Bike Barn. Rods and reels cost $13 per day; bait runs about $6.

CARIBBEAN BEACH AND CORONADO SPRINGS RESORTS: Private fishing excursions are offered at 7 A.M, 10 A.M., and 1:30 P.M. Bass boats accommodate the guide and up to two guests. The cost for each 2-hour trip (including equipment) is $235 for A.M. excursions and $200 for those in the afternoon.

Biking

While Fort Wilderness is prime territory for leisurely cycling, the World is filled with roads that wind within many of its resorts.

Bikes are available (about $9 per hour or $22 per day, with some variation) in precisely the spots where guests will want to ride them: Fort Wilderness, Wilderness Lodge, Old Key West, Port

Orleans Riverside, Yacht and Beach Club, Saratoga Springs, Caribbean Beach, BoardWalk, and Coronado Springs.

Boating

Guests looking to cruise, paddle, or even create a small wake on the pristine lakes and waterways of Disney World have nothing short of the largest fleet of pleasure boats in the country at their disposal. Resort marinas stand by with sailboats, kayaks, pontoon boats, Boston Whaler Montauk boats, canoes, pedal boats, and motorboats, all of which are available for rent on a first-come, first-served basis.

On the World's most expansive boating forum, the 585-acre body of water comprising Bay Lake and the adjoining Seven Seas Lagoon, watercraft from the Contemporary, Wilderness Lodge, and Fort Wilderness marinas converge with boats lighting out from the Polynesian and Grand Floridian. Other areas are more contained. Craft rented at the Caribbean Beach cruise around 45-acre Barefoot Bay. As boats on loan from the Downtown Disney Marketplace roam 35-acre Lake Buena Vista, small flotillas of rental craft drift in from the upriver marinas of Old Key West

and Port Orleans Riverside. Meanwhile, watercraft from the Yacht and Beach Club make ripples on Crescent Lake, while pedal boats, kayaks, Boston Whaler Montauk boats, and motorboats ply the 15-acre Lago Dorado at Coronado Springs.

Resort marinas are usually open from 10 A.M. until early evening (hours vary seasonally). No privately owned boats are permitted on WDW waterways. Renters must present a WDW resort ID card, a driver's license, or a passport. Some boat rentals carry other restrictions.

CANOEING: Paddling among the narrow channels of Fort Wilderness during the peaceful morning hours, canoers pass through forest and meadows, encountering the occasional quacking contingent along the way. Canoes (which run about $8 per half hour or $12 per hour) are available at the Fort Wilderness Bike Barn. Use of these watercraft is restricted to Walt Disney World canals. It's also possible to rent canoes at Coronado Springs and Caribbean Beach resort marinas.

CRUISING: For groups interested in taking a leisurely sunning, sightseeing, or party excursion on the water, motorized Boston Whaler Montauk boats and pontoon boats are the only way to go. Seventeen-foot Boston Whaler boats accommodating up to six adults (about $45 per half hour) and 21-foot pontoon boats holding 10 adults (about $45 per half hour) are available for rent at most marinas. Guests must be 18 years old to rent a pontoon boat or Boston Whaler boat. For information on special-occasion cruises, see page 176.

PEDAL BOATING: For those who prefer pedal-pushing to paddling, pedal boats (accommodating two pedaling passengers and two freeloaders) are available for about $7 per half hour or $11 per hour at most marinas. WDW resort guests can rent the boats at the Caribbean Beach, Old Key West, Swan, Dolphin, and Coronado Springs. The Swan, Dolphin, and Old Key West also rent Hydro Bikes (singles, $8 per half hour; doubles, about $16 per half hour), which resemble upright bicycles affixed to pontoons. Guests of Animal Kingdom Lodge, the All-Star resorts, Saratoga Springs, and Pop Century can rent boats at any WDW resort marina.

PERSONAL WATERCRAFT: Up for a "Jet-Ski–like" experience? You've come to the right place. Provided, that is, you've come to Sammy Duvall's Watersports Centre behind the Contemporary resort. The 3-seat, Jet Ski-style personal watercraft (PWC) may be rented between 9 A.M. and 5 P.M. daily. The cost is $75 plus tax per half hour; $125 per hour. That covers up to 3 people whose combined weight doesn't exceed 400 pounds. To drive, guests must be at least 16 years old and have a valid driver's license.

If you'd like a little live narration and a touch of guidance with your PWC experience, consider the Personal Watercraft Guided Excursion. Departing daily at 9 A.M., the excursion includes a knowledgeable guide who will offer driving tips, lead the group, and call attention to various points of interest on the tour of Bay Lake and Seven Seas Lagoon. Post-tour, guests may enjoy supervised "Free Ride" time. The maximum number of rental units per excursion is four. Price, age, and weight restrictions are the same as those mentioned above. Call 407-939-0754 or pay a visit to *www.sammyduvall.com* for information and reservations.

SAILING: Bay Lake and Seven Seas Lagoon offer pretty reliable winds and unparalleled running room. Sailing conditions are generally best in March and April. Sailboats may be rented at the Grand Floridian, Polynesian, and Caribbean Beach marinas. Rental fees range from $20 to $35 per hour.

MOTORBOATING: Among the most enjoyable ways to cool off at Walt Disney World is the legion of mini motorboats called Sea Raycers (which replaced Water Mouse boats). The boats' small hulls ride a choppy surface as though they were galloping steeds. (A bonus: Drivers must be at least 12 years old and at least 5 feet tall to pilot the boats.) Fort Wilderness Marina offers one of the more uncrowded arenas at WDW. While the boats seat two, adult boaters will reach greater speeds going solo (and creating tiny wakes for one another). Sea Raycer boats are restricted to lakes only and are available for about $30 per half hour at the Grand Floridian, Polynesian, Contemporary, Wilderness Lodge, Fort Wilderness, Yacht and Beach Club, Caribbean Beach, Port Orleans Riverside, Old Key West, Downtown Disney, and Coronado Springs marinas.

WATERSKIING, WAKEBOARDING, AND TUBING: Guests interested in hitching a ride around Bay Lake pay about $155 for tubing, wakeboarding, and waterskiing. That's for one hour, and it includes the boat and instructor. Cost is by the boatload, and up to five people can be accommodated at a time.

Trips depart from the Contemporary resort. Reservations must be made at least 24 hours in advance and can be made up to 180 days ahead of time. Call 407-939-0754 or visit *www. sammyduvall.com.*

Jogging

Despite pleasant terrain that looks like it's been spread with a rolling pin, Walt Disney World can be a rough place to pursue the world's most mobile form of exercise. From late spring through early fall, comfortable running conditions are fleeting, with early birds getting the best shot at an enjoyable run. In the cooler seasons, joggers have greater freedom to explore the many compelling choices here.

Ask about maps of the jogging trails and footpaths accessible from most Walt Disney World resorts at the hotel's Lobby Concierge desk. Courses range in distance. Port Orleans Riverside, Old Key West, and Fort Wilderness offer some of the most extensive venues.

Parasailing

If the notion of flying like a kite above Bay Lake with a panorama of the Magic Kingdom appeals to you, factor in a harness that allows you to sit in a reclined position, and you have an idea of the parasailing experience as it exists at Walt Disney World.

The flight lasts 7 to 10 minutes, and the landing is exceptionally soft, thanks to the parachute and the two-person crew's skillful handling (as one reels in the cord, the other slows the boat to just the right speed). You won't even get wet!

Parasailing excursions are offered at the Contemporary marina, with four-time World Overall Champion Sammy Duvall and his world-class instructors.

The cost is about $95 for single riders and $175 for tandem riders. Flights last 7 to 10 minutes. Make reservations up to 180 days in advance by calling 407-939-0754 or visiting *www.sammyduvall.com*. Guests must check in 20 minutes before departure. (If you're afraid of heights, this adventure will scare you silly. If you're a non-acrophobe, we recommend the experience. The views of the Magic Kingdom are stunning.)

Swimming

As if it weren't enough to have an inside track to two massive water parks (see "Other Pursuits" in the latter part of this chapter), Walt Disney World resorts are themselves bursting at the seams with watery playgrounds. With no fewer than 70 swimming pools spread throughout Disney's hotel

grounds, guests at each resort can be assured of easy access to at least one pool. However, it is important to note that, due to a policy initiated to prevent over-crowding, Walt Disney World hotel pools are open only to guests staying at that resort. Pool-hopping is permitted between sister resorts (the Yacht

and Beach Club; Port Orleans Riverside and Port Orleans French Quarter; All-Star Movies, All-Star Music, and All-Star Sports; and the Swan and Dolphin).

Stock Car Driving

The drone of stock cars burning up a one-mile oval sets most anyone's mind to racing. Ergo, a pumped-up Driver's Ed has been introduced at the WDW Speedway, near the Magic Kingdom parking lot.

The Richard Petty Driving Experience even welcomes back-seat drivers (or passenger-seat drivers, as the case happens to be). Prefer to keep your sweaty palms off the wheel? Try the Riding Experience, about $120 for three laps; no reservations necessary.

Want your foot on that gas pedal? If you can drive a stick shift (and can prove it), consider reserving the three-hour Rookie Experience (about $400). It includes instruction and eight high-speed laps. If that doesn't sound like enough of a challenge, perhaps the 18-Lap King's Experience (about $850) is more your speed. Or, finally, ponder the Experience of a Lifetime (about $1,250). It delivers three rounds of Petty practice. Prices quoted are seasonal and don't include tax. Expect to pay about $50 extra during peak times of year (holidays, school vacations, summer, etc.).

For additional information, or to get in the driver's seat, call 800-237-3889 or visit *www.1800bepetty.com.*

ESPN Wide World of Sports Complex

Should your definition of paradise include slam dunks, screeching fastballs, and the intoxicating aroma of steamed weenies, welcome to nirvana. ESPN Wide World of Sports complex, which sprawls over 220 acres, is one agile place. Capable of hosting a dozen events at once, the facility has an archery-to-wrestling lineup that can make for compelling competition.

The complex, which partnered with ESPN in 2009, serves as the spring-training ground for Major League Baseball's Atlanta Braves and the summer training camp of the National Football League's 2003 Super Bowl champion Tampa Bay Buccaneers. It also hosts the Amateur Athletic Union

Sports Complex Tips

- For a complete, updated sporting event calendar, call 407-828-FANS (3267) or pay a visit to *www.disneysports.com.*

- WDW resort guests may take buses from Disney's Hollywood Studios during park hours. Note that transfers can take quite a bit of time.

- Tailgating in the parking lot is not permitted. (Parking is free.)

- Take an umbrella to outdoor contests (the area's prone to afternoon showers), and know that games may be cancelled due to inclement weather.

- Want to be a part of the action? Volunteer to work at a Wide World of Sports event. Call 407-938-3880.

(AAU) as well as a veritable turntable of tournaments.

Despite its large size, the complex somehow comes off as almost quaint. Its old-time Floridian architecture harks back to a simpler time and place. It recaptures the essence of a neighborhood ballpark, beckoning friends and families to spend a lazy afternoon together.

The complex, near the junction of I-4 and U.S. 192, has an armory of box and bleacher seats to accommodate all manner of spectators. Among the facilities to observe are the 7,500-seat baseball stadium; a field house that hosts basketball, wrestling, and volleyball; a track-and-field complex; 10 clay tennis courts; and nine multi-purpose fields for football, soccer, lacrosse, and more.

About $13 (plus tax) will get you a general admission ticket on days when events are scheduled. It allows you to take in a number of nonpremium events—that is, competitions that are worth watching, but not quite major league. Tickets for all premium events, such as Atlanta Braves games, are available through Ticketmaster (800-745-3000; *www.ticketmaster.com*) and include license to roam the complex. Premium tickets may also be purchased at the complex's ticket office on the day of the event, if available.

For the whole lineup, visit the Wide World of Sports Web site: *www.disneysports.com* or call 407-WDW-GAME (939-4263). Queries about handicapped seating can be handled by calling the aforementioned phone number.

If an afternoon of cheering (pom-poms optional) and rooting for the next-best-thing-to-the-home-team leaves you with a linebacker-style appetite, head straight for the concession stand. Vendors offer snacks for those dining in their seats or on the run.

WDW's Most Striking Feature

Walt Disney World lies squarely within a band of Central Florida known as the Lightning Capital of the World. Prime striking season runs from May through September, peaking during July and August, when Mother Nature unleashes about 40 thunderstorms over just 62 days, according to National Weather Service figures. Most of these storms come and go rather quickly.

To protect yourself, seek shelter (the type with four walls and a roof) the moment you see a storm developing, and wait a good 15 minutes after the last rumble before resuming outdoor activity. Trees and umbrellas do not provide safe refuge. Guests are allowed back in resort pools 30 minutes after the last lightning strike. For a weather report, call 407-824-4104.

Health Clubs

Ten WDW resorts offer guests free access to health club facilities. They are: Animal Kingdom Lodge (Zahanati Fitness Center), BoardWalk (Muscles & Bustles Health Club), Contemporary (Olympiad Fitness Center), Coronado Springs (La Vida Health Club), Grand Floridian (Grand Floridian Spa & Health Club), Old Key West (R.E.S.T. Exercise Room), Saratoga Springs (Saratoga Springs Spa & Fitness Center), Wilderness Lodge (Sturdy Branches Fitness Center), Yacht & Beach Club (Ship Shape Health Club). What if you're not staying at one of these resorts? Provided that you are staying at another Disney-owned-and-operated resort, you can use any health club facility (based on availability) for a $12 fee per day. Note that the Polynesian resort does not have its own fitness center. Poly guests may use the adjacent Grand Floridian health club facility at no extra charge.

The bare-bones facility at the Swan is free for all Swan and Dolphin guests, and fine for on-the-road maintenance. Better equipped—more cardiovascular machines and saunas—are the Contemporary's Fitness Center, Muscles & Bustles at BoardWalk, La Vida at Coronado Springs, Sturdy Branches at The Villas at Wilderness Lodge, Ship Shape at

the Yacht and Beach Club (which has a whirlpool, steam room, and sauna), and Zahanati at Animal Kingdom Lodge (which boasts a steam room plus spa services including massage). R.E.S.T. at Old Key West is free for DVC resort guests. The BoardWalk and Yacht and Beach health clubs are available to their respective guests 24/7.

The best of the lot distinguish themselves by offering pleasant surroundings and the likes of personal trainers and strength and cardio machines. The Dolphin ($10 per day; free for Swan and Dolphin guests) offers aerobics, and the Grand Floridian Spa & Health Club comes with frills; for details, see this chapter's "Spas" section (page 177).

The well-appointed spa at Disney's Saratoga Springs resort could be a Life Fitness warehouse if not for its airy setting.

Which Way to the Beach?

WDW resort guests need not set out for the coast to find pretty strands to sunbathe on and get sand between their toes. Between the resorts fronting Bay Lake (the Contemporary, Wilderness Lodge, and Fort Wilderness) and those alongside Seven Seas Lagoon (the Grand Floridian and Polynesian), there are more than five miles of white-sand beaches. And that does not include the powdery white stretches at the Caribbean Beach, Yacht and Beach Club, Swan and Dolphin, and Coronado Springs resorts. The beach fronting the Polynesian's Tahiti guest building is among the more secluded shores. Beaches are reserved exclusively for guests staying at those properties. Swimming is not permitted.

SHOPPING

In Downtown Disney Marketplace

ARRIBAS BROTHERS: This shop offers crystal keepsakes (engraved on-site by cutters who demonstrate the age-old art of glass sculpting), porcelain figurines, glass slippers, and more.

THE ART OF DISNEY: If you skip this showroom filled with limited-edition art pieces, collectibles, and animation cels, you've missed

Downtown Disney, Defined

In addition to the World's best shopping, the Downtown Disney Marketplace offers restaurants, lounges, a marina, special events, and interactive fountains. Walkways link the Marketplace to its spirited neighbors: Pleasure Island and West Side. The three locales (and the stockpile of shops, shows, and restaurants therein) are collectively known as Downtown Disney—a district zoned exclusively for entertainment. Buses and boats service the area. Marketplace shops are described in this section (starting above), while Pleasure Island and West Side shops are summed up in the box on the next page. For further details, see our "Restaurant Guide" and "Nightlife Guide" in the *Dining & Entertainment* chapter, visit *www.downtowndisney.com*, or call 407-939-2648.

out on some of the most spectacular ogling to be had in all of Walt Disney World. A Disney artist is on hand daily to draw personalized sketches of favorite characters, as well as answer questions about the animation process.

BASIN: Scents make sense at this shop, which soothes body and soul with bath crystals, soaps, shampoos, lotions, custom candles, and gift baskets. Time seems to stand still here— the decor is reminiscent of a 19th-century shop.

DESIGN A TEE: Showcase your inner fashion designer and create a custom T-shirt. It's possible to personalize other merchandise here, too.

DISNEY'S DAYS OF CHRISTMAS: This is the World's largest excuse to say, "Ho, ho, ho." Rather than tick off the many delightful trimmings—both traditional and Disney style—proffered at this trove of decorative items, ornaments, and collectibles, we'll cut to the chase: Just add eggnog.

EARL OF SANDWICH: This Marketplace spot specializes in gourmet sandwiches and freshly made baked goods. Other savory snack items are available. (This shop does double-duty as a quick-service eatery.) If you can't get a seat inside, there's ample outdoor seating along the waterfront.

GOOFY'S CANDY CO.: A shop that aims to satisfy every sweet tooth—from simple to sublime. Expect to find all things gooey and sugarcoated. They even have a chocolate dipping kitchen. This makes us happy.

TEAM MICKEY ATHLETIC CLUB: This supersize shop specializes in sport-specific Disney character apparel, gear, and souvenirs that run the gamut from Goofy golf club covers to Minnie Mouse tennis whites. Customize sports gear in the Rawlings Making the Game section of the store.

WORLD OF DISNEY: The most comprehensive collection of Disney character merchandise available anywhere and a shopper's concierge desk equipped to locate any item in stock make this vast retail emporium an unbeatable venue for one-stop souvenir sprees. From limited-edition watches to stuffed animals, from intimate apparel to office accessories, and from

Beyond the Marketplace

The shops at Downtown Disney West Side are light on Mouse goods and heavy on offbeat items with adult appeal.

Starabilias peddles Hollywood memorabilia; Magic Masters offers crystal balls, linking handcuffs, and other magician's wish-list items; and Magnetron is the place for umpteen magnets (seriously, you could cover nearly every fridge in Florida with this supply!). Sosa Family Cigars offers premium smokes; and Pop Gallery features artist-signed, limited-edition sculptures and paintings, plus high-end gift items—and a champagne bar. House of Blues has a souvenir shop, too.

While at Downtown Disney Pleasure Island you'll find Fuego by Sosa Cigars, Harley-Davidson Orlando, and Curl by Sammy Duvall—because you never know when you will need a brand-new surfboard!

frames to photo albums—this place has it all. It also offers a discount to annual passholders. Bonus!

In the Parks
Magic Kingdom Standouts

AGRABAH BAZAAR (Adventure-land): This open-air marketplace was designed to resemble a Moroccan port, where merchants from around the world come to sell their vases, brass, and other exotic wares.

BRIAR PATCH (Frontierland): The specialty of the house is merchandise that showcases its neighbor—the crowd-pleasing Splash Mountain attraction. There's usually a selection of sweets, too.

CRYSTAL ARTS (Main Street): Presented by Arribas Brothers, this shop offers cut-glass bowls,

vases, plates, and clear-glass mugs and steins similar to those found at Arribas Brothers in the Downtown Disney Marketplace. Items can be engraved on-site, and guests have the opportunity to observe an engraver or glass-blower at work.

DISNEY CLOTHIERS (Main Street): Souvenir clothing earns big style points here, as various Disney characters appear on collared shirts, denim shirts, sweaters, jackets, and nightshirts. The selection is small but choice.

EMPORIUM (Main Street): The Magic Kingdom's largest gift shop offers an array of Walt Disney World logo and character merchandise (including lots of stuffed animals, T-shirts, sweat-shirts, and hats) whose variety is eclipsed only by that found at the Downtown Disney Marketplace. Be sure to get a glimpse of the display windows out front.

MAIN STREET ATHLETIC CLUB (Main Street): A nifty stash of sports-related character apparel

silver jewelry, or souvenir charms, this elegant catchall is the place. This is Main Street's primary collector-pin location, too.

YANKEE TRADERS (Liberty Square): A front porch with a rocking chair sets the tone for this cozy niche selling kitchen accessories and candy.

YE OLDE CHRISTMAS SHOPPE (Liberty Square): Although smaller than Disney's Days of Christmas at Downtown Disney Marketplace, this locale is a fine resource for traditional and character holiday decorations. Have a holly, jolly Christmas!

can be found here. If you want to score some great gear sporting classic Disney characters in action, don't pass.

MAIN STREET CONFECTIONERY (Main Street): The sweet-toothed fall in line for peanut brittle, fudge, and marshmallow crispy treats made on the premises. For hand-dipped caramel apples (which can be sectioned upon request), chocolate-covered Mickey-shaped pretzels, and creatively candy-coated marshmallows, this is the source. Who knows? You may even get to watch the candymakers in action.

UPTOWN JEWELERS (Main Street): If you're shopping for a character watch, 14-karat gold or sterling

Epcot Standouts

THE AMERICAN ADVENTURE (World Showcase): Heritage Manor Gifts waxes patriotic with Americana. Highlights include apparel, history books, and American memorabilia.

THE ART OF DISNEY (Future World): The Art of Disney serves as the park's repository for Disney animation cels and limited-edition art pieces and collectibles. It is one of five such showrooms to explore at Walt Disney World.

CANADA (World Showcase): A vast array of Canadian handicrafts and Indian artifacts puts the Northwest Mercantile on the essential-shopping circuit. There's an apparel selection, as well as Canadian perfumes, wine, syrup, candy, and hockey gear (of course!).

CHINA (World Showcase): Yong Feng Shangdian is so huge it's almost a province. The montage of paper fans, Chinese prints, silk robes, jade, vases, tea sets, aromatherapy products, snacks, and more is truly something to behold.

FRANCE (World Showcase): Boutiques offering lovely French wares. Our favorites are Plume et Palette (fragrances),

Les Vins de France (French wines, cookbooks, and some hand-painted dishes), and La Signature (Guerlain cosmetics and fragrances).

GERMANY (World Showcase): The little shops here are simply irresistible. Die Weihnachts Ecke is bursting with hand-crafted glass ornaments and other holiday items. Volkskunst features beer steins in all sizes, while Der Teddybär is a toy shop. Weinkeller boasts about 50 vintage varieties and holds daily wine tastings (for a fee). Kunstarbeit in Kristall offers steins and crystal treasures. Finally, Glas und Porzellan is a boutique stocked with Goebel's M.I. Hummel figurines.

ITALY (World Showcase): When in this multi-shop pavilion, we gravitate toward Enoteca Castello for Italian wines and wine accessories, plus some chocolates and handmade Venetian masks; La Bottega Italiana for decorative ceramics and glassware, plus masks from

Venice; and Il Bel Cristallo for Armani figurines, silk scarves, and leather purses and bags.

JAPAN (World Showcase): In the vast emporium known as the Mitsukoshi Department Store, kimono-clad dolls (priced from $20 to $500) merit special attention, as do colorful kimonos, origami kits, bonsai, candy, and children's toys. You will also find a variety of items with which to set the table and decorate the home.

MEXICO (World Showcase): At the Plaza de los Amigos you can find all things South of the Border, including Mexican liquor, salsas and hot sauces, sombreros, and a fine selection of ceramics and other handicrafts.

MOROCCO (World Showcase): At least half the fun of shopping in this pavilion's maze of Berber bangles, basketry, and clothing is never knowing just what awaits around the bend (we found a lovely little bottle filled with rosewater, known as *cortas*).

MOUSE GEAR (Innoventions, Future World): Epcot's best address for character merchandise also stocks a selection of souvenirs relating to surrounding pavilions (most notably, Spaceship Earth). This shop stays open about a half hour after the rest of the park. It's a great place to wait out the big exit crush.

NORWAY (World Showcase): The Puffin's Roost is undoubtedly Central Florida's best source for trolls and gorgeous Norwegian sweaters and other outerwear (bargains when compared to the cost of flights to Oslo). Jewelry, wine-themed items, and toys add to the purchase panorama.

UNITED KINGDOM (World Showcase): Some of Epcot's finest shops lie within this pavilion's borders. There's The Toy Soldier (where Winnie the Pooh and Thomas the Tank Engine star); The Crown & Crest (a British free-for-all); Sportsman's Shoppe (a bounty of sports apparel); The Queen's Table (with fragrances, soaps, jewelry, tartans, and other collectibles); and The Magic of Wales (rock 'n' roll-inspired merchandise). The Tea Caddy is a must-see for fans of English tea.

Disney's Hollywood Studios

ANIMATION GALLERY: One of five Walt Disney World venues showcasing limited-edition art pieces, collectibles, and animation cels from a variety of Disney movies. The difference here: the chance to watch an artist creating a work that will be for sale in the shop once it's finished. (Note that this doesn't happen all the time. That's part of what makes it special.)

KEYSTONE CLOTHIERS: Characters turn up on smartly styled men's and women's casual wear, luggage, and shoes, not to mention accessories of the character tie and boxer short sort.

SID CAHUENGA'S ONE-OF-A-KIND: Celebrity encounters abound in this den of movie and television memorabilia. There's lots of signed photos

and movie posters and, if you time it right, very belated premiere invitations to Disney animated films.

There's also an occasional opportunity to snap up hand-me-downs direct from the stars, so when someone compliments your handbag, you can say, "Yeah, Mae West liked it, too."

MOUSE ABOUT TOWN: This shop offers a well-heeled wardrobe of subtly (for the most part) Mouse-infused jackets, shirts, and sweatshirts, pajamas, and other apparel in colors a human-about-town would also appreciate. Christmas-themed items can also be found here.

ONCE UPON A TIME: . . . there was a little shop that offered a very classy clothing collection—with items ranging from classic to trendy. (And yes, most of it features a very familiar mouse.)

The Mouse Delivers

- Prowling the property but can't find the object of your obsession? Ask a park employee, and if that must-have Donald Duck screen saver or Tinker Bell tea set exists, he or she should be able to find out where it's sold.

- Have a sudden not-to-be-denied yearning for a watch or tie that you saw in a shop during your visit? Call WDW Mail Order at 407-363-6200.

- If your Disney cravings are still unfulfilled, call 818-265-4660 to find the Disney Store nearest you. Or browse through Disney offerings from the comfort of home at www.disneyshopping.com.

- Theme park shoppers may arrange to send purchases to a location near the gates for later pickup. Walt Disney World resort guests can have purchases delivered to their hotels free of charge. (Packages don't arrive until the next day, so don't ship anything for the day you plan to check out.) For an extra charge, shoppers may arrange to have packages shipped home.

SUNSET CLUB COUTURE: This purveyor of jewelry and limited-edition timepieces has the sort of incomparable selection that makes collectors' eyes widen. Consider gold pocket watches with conspicuous ears, marcasite pieces with stylized Mickey designs, and custom-made watches with tremendous face value (namely, your choice of characters, drawn and then sealed onto the watch's face).

THE WRITER'S STOP: A cozy commissary of cookies, cappuccino, stationery (and scrapbooking accessories), and Hollywood- and Disney-themed page-turners, this outlet provides a comfy pit stop (and shop).

Animal Kingdom Standouts

DISNEY OUTFITTERS (Discovery Island): Nature-themed apparel and gifts can be found here. Selections vary from everything you need to start your own backyard habitat to tinkling chimes, aromatic candles, and soothing fountains. Disney character merchandise is sold here, too.

ISLAND MERCANTILE (Discovery Island): The park's largest shopping oasis in a nutshell: stuffed animals on safari. Certainly, this is the last word in safari hat style, as interpreted by every Disney character that ever saw the embroidered front of a sweatshirt.

MOMBASA MARKETPLACE / ZIWANI TRADERS (Africa): Take one of the striking Kenyan-made walking sticks for an in-store test stroll, and you may well receive raves on your carving skills while perusing the soapstone elephants, hand-painted boxes, raku animal figurines, straw hats, colorful apparel, and other traditional African wares—as well as a selection of Disney character–inspired items.

Conservation Initiative

As anyone who has ever given a gorilla a dollar could tell you, animals aren't great money managers. Which is why initiatives like the Disney Worldwide Conservation Fund come in handy.

This fund was established to support conservation efforts worldwide. You can help by tacking on a dollar for the Conservation Fund when you make a purchase at any Animal Kingdom shop. If you're interested, pick up a brochure from a shop display for a list of nonprofit organizations assisted to date.

Expect a gentle solicitation at the cash register. Don't expect a gorilla looking for a handout.

Other Pursuits

You're at Walt Disney World, but you're not in the mood for a theme park, don't feel much like swatting a little ball or sitting poolside, and have already shopped (and dropped). You're up for something, but lack inspiration. What to do? Don't despair. Disney's got it covered.

Water Parks

Typhoon Lagoon

The centerpiece of this 61-acre water park—ostensibly a small resort town transformed by a big storm—is a surf lagoon larger than two football fields that incites happy pandemonium with every six-foot wave that comes along. But there are also three speed slides (which drop 51 feet at 30 miles per hour), three quick and curvy body slides, and a trio of raft rides that send tubers careening through caverns and over

Did You Know?

Pontoon boats may be chartered for a cruise at select times of day. The cost for a one-hour excursion starts at about $225 for up to 8 guests. The price includes a driver, snacks, and soft drinks. Call 407-WDW-PLAY (939-7529) for details.

waterfalls. Wanna know what your socks experience during the washing machine's spin cycle? Give Crush 'n' Gusher a whirl. It's the park's famous "water coaster" thrill ride. For a calmer alternative, hop in a tube and float along the lazy river that encircles the park.

KNOW BEFORE YOU GO: Typhoon Lagoon is near Downtown Disney. Pools are heated during winter, and the park may be closed for refurbishment for about two months each year (call 407-WDW-PLAY [939-7529] for exact dates). During warmer months, the masses arrive early, often filling the parking lot before noon. When capacity is reached, no one is admitted until crowds subside, often around 2 P.M. (Typhoon Lagoon is usually the second water park to reach capacity. Blizzard Beach is first.)

HOW TO GET THERE: Buses from all Disney resorts. (It's the Typhoon Lagoon/Downtown Disney line.)

WHERE TO EAT: Of the two main snack stands, Leaning Palms has a larger selection than Typhoon Tilly's. Picnic areas are close at hand. Outside food is welcome, but alcoholic beverages are not.

VITAL STATISTICS:
Hours vary, but are generally 10 A.M. to 5 P.M., with extended hours in effect during summer months (call 407-939-7529 for current times). Adult admission is about $45, not including tax. Entry to the Typhoon Lagoon water park is a "Water Park Fun and More" add-on (aka "plus") option with the Magic Your Way base ticket. It's included with a Premium Annual Pass, too. Dressing rooms are available, and lockers and towels may be rented. Singapore Sal's has beach basics.

Typhoon Lagoon Tips

- Call 407-WDW-PLAY (939-7739) to ask about (very) early-morning surf lessons.

- For time checks, look to the shrimp boat marooned atop Typhoon Lagoon's makeshift mountain; it sounds its horn and shoots a 50-foot blast of water into the air every 30 minutes.

- Bad weather or capacity crowds can prompt the park to close.

- Women will find that one-piece suits generally fare better on the slides here.

- Premium, cabana-like spaces known as Beachcomber Shacks are available for rental. They include an attendant, refreshments, towels, and more. Each shack accommodates up to six guests and costs about $250 a day. For details or to make a reservation, call 407-939-7529.

Blizzard Beach

Disney legend has it that this 66-acre water park—Walt Disney World's largest—is the melted remains of a failed Disney ski resort. Call it a not-so-little white lie. The bottom line on this place built around a "snow-covered" man-made peak called Mount Gushmore: It has some amazing runs. Chief among them is a ski-jump-turned-speed-slide that sends giddy riders down the watery equivalent of a double-black diamond run (a 120-foot drop at a 66-degree angle, in which speeds reach 60 miles per hour). A second slide plunges from 90 feet. Less intimidating highlights include a raft ride accommodating five people per raft, side-by-side "racing" slides, and flumes that slalom. For cool yet calm, there's a lazy floatable creek that encircles the park (though it does at one point run through a cave dripping with ice-cold water) and a free-form pool with gently bobbing waves.

KNOW BEFORE YOU GO: Blizzard Beach is located near Animal Kingdom, adjacent to Disney's Winter Summerland miniature-golf course. All pools are heated during the winter; the park is typically closed for refurbishment for at least one month or two each year. During the warmer months, the masses descend upon Blizzard Beach early in the day. When peak

Blizzard Beach Tips

- The chairlift that transports guests to the summit of Mount Gushmore affords a wonderful view, as does an observatory located at the summit itself.

- Women will find that one-piece suits fare better on the speed slides here.

- Inclement weather or maxed-out crowds can cause the park to close early.

- The concrete pathways can get hot, making water shoes a coveted commodity.

- Premium, cabana-like spaces known as Polar Patios are available for rental. They include an attendant, refreshments, towels, and more. Each patio accommodates up to six guests and costs about $250 a day. For details or to make a reservation, call 407-939-7529.

capacity is reached, no one is admitted until crowds ease up, usually around 2 P.M. The park may also close due to inclement weather.

HOW TO GET THERE: Buses are available from Disney's Hollywood Studios and all Walt Disney World resorts.

WHERE TO EAT: Of the four snack stands, Lottawatta Lodge is the largest and most centrally located. Picnic areas are nearby.

VITAL STATISTICS: Hours vary, but are generally from 10 A.M. to 5 P.M., with extended hours in effect throughout the summer months. Adult admission is $45, not including tax. A Blizzard Beach/Disney's Winter Summerland pass, including Blizzard Beach admission and a round of mini golf, may be offered, too. Entry to Blizzard Beach is a "Water Park Fun and More" add-on (aka "plus") option with the Magic Your Way base ticket. It's also included with a Premium Annual Pass. Dressing rooms are available, and lockers and towels may be rented. The Beach Haus stocks essentials.

Natural Distraction
Fort Wilderness

Simply put, no place on Disney property is better equipped to satisfy most yens related to the great outdoors than this resort and recreation area, set on 750 forested, canal-crossed acres on the shore of the World's largest lake. Between its scenic canals and its guided fishing excursions, Fort Wilderness gives anglers unparalleled access to Bay Lake's largemouth bass. Since the lake was stocked with more than 70,000 bass in the 1960s, this waterway is teeming with fish that are ready and waiting to tangle with your line.

A marina invites guests to rent all manner of boats for explorations of the lake. (See "Sports" earlier in this chapter for more details on fishing and boating excursions.) Escorted trail rides and a hiking path deliver nature lovers into peaceful areas where it's not uncommon to see deer, armadillos, and birds. Myriad pathways provide inspiring venues for joggers and cyclists (bikes are available for rent), and tennis, volleyball, and basketball courts are scattered about the property. There's also a pony farm, blacksmith shop (where you can meet the man who shoes the horses that pull the trolleys

on Main Street, U.S.A.), and a funky tree that has mysteriously grown around a lawn mower. The two swimming pools are open only to campground guests. In the evenings, carriage rides and wagon rides (see pages 65 and 176 for more information), Mickey's Backyard Barbecue (seasonal), and the popular dinner show the Hoop-Dee-Doo Musical Revue keep things humming. Note that the beach is for sun-bathing only.

HOW TO GET THERE: This isn't the easiest place to get to—but there are several travel options. The quickest way is generally by car. But know that guests staying at any Walt Disney World–owned property may take boat launches from the Magic Kingdom park, Wilderness Lodge, or the Contemporary resort. Buses also transport guests here from

Downtown Disney and the theme parks.

GETTING AROUND: Only vehicles bound for campsites and cabins are permitted beyond the guest parking lot. Fort Wilderness is serviced by an internal bus system that links all recreation areas, campsites, and cabins (buses circulate at 20-minute intervals from 7 A.M. to 2 A.M.). Guests who prefer greater independence may rent bikes from the Bike Barn or electric carts at the Reception Outpost.

WHERE TO EAT: The Settlement Trading Post and the Meadow Trading Post stock a tiny supply of staples and prepared sandwiches; there's also Trail's End restaurant for all-day dining.

VITAL STATISTICS: Admission is free for Disney resort guests. The Bike Barn in the Meadow Recreation Area is the place to pick up trail maps and rent bikes (about $9 per hour, $22 per day), canoes ($7 per half hour, $11 per hour), rods and reels (for a fee), fishing poles (for a fee), and electric carts (about $49 for 24 hours; reservations necessary; call 407-824-2742). Wagon rides depart twice nightly at 5:30 P.M. and 9:30 P.M. from Pioneer Hall

Fort Wilderness Tips

- You can survey the beauty of Fort Wilderness via bicycles rented from the Bike Barn for about $9 per hour or $22 per day.

- Getting to and from this area can take a lot of time—inquire at the Lobby Concierge as to the most efficient route. Build in extra commuting time if you're planning to attend the Hoop-Dee-Doo Musical Revue.

and last about an hour. The ride costs about $8 per person.

Fort Wilderness carriage rides depart every thirty minutes, from 5:30 P.M. until 9:30 P.M. Each 30-minute ride begins in front of Crockett's Tavern at Pioneer Hall and costs $45 (credit cards are not accepted; Disney hotel IDs, cash, and Disney Dollars are). Tickets are sold by the carriage drivers. Small carriages fit two guests; larger ones can accommodate four. For more information, call 407-939-7529.

Guided 45-minute trail rides depart four times daily from the Tri-Circle-D Livery near the visitor lot; reservations suggested ($46; call 407-WDW-PLAY [939-7529] up to 180 days ahead).

Romantic Excursions and Specialty Cruises

Grand I

This sleek 52-foot Sea Ray yacht, completely furnished with bedroom, bathroom, kitchen, and living/dining room, is the sort of craft that escorts VIPs on private tours of the Seven Seas Lagoon and Bay Lake before nightfall, pausing in just the right spot as the Wishes fireworks show (when available) explodes above Cinderella Castle. But don't be misled: The *Grand I* defines VIPs quite broadly, to encompass any group of up to 18 passengers lucky enough to snare a reservation. Although providing vistas of the Magic Kingdom fireworks (with audio) is the *Grand I*'s specialty, the craft can be booked for most any hour, most any day. You may content yourself with feasting merely on the fireworks and the stars, or you may have your excursion catered, courtesy of chefs at the Grand Floridian. Thus, the possibilities extend from a private cruise for two, complete with dinner and champagne, to a cocktail party for 18, with shrimp, chips and salsa, wings, beer, and wine. And yes, it is always an option for a small-but-elegant wedding reception.

RATES: You'll pay $480 an hour to rent the *Grand I*. Cost is per boat-load (up to 18 passengers); driver and deckhand are included, refreshments are not. The price is higher if you add butler service.

RESERVATIONS: Reservations for excursions on the *Grand I* may be made up to 180 days in advance; they must be made at least 24 hours ahead. Call 407-939-7529 to book the *Grand I*.

Pontoon Boats

No one will ever confuse a pontoon boat with a fancy yacht, but when it comes to specialty cruises, no one's looking at the boat, anyway. What matters: comfort, a great vantage point, and timing. So it is that Walt Disney World's pontoon boats, which accommodate up to eight or ten people on private one-hour cruises, provide some of the best seats around for the Wishes fireworks show (Magic Kingdom) and Epcot's IllumiNations (when available). Wishes fireworks cruises ply the Seven Seas Lagoon and Bay Lake, making quiet ripples on the water outside the Magic Kingdom. Some pontoon boats even have audio. IllumiNations excursions prowl the waters of Crescent Lake.

RATES: Cost for Wishes (Magic Kingdom) and IllumiNations cruises start at about $250 (for up to eight passengers); premium cruises run about $275 for up to ten people. A driver is provided, as are snacks and soft drinks.

RESERVATIONS: Specialty cruises must be reserved at least 24 hours ahead; advance reservations, accepted up to 180 days ahead, are strongly recommended (especially during peak times of the year). Call 407-WDW-PLAY (939-7529).

Spas
Grand Floridian Spa & Health Club

Although more pocket-size than palatial, this low-frills peach-and-aqua-hued retreat has ample space to coddle 17 people at once—provided that there's a twosome being pummeled to contentment in the couple's treatment room. His-and-hers lounges, saunas, steam rooms, and whirlpools make worthy hangouts of the locker rooms. Services have included baths steeped in native Floridian flowers and a deluxe facial complete with two masks and hand and foot massages. A cooling wrap incorporating lavender oil and calendula soothes the sunburned. Ultimate Relaxation pairs a traditional massage with a soak in hydrotherapy. The facility is much less opulent than one might expect at this resort, but it delivers a relaxing respite.

WORTH NOTING: The treatment menu includes aromatherapy; reflexology; shiatsu; Swedish body services; as well as a relaxing massage designed especially for expectant mothers. Massages last 25 to 80 minutes. Manicures, pedicures, and soothing hand and foot treatments are administered in the comfort of chairs that massage the lower back; feet are soaked in whirlpool baths. The spa offers a variety of body wraps and scrubs; an array of facials, including one especially for men; and several aromatherapy baths. Couples may receive side-by-side aromatherapy massages or a hands-on massage lesson in the spa's couples room.

KNOW BEFORE YOU GO: The Grand Floridian Spa is next to the health club at its namesake hotel, near the Magic Kingdom theme park. Hours are usually from 8 A.M. to 7 P.M. For information, visit *www.relaxedyet.com*. Reservations are accepted up to one year ahead; call 407-824-2332.

HOW TO GET THERE: Monorail and boat transportation are available to Walt Disney World resort guests from the Magic Kingdom park. Guests may also take the monorail from Epcot and the Transportation and Ticket Center (TTC), and buses from Downtown Disney, Disney's Hollywood Studios, and Animal Kingdom.

RATES: Expect to pay about $120 for a 50-minute massage and about $130 for a facial. Prices do not include gratuity. We recommend a tip of 18 to 20 percent for quality service.

PACKAGES: Both half-day and full-day options are available. Packages range from the Citrus Zest Collection (which includes all of the signature Grand Floridian spa services) to the Relaxed Yet? package (five hours of treatments, plus lunch).

Did You Know?

You're not only welcome, you are encouraged to show up at least 30 minutes before your scheduled spa service to lounge in the sauna, steam room, and whirlpool. Similarly, all three spas are linked to first-rate health clubs, which you can use before or (yeah, right) after your treatment.

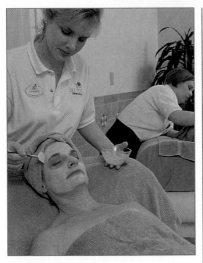

The Spa at Disney's Saratoga Springs Resort

This sweat-free zone within Sweat Central (aka the Saratoga Springs Fitness Center) is a realm of unaffected calm.

Services include soothing massage, hydrotherapy, reflexology, aromatherapy, deluxe and stone facials, plus hand and foot treatments. Also on the menu is a series of signature Mystical Forest treatments and a Maple Sugar Body Polish. The locker rooms are each equipped with a steam room, sauna, and whirlpool. Ordering a spa cuisine lunch is an option in the spa's co-ed lounge. Specifics may change.

WORTH NOTING: The treatment lineup runs from sports and Swedish massages to couples treatments. Massages last about 25 to 80 minutes. The selection of body wraps and scrubs is designed to promote harmony while achieving optimum benefits for the entire body. In addition to specialty manicures and pedicures, this spa offers an array of facials.

KNOW BEFORE YOU GO: The spa is tucked within the resort's fitness center. Treatment hours are from 8 A.M. to 8 P.M. daily. Reservations are taken up to one year ahead. Health club hours are 6 A.M. to 9 P.M. daily. For more information, visit *www.relaxedyet.com*. For reservations, call 407-827-4455.

HOW TO GET THERE: Buses transport WDW resort guests from the theme parks and Downtown Disney. There are footpaths to the spa from the Downtown Disney Marketplace and West Side. (It's about a five-minute walk.)

RATES: It costs about $120 for a 50-minute massage and about $130 (plus gratuity) for a facial.

PACKAGES: Full- and half-day packages are available. They range from the "Mystical Forest Retreat" for about $330 to the "Adirondack Adventure," which is about $405.

The Spa at Buena Vista Palace

Opposite Downtown Disney Marketplace, this peaceful piece of the Buena Vista Palace offers a pampering repertoire of more than 75 treatments that are about as deep and diverse as they come. Features include a landscaped outdoor whirlpool and 13 treatment rooms. The cool-mud Theme Park Leg Relief Wrap shows the spa's lighter side. Speaking of light, spa cuisine can be delivered poolside. Now that's indulgent.

WORTH NOTING: Treatments include aromatherapy, shiatsu, Swedish, deep-tissue, reflexology, and hot stone massages lasting from 25 to 80 minutes. An adjoining full-service salon offers the usual services; normal pedicures and manicures are eclipsed by the likes of the 80-minute Sports Pedicure, complete with whirlpool footbath, heated mud pack, aromatherapy, paraffin dip, and foot massage.

The spa offers a variety of facials, including one to relieve sun-stressed skin. Body scrubs and wraps incorporate cool and warm mud, sea salt, aromatic oils, tea, seaweed, exotic plants, brown sugar, and even chocolate.

KNOW BEFORE YOU GO: Buena Vista Palace Hotel & Spa is located on Buena Vista Drive, across from the Downtown Disney Marketplace. Hours vary, but are usually from about 8 A.M. to 8 P.M. Call 407-827-3200.

HOW TO GET THERE: The resort is across the street from the Downtown Disney Marketplace, which can be reached from any Disney resort via bus.

RATES: A 25-minute "Meeting Relief" massage is about $75, and facials cost about $110 (a 20 percent gratuity is added to single spa services).

PACKAGES: The 2- to 5-hour options include, among others, the Golden Door Experience (pineapple body scrub, Golden Door Harvest facial, spa cuisine

Spa 101

As a rule, aromatherapy massages are the lightest (and most aromatic); reflexology (hands and feet) and shiatsu involve precise pressure points rather than the (light or deep) kneading motions of Swedish massage; hydrotherapy massage (delivered by jets or a water-jet wand as you float in a tub) is as soothing as it gets.

lunch; $230) and the Gentlemen's Special (deep-tissue massage, facial, and aromatherapy salt glow; $265).

Mandara Spa

As guests enter this, Walt Disney World's newest and most elaborately themed spa, they are instantly immersed in an atmosphere of serenity. The peaceful retreat, housed in the Dolphin resort, reflects "the beauty, spirit and traditions of both Eastern and Western cultures."

The spa menu showcases, among other things, Mandara's signature Balinese massage. Developed in Bali, it is an eclectic variation of the traditional Swedish massage ($125 for 50 minutes). Other luxurious treatments include Mandara Four Hand massage ($240 for 50 minutes), Elemis aroma stone therapy massage ($185 for 75 minutes), the Elemis visible brilliance facial ($160 for 50 minutes), and the Elemis coconut rub and milk ritual wrap with a 50-minute massage ($220). Relaxing "rituals" include a 2½-hour Sunrise Awakening ($270) and the 3½-hour Zen for Men ($315). There is a full-service hair and nail salon on-site, as well as a tea

Spa Tips

- Reserve treatments well in advance; confirm your appointment before you arrive.

- Request a female or male spa therapist if you have a preference. The spa will honor your wishes, if at all possible.

- Jewelry and spa treatments don't mix. Plan ahead and leave yours in a safe at your hotel.

- Arrive about 15 minutes before your appointment. That'll give you time to shower and change.

- It's a good idea to jump in the shower before any spa treatment—especially during summer.

- Clean slippers are available to all spa customers. Wear 'em.

- If it's a body treatment, you may or may not leave underwear in the locker. It's all about your comfort level. Robes provided are sized for modesty, and therapists are trained to discreetly cover private areas during treatments.

- Bathing suits are optional for the separate men's and women's saunas and whirlpools.

- Drink plenty of water to counter dehydrating effects of treatments.

- Take time to enjoy the glow: All Walt Disney World spas have a peaceful area in which guests may relax post treatment.

- Silence your cell phone.

garden and a meditation garden.

For additional information on the sensational Mandara spa and how to book a treatment, visit *www.swandolphin.com.*

181

From casual to posh, Disney dining offers a delicious world of possibilities.

Dining & Entertainment

It's late in the book, and we're sure you must be dying of hunger by now, so we'll begin by running through the food specials. But first, you'll be happy to hear that the outfit you are wearing at this moment, plus shoes, will be just fine for most any WDW restaurant (assuming that you didn't get all gussied up to read this chapter or that you're not in your pajamas). And second, atmosphere is a specialty of the house (you won't simply dine on seafood here, you'll do it cheek-to-cheek with a bustling coral reef or within the effervescent context of a New England clambake). Sampler platters include such unfamiliar cuisines as Norwegian and Moroccan. And if you're looking for some sophisticated eats, you're in luck.

In response to patrons' requests for fresher, more imaginative fare, Disney has given its chefs greater freedom. As an example of the quality of dining that can now be found at Walt Disney World, consider Artist Point restaurant, which features the likes of just-hooked king salmon, creatively prepared and served with hard-to-find pinot noirs from the Pacific Northwest. But we're getting carried away, and you're hungry and need to make some decisions. Our "Restaurant Guide" will help. It cuts to the chase and describes the best dining spots for adults in the World.

Of course, you also need to be thinking about what you want to do later in the evening. Please, take your time, and when you're ready to think about after-dinner entertainment, know that this chapter's "Nightlife Guide" provides the complete scoop on Downtown Disney and BoardWalk, as well as some of the more compelling spots in the theme parks and resorts.

Enjoy!

RESTAURANT GUIDE

We're happy to report that Walt Disney World has more tempting cuisine for the sophisticated palate than ever before, as behind-the-scenes improvements—from fresher, more flavorful ingredients to stronger wine lists—have quietly pushed the epicurean envelope. Healthier, more interesting grazing options in the theme parks can provide inexpensive treats that help subsidize the sit-down meals.

To ease the task of deciding among the many eateries, we've whittled the list down to the full-service restaurants and more casual noshing spots we recommend as the best adult bets.

Under the heading "Standouts," you'll find stellar places to grab a great bite on the quick, moderately priced restaurants with exceptional flair, and extra-special havens worth every hard-earned dollar for their distinctive food and settings. Under the designation "Good Bets," we've corralled additional locales, also highly regarded, that we've come to know as fine places to have a meal. Because Disney's theme parks are unique terrain calling for both firm arrangements and flexible eating plans, we have included recommendations for fast-food and full-service options.

THEME PARKS
Table Service
Standouts

BISTRO DE PARIS (France, Epcot's World Showcase): An intimate bistro that puts on romantic airs rather than the usual bustle. If you think the elegant decor, with its evocative interplay of brass sconces, milk-glass chandeliers,

Reservations Explained

A Disney World reservation is far from traditional. The system was devised to minimize wait times, while allowing for walk-ins (who are willing to wait). When you make a reservation, you will receive a seating time, but it's not a guarantee that you'll get a table at that time. Instead, you'll be asked to check in at the restaurant at your reservation time and will then become eligible for the next available table. (Our advice: Arrive early.)

Here's how the system works: (1) Those with a reservation will be seated at or near their assigned time, and (2) walk-ins will have a shot at any open tables. To make arrangements, call 407-WDW-DINE (939-3463) up to 180 days ahead* of your preferred dining date. Hours are daily from 7 A.M. to 10 P.M. It's best to confirm policies with 407-WDW-DINE. And be sure to bring your confirmation number.

Do you have a confirmed reservation at a Disney–owned–and–operated resort? If so, you are entitled to one very special perk: Call 180 days prior to the first day of your reservation and you can make dining reservations for up to 10 days of your stay. That's like getting a 1- to 10-day jump on everyone else! (Stays longer than 10 days will require a second call.) Have your resort confirmation number handy when you contact 407-WDW-DINE.

mirrors, and leaded glass, is convincingly French, wait until you swallow your first morsel. This is hearty dining, so you might want to stroll around the promenade to walk off your escargots, rack of lamb, and warm chocolate cake. The impressive wine list is *très* French. Reservations are suggested. **D $$$-$$$$**

CHEFS DE FRANCE (France, Epcot's World Showcase): "Bright lights, big dining room" describes this airy restaurant. With three of France's best chefs—Paul Bocuse, Roger Vergé, and pastry guru Gaston Lenôtre—keeping tabs on this *nouvelle* French kitchen, the broth is far from spoiled. We love the mere thought of the Lyon-style onion soup and the ways in which they fill a puff pastry. Wine pairings are suggested from the modest list. Reservations are suggested. **L D $$$-$$$$**

THE CRYSTAL PALACE (Main Street, Magic Kingdom): A landmark of sorts, this restaurant—one of our favorites in the Magic Kingdom—could be a Victorian garden if not for the walls and

How to Book a Table

- In the theme parks: Reservations are suggested for nearly all table-service restaurants; simply call 407-939-3463, or visit *www.disneyworld.com/dining/*. For same-day arrangements in the Magic Kingdom, report to City Hall; in Epcot, head to Guest Relations; in Disney's Hollywood Studios, go to the corner of Hollywood and Sunset; and in Animal Kingdom, ask at Guest Relations in The Oasis (go to Rainforest Cafe for a table at the restaurant itself). Same-day plans can also be made at all park restaurants or by dialing *88 from a pay phone within a theme park.

- In WDW resorts: Reservations for Disney resort restaurants may be made by calling 407-WDW-DINE (939-3463) or by dialing 55 on any house phone.

- Unless otherwise noted, reservations at Downtown Disney and the Hotel Plaza Boulevard resorts may be made by calling 407-WDW-DINE (939-3463).

various sides for dinner. Friends from the Hundred Acre Wood wander about during all meals. Though the name "Crystal Palace" tends to conjure up images of serenity, that's not quite the case. As a character affair, this joint is always jumping. Reservations are suggested. **B L D $$-$$$**

50'S PRIME TIME CAFE (Disney's Hollywood Studios): In a word: cool. This good-humored retreat to the era of *I Love Lucy* is an amusing amalgam of comfort food, kitschy 1950s-style kitchen nooks, and attentive servers of

ceiling. The views (of Main Street and Cinderella Castle) are a feast for the eyes, and the all-you-can-eat buffet is easily the most bountiful (if not terribly creative) spread of any meal in the park. It's driven by fresh produce, including a salad bar, and adds carved meats, fish, and

the "No talking with your mouth full" ilk. Expect Mom or her favored offspring to meddle in your affairs here ("Did you wash your hands? All right, then; what color was the soap?"). And recognize that the best fun is had by doing some regressing of your own. As for the fare, it's tasty home cooking as it used to be (heavy on the meat and potatoes), served in generous-to-the-point-of-grandmotherly portions. Most guests find that it honors their memory of fried chicken, meat loaf, s'mores, and peanut-butter-and-jelly milk shakes. A full bar is available. Reservations are suggested. **L D $$-$$$**

CORAL REEF (Epcot, Future World): It's all about sneaking bites of fresh fish under the watchful eyes of sea turtles, dolphins, and gargantuan groupers. Every table has a panoramic view of the living coral reef; some are right up against the glass. Menu items run the gamut, but include traditional seafood dishes such as seared salmon and grilled mahimahi. Grilled New York strip and wild mushroom lasagna are available for those who prefer to just watch the fish. Reservations are suggested. **L D $$$**

HOLLYWOOD BROWN DERBY (Disney's Hollywood Studios): The Studios' most gracious dining is found at this faithful revival of the original cause célèbre, which opened on Hollywood and Vine back in 1926. Dressed to the nines in chandeliers and celebrity caricatures, the restaurant stokes the appetite with its finely chopped signature Cobb salad and fabulous grapefruit cake. The New World wine list is excellent. Reservations are suggested.

Note: Park guests can take advantage of the Fantasmic! Dining Opportunity. Special seating for the evening's performance of Fantasmic is offered, but is not guaranteed—plan to arrive at the theater 60 to 90 minutes early. The Fantasmic! Dining Opportunity can—and should—be booked in advance; call 407-WDW-DINE (939-3463). **L D $$-$$$**

Smoker's Alert

With the exception of designated areas, public parts of Walt Disney World are all nonsmoking. Same goes for the rest of the state, as it is now a Florida law. Check park guidemaps for areas where smoking is permitted, or inquire at your resort's lobby concierge desk.

TUSKER HOUSE (Africa, Animal Kingdom): Wild elephants could not keep us away from this grazing option. The ample buffet fare here is a big draw. That said, the morning meal is a character affair, so it's hardly a relaxing respite. Lunch and dinner, however, are character free. We dig the carved chairs inside, but somehow the Safari Amber beer tastes better outside. (There is seating both in- and outdoors.) Reservations are suggested. `B L D` $$–$$$

Good Bets

BIERGARTEN (Germany, Epcot's World Showcase): Prepare for the best of the wurst. A buffet of traditional German cuisine (don't miss the red cabbage, spaetzle, or sauerbraten) is the main attraction in this charming makeshift courtyard. Adding to the fun are communal tables, steins of beer, a selection of German wines and liqueurs, and live entertainment (at both lunch and dinner). Follow it up with apple strudel. Reservations are strongly suggested. `L D` $$–$$$

CINDERELLA'S ROYAL TABLE (Cinderella Castle, Magic Kingdom): Normally we would not flag an all-character-meal-all-the-time eatery as a grown-up destination, but the thrill of dining in the Castle combined with the quality of the royal fare makes this spot a Magic Kingdom treasure. Specialties have included roast prime rib, herbed chicken, and salmon. The majestic blue goblets, or the "milady" and "milord" salutations from our waiter always make us feel like queen and king for a day (or a meal).

Cinderella mingles with guests in the lobby while her princess friends visit each table during breakfast and lunch. Fairy Godmother works the room at dinner. Reservations are necessary for all meals. (It is one tough ticket! Call 180 days in advance, first thing in the morning [407-939-3463], and keep your fingers crossed.) A photo package is included with the

| B breakfast | L lunch | D dinner | S snacks | $ $15 | $$ $15-$36 | $$$ $36-$60 | $$$$ $60 and up |

package, so be sure to primp before you arrive. Payment in full is due at booking. Cancellations must be within 24 hours for a full refund. B L D $$$

GARDEN GRILL (Epcot, Future World): When your assigned reservation time comes due at this lazy-Susan-turned-dining-area (it rotates very slowly above the rainforest, desert, and prairie scenes visited by the Living with the Land boat ride below). Chip, Dale, and pals make the rounds at each meal. The vittles, which are served family style, actually feature some vegetables grown in The Land's greenhouses, plus fried fish, rotisserie meats, and grilled flank steak. Reservations are suggested. D $$-$$$

HOLLYWOOD & VINE (Disney's Hollywood Studios): This Art Deco–style buffet restaurant has Tinseltown flourishes. Spirits are available, too. Breakfast and lunch are Playhouse Disney character affairs. Dinner is character free.

Note: Park guests can take advantage of the Fantasmic! Dining Opportunity. Special seating for the evening's performance of Fantasmic is offered, but is not guaranteed—plan to arrive at the theater 60 to 90 minutes early. The Fantasmic! Dining Opportunity can—and should—be booked in advance; call 407-WDW-DINE (939-3463). L D $$-$$$

LE CELLIER STEAKHOUSE (Canada, Epcot's World Showcase): We love retreating to this wine cellar-like spot, a favorite place for a hearty meal. The menu has featured filet mignon, prime rib, and New York strip steaks. Cheddar cheese soup is another specialty of the house. Then there's potential for crème brûlée. Microbrew beers from Quebec and Canadian lagers are served. Reservations are necessary. L D $$-$$$

Dining Plan

If you are planning to book a Magic Your Way vacation package (see page 16), you may also purchase the Disney Dining Plan. Offered at regular and premium levels, the basic plan allows you to pre-pay for one counter-service meal, snack, and table-service meal per day. It is also possible to get a "quick-service only" plan. It includes two meals a day and a resort refillable mug.

The dining plans do not include gratuity and are subject to change in 2010. Regardless of which plan you opt for, it must be purchased for your entire trip. At press time, roughly 140 Walt Disney World eateries were participating in the program. Note that some menu items carry an additional surcharge, and "table-service" doesn't necessarily mean high end. In order to dine at a "signature" spot (think California Grill or the Hoop-Dee-Doo), you'll need to exchange two table-service meals. We did the math—and, though the selection of venues is a bit restrictive—the Disney Dining Plan really can save you a chunk of change. Which explains the program's loyal following.

MAMA MELROSE'S RISTORANTE ITALIANO (Disney's Hollywood Studios): A pleasantly removed bastion of movie-star photographs and thin-crust pizzas. The menu offers Italian favorites, meats, and seafood cooked in an oak-burning oven. The wine list includes selections from California and Italy. Reservations are suggested.

Note: Park guests can take advantage of the Fantasmic! Dining Opportunity. Special seating for the evening's performance of Fantasmic is offered, but is not guaranteed—plan to arrive at the theater 60 to 90 minutes early. For information or reservations, call 407-939-3463. L D $$-$$$

MARRAKESH (Morocco, Epcot's World Showcase): It's not every day that you can slip into an exquisitely tiled Moroccan palace and expect to be entertained by belly dancers and musicians as you polish off a sampler plate of Moroccan cuisine, such as couscous or kebobs. The music isn't always subtle. Reservations are suggested. L D $$$

PLAZA RESTAURANT (Main Street, Magic Kingdom): Frozen desserts outnumber the burgers and sandwiches on the menu in this under-appreciated-yet-ever-so-charming spot. Consider this ratio a hint to rope off stomach space for one of the sundaes or floats. Reservations are suggested. L D S $$

RAINFOREST CAFE (Animal Kingdom and Downtown Disney Marketplace): Lush (and loud) as a jungle, this place is thick with tropical vegetation and fish-filled aquariums (not to mention the occasional thunderstorm). Dishes answer to names like Mogambo (pasta with shrimp), Plant Sandwich (veggies), and Mojo Bones (barbecued ribs). Appetizers and desserts can be shared. Reservations are suggested at both locations (these eateries are quite popular). B L D S $$-$$$

ROSE & CROWN PUB & DINING ROOM (United Kingdom, Epcot's World Showcase): The menu ventures only a tad beyond (tasty) fish-and-chips, but we've never been disappointed. Outdoor tables offer a front-row view of the lagoon (and the nightly presentation of IllumiNations), and the indoor pub is downright neighborly. A pianist occasionally provides live entertainment. Reservations are suggested. L D S $$$

SCI-FI DINE-IN THEATER (Disney's Hollywood Studios): The salads, sandwiches, entrées, and desserts here are more creative than at your average drive-in, but the food takes a backseat to the campy setting. Parking

Special Dietary Requests

Most Disney restaurants that accept reservations try to accommodate special dietary requirements (such as allergies to gluten or wheat, shellfish, soy, lactose, peanuts, tree nuts, fish, or eggs). Such places may cater to lifestyle dietary needs (such as no sugar added, low fat, low sodium, or vegetarian), as well. Discuss your needs with your server when you arrive at the restaurant. To make reservations, call 407-939-3463, and ask to note the food allergy or intolerance on the reservation. If you have additional questions or requests after making a reservation, contact *specialdiets@disneyworld.com* at least 14 days prior to arrival.

Similarly, guests who require kosher meals may also have their needs met. Make your kosher requests known when you book your table at least 24 hours ahead. While a credit card is necessary to guarantee the order, it won't be charged if the reservation is canceled at least 24 hours before the reservation time.

The following theme park spots offer kosher selections: Liberty Tree Tavern and Cosmic Ray's Starlight Cafe at the Magic Kingdom; Liberty Inn at Epcot; ABC Commissary at Disney's Hollywood Studios; and Pizzafari at Animal Kingdom.

attendants lead guests to their cars (the tables resemble 1950s-era convertibles). Science-fiction and horror trailers play in a continuous loop on a large screen. A full bar is available. Reservations are suggested. L D $$-$$$

SAN ANGEL INN (Mexico, Epcot's World Showcase): The lights are low, the mood is romantic, and there is a volcano poised tableside. If that's not enchantment enough, there's a mystical pyramid and a moonlit river. The menu? You might need to bring it closer to read it, but you'll find Mexican fare from margaritas to chicken mole. Reservations are suggested. L D $$$

TEPPAN EDO (Japan, Epcot's World Showcase): Already known as one of Epcot's more

enticing pavilions, Japan has become even more so—thanks to the addition of this eatery. Filling the space formerly occupied by Teppanyaki Dining Room, the motif for this newcomer was inspired by Japan's Edo period (which is considered by many to be one of the most tranquil periods of time in human history). Here the spirit of authentic Japanese cuisine is demonstrated through the culinary feats of the Teppan chefs. Reservations are suggested. L D $$$

No Reservations?

If you're caught without dining reservations in the theme parks (not a good idea!), you *might* snag a place at one of these eateries (if you're willing to wait):

- Hollywood Brown Derby (Disney's Hollywood Studios)
- Marrakesh (Morocco, Epcot's World Showcase)
- The Plaza (Main Street, Magic Kingdom)
- Rainforest Cafe (Animal Kingdom)
- Biergarten (Germany, Epcot's World Showcase)
- Yak & Yeti (Animal Kingdom)

B breakfast L lunch D dinner S snacks $ $15 $$ $15-$36 $$$ $36-$60 $$$$ $60 and up

TUTTO ITALIA (Italy, Epcot's World Showcase): Located in the space long occupied by L'Originale Alfredo Di Roma Ristorante, this spot specializes in Mediterranean favorites. Despite its steep prices, Tutto Italia is one of the most popular World Showcase dining spots. Reservations are a must. `L D` `$$$-$$$$`

Quick Service
Standouts

BACKLOT EXPRESS (Disney's Hollywood Studios): Shady and inconspicuous (it's tucked away by the Indiana Jones attraction), this sprawling spot has indoor and outdoor seating. Paint-speckled floors and movie prop debris give you an idea of the decor. Grilled turkey sandwiches, chicken strips, and assorted desserts are available. `L D S` `$`

BOULANGERIE PATISSERIE (France, Epcot's World Showcase): The chocolate croissants, blueberry tarts, apple turnovers, and such are timeless. Follow your nose, and don't neglect to notice the sweet temptation aptly known as the Marvelous. Kronenbourg beer and French wines are also offered. `S` `$`

LA CANTINA DE SAN ANGEL (Mexico, Epcot's World Showcase): Forget for a moment the *churros*, the frozen margaritas, and the Dos Equis drafts: This place has south-of-the-border charm. When the weather cooperates, the outdoor lagoonside seating makes the experience even better. `L D S` `$`

COLUMBIA HARBOUR HOUSE (Liberty Square, Magic Kingdom): This spot distinguishes itself from the rest of the fast-food crowd by emphasizing things from the sea— among them clam chowder, fried fish, salads, and harpoons (which are strictly for decor). If you get salad, request the dressing on the side (we do). When it's open, we head for the upstairs dining room. `L D S` `$`

KRINGLA BAKERI OG KAFE (Norway, Epcot's World Showcase): A super place for a sweet fix or a light lunch. Among the choices here are sandwiches (roast beef, chicken salad, and salmon and scrambled eggs), sweet pretzels called kringlas, and vaflers (heart-shaped waffles freshly made and topped with powdered sugar and preserves). The outdoor seating area is shaded by a grass-thatched roof. L D S $

MAIN STREET BAKERY (Main Street, Magic Kingdom): This dainty spot is renowned for quick breakfasts (from bagels to warm cinnamon rolls) and enormous, fresh-from-the-oven cookies (we love the chocolate chip). The ice-cream cookie sandwiches make good use of flavors from the Plaza Ice Cream Parlor next door. We give high praise to the frozen latte, too. B S $

SOMMERFEST (Germany, Epcot's World Showcase): Here, quick sustenance takes such classic forms as bratwurst, soft pretzels, Black Forest cake, German chocolates, beer, and German wine. There's shaded outdoor seating. L D S $

STARRING ROLLS CAFE (Disney's Hollywood Studios): Have croissant and cappuccino, will travel. This is the place to get the day off

Cheap Eats

Our suggestions for spur-of-the-moment fast food:

- Backlot Express (Disney's Hollywood Studios)
- Casey's Corner (Main Street, Magic Kingdom)
- Flame Tree Barbecue (Discovery Island, Animal Kingdom)
- Columbia Harbour House (Liberty Square, Magic Kingdom)
- Pecos Bill Cafe (Frontierland, Magic Kingdom)
- Starring Rolls Cafe (Disney's Hollywood Studios)
- Sunshine Seasons (The Land, Epcot's Future World)
- Wolfgang Puck Express (Downtown Disney Marketplace)

to a sweet start or to take a cookie or coffee break under umbrella-shaded tables. Added bonus for coffee connoisseurs: They grind their own beans! B L S $

SUNSHINE SEASONS (Epcot, Future World): This bumper crop of dining opportunities, located on The Land pavilion's frenetic lower level, is the best place in Epcot to strap on the ol' feed bag and graze. For dining on the lighter side, select from fresh salads, soups, and sushi (California

B breakfast L lunch D dinner S snacks $ $15 $$ $15-$36 $$$ $36-$60 $$$$ $60 and up

rolls). Heartier fare comes in the form of pastas, sandwiches, rotisserie meats, and noodle bowls. Don't be surprised by the more creative selections, such as roasted beets and goat cheese salad and grilled salmon with kalamata olive pesto sauce. Baked goods—including Soarin' Crème Brûlée—ice cream, and libations round out the options. The eating's more peaceful here outside prime dining hours. **B L D S $**

Good Bets

COSMIC RAY'S STARLIGHT CAFE

(Tomorrowland, Magic Kingdom): Burgers, veggie burgers, salads, and rotisserie chicken are among the offerings here. Oddity of note: It isn't one-stop shopping. You may have to stand on several different lines to fill your order. There is a nice selection, though. An Audio-Animatronics lounge lizard performs throughout the day. **L D S $**

FLAME TREE BARBECUE (Discovery

Island, Animal Kingdom): Take a good gander and you'll see fingers being licked at the riverfront tables bounding this pulled-pork and barbecued-brisket hut. **L D S $**

PIZZAFARI (Discovery Island, Animal Kingdom): When the name of the craving is pizza, consider a spot that still prefers plain old pepperoni to nouveau toppings. The menu strays a bit more than the average pizza place (with the likes of grilled chicken Caesar salad), but we stick to the basics. **L D S $**

PLAZA ICE CREAM PARLOR (Main Street, Magic Kingdom): Simply the park's most bountiful stash of ice cream. Head here when you'd like to have a choice of flavors. **S $**

YAKITORI HOUSE (Japan, Epcot's World Showcase): This pleasant spot (named for the specialty of the house, a savory skewered chicken) is set beside one of the most relaxing settings in all of Epcot for a quick and satisfying bite. Sake and Kirin beer are available. **L D S $**

In the Resorts
Standouts

ARTIST POINT (Wilderness Lodge): The Pacific Northwest theme of this restaurant is announced in landscape murals, while tall, red-framed windows look out to Bay Lake. The cavernous dining room is by no means intimate, but it's not without a certain charm.

Artist Point's hallmark is its knack for translating fresh seasonal ingredients from the Pacific Northwest into flavorful creations. An excellent example is the salmon served on a smoking cedar plank.

The desserts are worth saving room for, no matter how full you think you are. It's just the fork-licking finale you'd expect from a restaurant of this caliber. The wine list features some of the best Syrahs and pinot noirs coming out of Oregon and Washington State right now. The cumulative effect is an artist's palette for the sophisticated palate. Reservations are strongly suggested. D $$$

BIG RIVER GRILLE & BREWING WORKS (BoardWalk): A standout for its fresh-brewed ales alone, this unassuming place delivers huge portions of pub grub. The straightforward menu runs from salads and (huge) sandwiches to burgers and steaks.

This restaurant tends to be more low-key than the other BoardWalk eateries, and makes

Coffee Talk

For java as main course, skip the usual cup of Nescafé and head to one of these coffeehouses—they know double lattes from skim mocha cappuccinos.

- American Adventure (Epcot's World Showcase, a stand in the front of the pavilion)
- Contemporary Grounds (Contemporary resort)
- Kona Cafe (Polynesian resort)
- Jiko—The Cooking Place (Animal Kingdom Lodge)
- Starring Rolls Cafe (Disney's Hollywood Studios)
- Picabu (Dolphin resort)
- Ghirardelli Soda Fountain and Chocolate Shop (Downtown Disney Marketplace)
- The Writer's Stop (Disney's Hollywood Studios)

for a peaceful retreat during the day. Seating is available outside on the boardwalk. First-come seating. L D S $$

CALIFORNIA GRILL (Contemporary): The fresh, seasonal ingredients credo gets an artistic interpretation at this casual feast for the eyes (as well as the stomach) on the Contemporary resort's 15th floor. Chefs here keep no culinary

B breakfast   L lunch   D dinner   S snacks $ $15 $$ $15-$36 $$$ $36-$60 $$$$ $60 and up

secrets as they prepare dishes in an exhibition kitchen.

The West Coast theme shines through in such dishes as grilled pork tenderloin with goat cheese polenta, button mushrooms, and a zinfandel glaze; pan-roasted grouper filet; and a crab salad with avocado and Florida citrus. If there's a bit of a din in the dining room, it's partly because of unsuppressible raves and the waitstaff's collective ability to elaborate on any dish, ingredient, or wine.

The star-studded wine list is a striking mix of greatest hits and good finds. (At press time, six vintages were available by the glass, but that may change.) Also drawing a crowd: the Grill's divine California-style flatbread, fabulous sushi bar, and a host of vegetarian choices. The goat-cheese ravioli appetizer is a crowd favorite.

Fresh desserts along the lines of butterscotch crème brûlée provide the finishing touches, as do sweeping views of the Magic Kingdom (from select seats). Reservations are strongly suggested. **D** $$$-$$$$

CAPE MAY CAFE (Beach Club): The popular, all-you-can-eat New England–style clambake held nightly in this beach-umbrella-decked dining area is among the better values at Walt Disney World. The lineup includes mussels, fish, clams, peel-and-eat shrimp, corn, ribs, red-skin potatoes, chowder, salad, and desserts. Breakfast is a character affair (hosted by Goofy and friends). Reservations are strongly suggested. B D $$-$$$

CITRICOS (Grand Floridian): From the aromas wafting from the open kitchen, it's clear that the chef has vowed to wow you with Mediterranean cuisine herb by fragrant herb. Even if the kitchen were sealed off from view and scent and there were no pastry chefs at work in the dining room, no loaves of bread baking, no private party room or artful wine pairings or potential for a fall-off-the-bone veal shank, we'd still . . . Strike that. There's no changing the essence of Cítricos. Reservations are suggested. D $$$-$$$$

FLYING FISH CAFE (BoardWalk): Expect an earful when you ask about the catch of the day at this compelling eatery bound and determined to serve seafood "so fresh it has an attitude." Fun, sophisticated decor from the designer of the Contemporary's California Grill elevates the appeal. As an example of the (exhibition) kitchen's knack for light, creatively prepared dishes, oak-grilled Maine diver scallops

and potato-wrapped snapper are dishes to consider. The menu items vary daily, but steaks and vegetarian choices are usually offered. Save room for dessert. Note that the fare tends to be more impressive than the service. There is a counter for solo diners. Reservations are strongly suggested. D $$$-$$$$

IL MULINO NEW YORK TRATTORIA (Swan): This elegant eatery offers upscale Italian cuisine in a relaxed yet vibrant bistro-like setting. Specializing in *piatti per il tavolo*, or family-style dining, the spot is ideal for groups. The seasonal menu is characterized by blends of seasonal ingredients suggestive of the Abruzzi region of Italy. Signature items include *gamberi al mulino* (jumbo shrimp with spicy cocktail sauce); *gnocchi bolognese* (potato dumplings

We (Almost) Never Close

The following hotel eateries offer limited menus 24 hours a day during busy seasons (hours may change):

Capt. Cook's (Polynesian)

Gasparilla Grill & Games (Grand Floridian)

Picabu (Dolphin)

with meat sauce); *pollo fra diavolo* (chicken in a spicy red sauce); and *branzino* (sea bass) cooked with cherry tomatoes, garlic, pancetta, and white wine.

All dinners begin with an antipasti tasting, on the house. Enjoy it while perusing the wine list's 250 or so Italian varietals.

Dinner is served from 5 P.M. until 11 P.M. The lounge serves light fare and cocktails from 3 P.M. till about 2 in the morning.

For more information or to make a reservation, call 407-934-1199 or visit *www.swandolphin.com*.
`D` `S` **$$$-$$$$**

JIKO—THE COOKING PLACE

(Animal Kingdom Lodge): One of the most unusual Walt Disney World dining experiences, Jiko's cuisine is inspired by the tastes of South Africa, with influences from around the globe. Start with one of the paper-thin flatbreads, like kalamata olive with five cheeses, or the unusual cucumber, tomato, and red-onion salad with a watermelon vinaigrette. Chermoula chicken is a signature dish, but you'll always find filet mignon and braised pork shank on the menu, too. End your meal with a

fabulous cheese course, pistachio crème brûlée, or Tanzanian chocolate cheesecake. The impressive wine list is exclusively South African, one of the most extensive collections in the U.S. The ethereal dining room was designed by Jeffrey Beers, in a nod to the opening scenes of *The Lion King*. Reservations are required. `D` **$$$-$$$$**

Dinner in Bed

Sometimes it doesn't matter how great a restaurant's ambience is. You want the next knock on the door to be a person with a platter. Room service at Disney's deluxe hotels is as grand as you want it; ask nicely and your appetite for most anything on a house restaurant menu can be sated. With the exception of Wilderness Lodge, BoardWalk, and the Polynesian (last knock: midnight), the deluxe hotels will rustle something up around the clock. Even at moderate and value hotels, room service isn't just about breakfast; from 6 P.M. to 11 P.M. you can order sandwiches, pizza, salads, and the like. Note that deliveries generally, but not always, come within an hour.

NARCOOSSEE'S (Grand Floridian): Within the conspicuous octagonal building that looks out over Seven Seas Lagoon, you'll find a casual restaurant whose open kitchen presents such not-so-casual fare as filet mignon and garlic-stuffed Maine lobster. Yet on the seasonal menu, you may also discover wild salmon and a penne pasta with sautéed vegetables. The food is excellent, and the international wine selection is quite good—you might even enjoy a predinner glass on the veranda. Reservations are strongly suggested.
D $$$

OLIVIA'S CAFE (Old Key West): We thoroughly enjoy the Key Western manner with which Olivia's approaches its theme; certainly, the laid-back setting and menu convey the spirit of the leisure-centric locale. Menu items include salads, conch chowder, baked mahimahi, conch fritters, and seven-layer fudge cake. Wine, beer, and cocktails are served. The menu changes seasonally. Reservations are suggested. **B L D $$**

SANAA (Animal Kingdom Lodge): With a Swahili name that translates to "artwork," this

---

Cook Nook

You're on vacation from cooking, but you still might relish some time in the kitchen. No stirring, roasting, or chopping is required. Victoria & Albert's Chef's Table in the Grand Floridian lets you chat up the masters in the kitchen as they prepare culinary delights. To book this aromatic roost, call 407-WDW-DINE (939-3463) six months in advance. The Chef's Table costs $150 per person (plus tax); with wine pairings, it's $215 per person.

150-seat spot aspires to wow you with its artful African-Indian cuisine. The menu features signature dishes such as chicken or shrimp curry or beef short ribs slow-cooked in a tandoor oven. For lunch, we recommend the interesting salad sampler. Indian-style breads and chutneys, pickles, and raita (yogurt dip) make nice accompaniments. Desserts introduce new tastes, from mango pudding to cardamom butter cake. Reservations are suggested.
L D $$$-$$$$

VICTORIA & ALBERT'S (Grand Floridian): Indulgent without being too haute to handle, this is considered by many to be the grande dame of the Walt Disney

---

B breakfast L lunch D dinner S snacks $ $15 $$ $15-$36 $$$ $36-$60 $$$$ $60 and up

World dining scene. The seven-course prix fixe menu changes daily, always offering a selection of fish, poultry, beef, veal, and lamb dishes as well as a choice of soups, salads, and desserts.
The $125-per-person adventure begins with the arrival of hors d'oeuvres. As an example of what could follow, consider Oriental shrimp dumplings, chicken consommé with pheasant breast, poached Maine lobster with passion fruit butter, mixed field greens with raspberry–pinot noir vinaigrette, and a dark chocolate and strawberry soufflé. Perfect portions keep it all surprisingly manageable. The strains of a harp or violin provide a romantic backdrop. The wine list is positively encyclopedic. (Wine pairing costs $65 per person.) At the end of the meal, guests are presented with a souvenir menu and a red rose (ladies only). In sum, though the experience is an extremely expensive one, for many it is also quite special. Men must wear jackets. Reservations are a must. **D $$$$**

YACHTSMAN STEAKHOUSE (Yacht Club): Quite simply, a carnivore's paradise. The generous portions begin with massive rolls and continue with sensational seared Maine diver scallops. Of course, there's no skimping on the excellent and expertly prepared aged beef entrées (New York strip steak, filet mignon, and chateaubriand for two, to name a few), so good luck finding room for crème brûlée. The menu also includes chicken and seafood dishes. This restaurant has dining nooks suited for special occasions and can accommodate large groups. Reservations are strongly suggested. `B L D` **$$$**

Good Bets

BOATWRIGHT'S DINING HALL (Port Orleans Riverside): Reasonably priced Southern specialties are the big draw at this unique eatery, where the centerpiece is a riverboat under construction, boat-making tools are mounted on the walls, and tables are set with condiment-filled toolboxes. Try the prime rib and jambalaya. Full bar. Reservations are strongly suggested. `B D` **$$-$$$**

GRAND FLORIDIAN CAFE (Grand Floridian): Wall-length windows incorporate the hotel's central courtyard into this inviting spot's potted-palm greenery. A pleasant experience any time of day, it's a reasonably priced way to check out the World's poshest resort.

Seasonal dishes feature traditional American comfort food; past selections have included hamburgers and pork chops. Try the French toast with cinnamon or the crab cakes with mango relish. Excellent wine selection. Reservations are suggested. `B L D` **$$$**

KIMONOS (Swan): This is the place for good sushi and tempura in a lounge styled with bamboo and kimono accents. A wine selection is complemented by sake, Japanese and domestic beers, and cocktails. The calm is occasionally interrupted by a cacophony of karaoke (a big draw at night). Reservations are accepted. `D S` **$$-$$$**

Dining Guide

This is not a comprehensive listing of the World's eateries—for that, we immodestly recommend *Birnbaum's Official Guide to Walt Disney World Dining 2010.* Instead, this chapter is a selective roundup of the best adult dining and snacking venues.

Those restaurants designated as "Standouts" are dining rooms and fast-food places whose exceptional flair, distinctive fare, and/or terrific settings have earned our highest recommendation. "Good Bets" are additional locales that offer consistently rewarding dining experiences.

Secrets to Success

Hungry and in no mood to wait in line? To avoid the crunch, plan to eat an early (or late) meal. Table-service restaurants are usually less crowded at lunch than at dinner, so you might want to make lunch the main meal of the day. But if it's a dinner spot you relish, choose a place where reservations are available (see page 185 for details). Know that Disney's reservations system does allow for walk-ins. But, because there's often a wait involved, show up before you're starving.

'OHANA (Polynesian): The beauty of 'Ohana's family-style dining experience—a South Pacific feast prepared in the restaurant's prominent open-fire cooking pit—is that the oak-grilled skewers of turkey, pork, and beef just keep coming. Fresh coconut bread pudding, served à la mode with bananas Foster sauce, makes for a fine dessert.

To make the most of 'Ohana's setting, which features exotic wood carvings under a vast thatched roof, request a table that's right up against the windows overlooking the Seven Seas Lagoon. (The number of tables there is limited, but it's worth a shot.) This puts you a comfortable distance from the grill and the route where the coconut-

rolling contest is held, but still in prime position to be serenaded with Polynesian songs. Breakfast is a character affair. Reservations are strongly suggested. B D $$$

WHISPERING CANYON CAFE (Wilderness Lodge): For savory eating that does not stop until you say "when," consider this family-style restaurant a good candidate. (Don't be fooled by the name. This place can be downright rowdy.) At dinner, menu items such as oven-roasted chicken, smoked ribs, and pulled pork are sure to satisfy. Home-made desserts come with an extra charge. (Breakfast, lunch, and dinner selections are also available à la carte.) Reservations are strongly suggested. B L D $$$

Other Options in the World
Standouts

FULTON'S CRAB HOUSE (Downtown Disney Pleasure Island): Walk the gangway onto this would-be riverboat, and with one glance around you're prepared to book passage. Still, the polished woods, brass detailing, and nautical nostalgia of the restaurant are secondary to the fresh seafood served therein.

B breakfast   L lunch   D dinner   S snacks $ $15 $$ $15-$36 $$$ $36-$60 $$$$ $60 and up

The extensive (albeit pricey) dinner menu changes with the day's arrivals. It's not unusual for Hawaiian albacore tuna (accompanied by, say, crab Bordelaise and corn-whipped potatoes) to be seen next to Great Lakes walleyed pike (with garlic chips and herbed rice). Standbys include crab cakes; cioppino, a stew of seafood in a tomato broth; garlic chicken; crab and lobster platters; and filet mignon.

For a quicker, possibly more satisfying fix, visit the ravishing raw bar at the adjoining Stone Crab Lounge. For a reasonably priced lunch, it's lounge or bust. Reservations are suggested.
L D S $$$$

HOUSE OF BLUES (Downtown Disney West Side): An eclectic menu with New Orleans taste buds (think étouffée, jambalaya, barbecue, and crispy catfish nuggets) distinguishes this folk art–studded restaurant.

It's a good spot for a late-night bite. Those craving the illusion

Knockout Views

Big River Grille & Brewing Works (BoardWalk)

California Grill (Contemporary)

Cantina de San Angel (Mexico, Epcot's World Showcase)

Cap'n Jack's Restaurant (Downtown Disney Marketplace)

Cinderella's Royal Table (Magic Kingdom)

Coral Reef (The Seas, Epcot's Future World)

Flame Tree Barbecue (Discovery Island, Animal Kingdom)

Narcoossee's (Grand Floridian)

Rose & Crown Pub and Dining Room (United Kingdom, Epcot's World Showcase)

Sci-Fi Dine-In Theater (Disney's Hollywood Studios)

Stone Crab Lounge (Inside Fulton's Crab House, Downtown Disney Pleasure Island)

B breakfast   L lunch   D dinner   S snacks $ $15 $$ $15-$36 $$$ $36-$60 $$$$ $60 and up

of being outdoors will enjoy the atmospheric, enclosed Voodoo Garden (it's in the back of the restaurant). The lively Sunday gospel brunch is a winner. Reservations are suggested.
`L D S` `$$`

WOLFGANG PUCK CAFE (Downtown Disney West Side): This eatery marked the Los Angeles chef's Florida debut and brought trendy California cuisine to the fore.

There are actually three dining arenas here—an express counter, a cafe, and a formal dining room on the second floor—plus a sushi bar. All feature the famous chef's signature gourmet pizzas, rotisserie chicken, and other specialties prepared in the display kitchen.

The **Wolfgang Puck Express** counter here (there's also one at the Marketplace) offers wood-fired pizzas, Chinois chicken salad, and focaccia sandwiches that defy most definitions of fast food. First-come seating. `L D S` `$`

At **Wolfgang Puck Cafe** the menu includes (excellent, if a tad tuna-heavy) sushi, Asian hoisin barbecued ribs, and pumpkin ravioli with brown butter and sage. Reservations are suggested.
`L D S` `$$-$$$`

Wolfgang Puck Cafe—The Dining Room puts hunger pangs to rest with such dishes as Puck's original veal weinerschnitzel and shrimp scampi risotto, plus a wine list well suited to the cuisine. Reservations are suggested.
`D` `$$$$`

Good Bets

CAP'N JACK'S RESTAURANT (Downtown Disney Marketplace): This pretty pier house perched over

Scenic Cocktail Spots

Big River Grille & Brewing Works (BoardWalk, outdoor tables)

Cantina de San Angel (Mexico, Epcot's World Showcase)

Outer Rim (Contemporary)

Stone Crab Lounge (Fulton's Crab House, Downtown Disney Marketplace)

Top of the Palace (Buena Vista Palace)

B breakfast L lunch D dinner S snacks $ $15 $$ $15-$36 $$$ $36-$60 $$$$ $60 and up

Lake Buena Vista is the place to socialize over cold drafts and seafood. The strawberry margarita is tops, as are the clam chowder and crab cake starters. Or try the fresh fish and seafood pasta entrées. The Captain has been satisfying hungry Walt Disney World visitors since the '70s. Reservations are suggested.

`L D S $$`

OUTBACK (Buena Vista Palace, Hotel Plaza Boulevard; 407-827-3430): Despite its similar meat-and-potatoes inclinations, this establishment has no relation to the chain of the same name. Go for the baby back ribs, shrimp, and steak. Reservations are suggested. `D $$`

PLANET HOLLYWOOD (Downtown Disney West Side): This casual restaurant is ensconced in a 120-foot-diameter sphere and surrounded by a three-dimensional collage of movie memorabilia. The menu has simple, creative flair and depth (consider the blackened shrimp, a Shanghai chicken salad, or the old reliable burger and fries). Reservations are suggested.

`L D S $$-$$$`

NIGHTLIFE GUIDE

In the pages that follow, we present the best nightlife in Walt Disney World. You'll receive an overview of Pleasure Island; next, an introduction to Downtown Disney West Side; and a briefing on the clubs found along the BoardWalk.

The final section of this guide completes the nightlife picture with our report on other recommended clubs and lounges located on Walt Disney World property. Cheers!

Downtown Disney Pleasure Island

This bustling metropolis is a six-acre island consumed by restaurants, shops, and a lounge or two. (Its nightclub scene moseyed off into the sunset in 2008—and with it went Mannequins, Motion, The Adventurers Club, Comedy Warehouse, BET Soundstage, and 8Trax.) The legal drinking age in Florida is 21, and a valid, government-issued, photo ID is required.

 breakfast   L lunch   D dinner   S snacks $ $15 $$ $15-$36 $$$ $36-$60 $$$$ $60 and up

Although the clubs are gone, there is still much fun to be had in these parts. Kick things off with a visit to **Raglan Road**. This jovial joint is an authentic Irish pub. The cozy-yet-rollicking pub is a meticulously decorated Emerald Isle oasis—complete with freshly prepared Irish cuisine and live entertainment. Oh, and of course, pints of stout and other spirited beverages. An evening here leaves most eyes—Irish or otherwise—smiling. Top o' the evenin' to ya.

When you leave Raglan Road, you're on course for **Fuego Cigars by Sosa**. A funky cigar bar—yes, it's okay to puff away inside here—Fuego features premium house-branded cigars, as well as cocktails. Guests must be 18 years old to smoke, 21 to drink. It gets pretty hazy in here—non-smokers may want to imbibe elsewhere.

Cha, Cha, Cha Changes

The patch of Walt Disney World known as Pleasure Island is undergoing a *major* metamorphosis. The most dramatic change? The dance clubs are no more. (However, guests who wish to exercise their happy feet can still do so at BoardWalk's Atlantic Dance—see page 209.) What's in store for our old friend Pleasure Island? Well, that's in the hands of Disney's Imagineers. At press time, we were told to expect, among other things, "an extraordinary mix of dining and shopping." P.I. may be in flux, but one thing is certain: When the dust settles, this will still be an island we wouldn't mind being stranded on.

Downtown Disney West Side

The West Side merges with the Marketplace and Pleasure Island to make a triple-header of the distraction zone known as Downtown Disney. It's a colorful lakeside strip of restaurants, shops, and energy. Here, guests pay as they play, springing for cover charges only at places they patronize.

Puffer's Alert: Smoking is allowed in designated areas only. Ask at the venue for the nearest spot. Night Owl's Alert: Raglan Road, Planet Hollywood, Bongos, and House of Blues serve until the wee hours (well, at least until around midnight).

The easternmost spot at the West Side is the AMC Theatres, a celebration of the silver screen (make that screens—there are 24 of them). The marquee is *au courant*, the seats are roomy (not to mention stadium style), and the sound system, developed by George Lucas, is first-rate.

Call 407-298-4488 for show-times, the earliest of which is about 1 P.M. And bring a sweater. The air-conditioning here is powerful, to say the least.

If you prefer a diversion with an added dimension, start a conga line and head for the three-story pineapple directly across the promenade. **Bongos Cuban Cafe**, created in part by singer Gloria Estefan, is a bright, boisterous restaurant that parades the flavors and rhythms of Cuba and other Latin American countries.

More Reasons to Go West

Downtown Disney West Side has more than just restaurants, night-clubs, and movie theaters. It's also home to interesting shops (open until 11 P.M.; see page 163 for details) and DisneyQuest (see page 214). Most notably, it has a perma-nent tent for a Cirque du Soleil show called La Nouba. Wipe out all thoughts of Bozo-style antics; this circus ensemble is not your typical ringmastered, big-top production. Cirque features a cast of 60 per-forming a mix of acrobatics and modern dance. Wild costumes and dramatic original music add to the fun. Cirque fans consider it The Greatest Show in Downtown Disney. Call 407-939-7600 or go to *www.disneyworld.com* for tickets (up to six months in advance). Cirque du Soleil is usually dark on Sunday and Monday.

When you've had your fill of the fruit-fly fandango, plot a moonlight stroll along the peaceful shore of Village Lake. Melt away the Miami mentality with a dose of cool: **House of Blues**. It has capacity for 2,000 soul men and women. Inspired by one of America's proudest musical traditions, the club also serves up country, with an occasional mix of R&B, gospel, or rock.

You may buy tickets through Ticketmaster (407-839-3900; *www.ticketmaster.com*) or at the box office up until showtime; ticket prices vary, depending on the act.

BoardWalk

While merely strolling the boards of this nostalgic entertainment district a short walk from Epcot provides a delightful escape to simpler times, the temptations en route are tough to resist. Cotton candy vendors, savory dining, and surrey bike rides aside, BoardWalk gives the World things it has long needed—a sports bar, a brewpub, a sing-along piano bar, and more. In addition to being an appealing resort (see *Checking In* for a complete description), BoardWalk is a great adult hangout. Although there's no general admission fee, **Jellyrolls** charges a cover after 7 P.M. (about $8–$10), while **Atlantic Dance** is usually cover free. You must be 21 or older to enter both venues. Valet parking ($10) is available. All of the bars and clubs described below stay open until 2 A.M. With the exception of Atlantic Dance, which is open Tuesday through Saturday, all bars and clubs are open seven

days a week. Smoking is permitted in designated spots only.

Sitting high on the hit list is **ESPN Club**, a sports bar so over-the-top it practically has referees. Between the live sports commentators, the ballpark fare, and the more than 100 televisions (some in the restrooms) broadcasting any number of games, no unnecessary time-outs are taken. Note that this spot does not take reservations. If you want a seat for a big game, get there very early!

Several first downs away, the **Big River Grille & Brewing Works** invites you to bend the ol' elbow right under the brewmaster's nose. Five specialty ales, including two that change with the seasons, are crafted on the premises. It's a tough job, but someone's got to polish off the beer

bread and raise a glass to the brew maestro. After trying the beer sampler (tastes of all five ales for about $5), we recommend the Tilt Pale Ale house brew. Hot beer pretzels and other appetizers from the restaurant menu are available at the bar until the kitchen closes, at around 11 P.M., providing fitting accompaniments to tastings.

Walk a few short strides into the dueling-pianist realm of **Jellyrolls** and you're soon crooning and swaying along with the rest of the congregation to songs from the 1970s to the present. As an example of the musicians' versatility, consider this sampling of one set: "King of the Road," "Joy to the World," and a rousing medley of TV theme songs—including odes to *The Brady Bunch* and *The Jeffersons*. The music comes uninterrupted (except by the wisecracking pianists themselves). Soon you're wondering how you got so hoarse.

So you head next door to **Atlantic Dance**, an elegant club that is perpetually reinventing itself. A deejay supplies a sound track to groove to, with a live band filling in on auspicious nights. You're free to dance, and, if you like, enjoy a specialty drink on a balcony overlooking the water. From this perspective, the

Two for Tea

Teatime with all the trimmings—scones, tiny sandwiches, and pastries served on bone china—is 2 P.M. in the Garden View Tea Room at the Grand Floridian. A large selection of teas and tasty accompaniments is offered every day until 6 P.M. (reservations recommended). Call 407-939-3463.

game highlights on ESPN Club's monitors seem miles away. But they're not, and so, when your mood shifts, you can easily venture back to check the scores. Such is an evening at BoardWalk.

Other World Options
Standouts
CALIFORNIA GRILL LOUNGE

(Contemporary): The tiny lounge in the California Grill offers what amounts to box seats for the Magic Kingdom fireworks. You can order from the California Grill menu, too. Last call: 11:45 P.M.

After-Dark Dazzle

- The Magic Kingdom's extended curfew during busy seasons (generally summers and holiday periods) means the relaxed atmosphere and romance of the park in the early evening hours are more accessible. After-dark also means nightly fireworks and performances of the nighttime parade.

- The fireworks show is a pyrotechnics display worthy of a Fourth of July finale. And the evening parade is not to be missed; if there are two performances, aim for the later one, when the prime viewing spots (anywhere on Main Street) are easier to snare, thanks to the little ones' need to go beddie-bye.

- Epcot's World Showcase, which stays open until at least 9 P.M. year-round, assumes a sparkling beauty at night. For this reason, Disney presents a special show, IllumiNations. This simulation of our planet's evolution features a three-story globe, intense fireworks, and stirring music. The 13-minute show, typically ignited at closing time, is visible from any point along the promenade.

- Sure to top the after-dark A-list is Fantasmic!, served up in an amphitheater behind The Twilight Zone Tower of Terror at Disney's Hollywood Studios. The 26-minute show takes you inside Mickey's dreams as he conducts dancing fountains, swirling stars, and a delightful musical score. Animation projected onto water screens on the lake helps tell the story, which climaxes with a visit from Disney villains. A battle powered by flaming special effects leads to a character-filled finale.

- The Electrical Water Pageant, a 1,000-foot-long string of illuminated floating creatures, makes its way around Bay Lake each night. You can usually view the pageant at 9 P.M. from the Polynesian, 9:15 P.M. from the Grand Floridian, 9:35 P.M. from Wilderness Lodge, 9:45 P.M. from Fort Wilderness, and 10:05 P.M. from the Contemporary. Times may change.

CREW'S CUP (Yacht Club): When it comes to beer, the Crew's Cup runneth over with nearly 30 international brews. Consider the warm copper-accented decor, the scintillating aromas wafting in from the neighboring Yachtsman Steakhouse, and the potential for savory snacks (from 6–10 P.M.), and you have an even better idea of why we are putty in this joint's hands. Doors close: about midnight.

IL MULINO NEW YORK TRATTORIA LOUNGE (Swan): A vibrant addition to the local lounge lineup, this sleek and spacious spot serves Italian wines (the wine list is excellent), cocktails, and light fare. Doors close: about 2 A.M.

Information, Please

For more on Downtown Disney happenings—from retail to concerts to the AMC 24-movie lineup—call 407-WDW-2-NITE (939-2648).

KIMONOS (Swan): Care for a sake with a karaoke chaser? You've come to the right place! In addition to nightly songfests, this festive lounge serves loads of lip-smacking libations. Not to mention swell sushi. Doors close: about 1 A.M. depending on just how much the joint jumps as the night wears on.

MARTHA'S VINEYARD (Beach Club): Although appetizers are served, the main reason you're here is the wine. Selections from a real Martha's Vineyard winery,

as well as some from California, Long Island, and European vineyards, make for tough decisions, but it helps to know that wine can be ordered in sample sizes, as well as full glasses. There's a full bar, too. Last call: 11:45 P.M.

ROSE & CROWN PUB (United Kingdom, Epcot's World Showcase): We've always loved this cheeky classic—for its polished-wood and brass decor; its rich Irish, Scottish, and British drafts; and its neighborly feel. So we weren't too surprised during one of many visits to overhear a gentleman asking a fellow behind the bar to please let Jerry (a bartender not present) know that he was sorry he'd missed him. "Next time," he said hopefully. You needn't be a fan of shandies or black and tans to appreciate that. Doors close: at park closing. Note that specifics are apt to change.

STONE CRAB LOUNGE (Fulton's Crab House, Downtown Disney Marketplace): Like the local heartthrob who happens to be loaded, this gorgeous riverboat bar stacks the odds even more in its favor with an excellent raw bar, prime water views, and a honey-wheat house brew. It doesn't just make Bloody Marys

from scratch (as in hand-squeezed tomatoes and fresh horseradish), it garnishes them with shrimp. Doors close: 11 P.M.

TERRITORY LOUNGE (Wilderness Lodge): This rustic spot is marked by wood-carved grizzlies and a muraled map of the Western frontier that "unfolds" over the ceiling.

While this spot can be swamped with diners-in-waiting during prime mealtimes, it more often inspires lingering. Appetizers and snacks add to the appeal. Doors close: about midnight.

TUNE-IN LOUNGE (Disney's Hollywood Studios): This Formica-laden spot, the family den to 50's Prime Time Cafe, serves Dad's Super Snacks and spirits from Dad's Liquor Cabinet, while vintage TVs show clips from the decade's most popular sitcoms (all food related, of course). A baby boomer's paradise, it's an excellent spot to cool off and regroup. Doors close: at park closing time.

Virgin Daiquiri, Anyone?

Soft drinks, fruit juices, and tasty specialty drinks *sans* alcohol are available at all Walt Disney World clubs. Just ask the bartender.

DisneyQuest: A Virtual Toy Box

Call it a virtual-reality check. An ode to flippers and joysticks. A bumper-car blast from your arcade past. DisneyQuest at Downtown Disney West Side is five stories of rampant interactivity that could test the supple wrists of The Who's Pinball Wizard. A sampling: You paddle a buoyant raft around rugged rocks, not to mention dinosaurs, on the Virtual Jungle Cruise. After rediscovering Centipede, you ride a simulated self-made roller coaster—a hair-raising excuse for a Virtual Makeover at Magic Mirror. DisneyQuest is open from 11:30 A.M. to 10 P.M. Sunday through Thursday, 11:30 A.M. to 11 P.M. Friday and Saturday. One-day admission is about $40, not including tax (prices may change).

Good Bets

CAP'N JACK'S RESTAURANT (Downtown Disney Marketplace): This pier house jutting out over Village Lake scores with a convivial atmosphere and strawberry margaritas. It also offers reasonably priced sunsets and beautiful seafood (or is it the reverse?). Solo diners note: A full menu is offered at the bar. Doors close: 10:30 P.M.

MIZNER'S (Grand Floridian): If you look past the house orchestra that sets up shop nightly outside this second-floor alcove, you'll find a mahogany bar with fine ports, brandies, and appetizers. It's popular with the business set. Doors close: 1 A.M.

NARCOOSSEE'S (Grand Floridian): You've got to love a lounge that's thoroughly steeped in Victoriana on the inside and framed by a lake that lies like a picnic blanket beneath the Magic Kingdom fireworks on the veranda. Worldly wines by the glass, as well as traditional cocktails and specialty drinks. Doors close: 10 P.M.

RAINFOREST CAFE (Two locations—Downtown Disney Marketplace and Disney's Animal Kingdom): The latter has two entrances—one outside the park entrance and another inside the turnstiles. When the restaurant is mobbed, we like to take in the thunderstorms and waterfalls from the central mushroom-capped bar. We simply saddle an unwitting zebra or giraffe (the

animal bar stools are strictly hooves-to-hips) and chase our tails. The festive, if bustling, "natural" ambience is intoxicating. Doors close: 11 P.M., weekdays; midnight, weekends.

RIVER ROOST (Port Orleans Riverside): This one's nothing fancy. Just your average, unassuming nook that happens to have a fireplace and ready access to chicken wings and spicy Cajun onion straws. Drinks stop at midnight.

SHULA'S (Dolphin): Enjoy your cocktail of choice in either the bar or cozy lounge areas of this restaurant that proclaims itself to be "one of the Top 10 steak houses in America." Who are we to argue? Former Miami Dolphins coach Don Shula scores big with appetizers ranging from barbecued shrimp to steak soup. There's a TV in each room, too. Expect the big sporting event du jour to be playing. Doors close: 11 P.M.

Dinner Shows

If you're looking for a side of entertainment to complement your meal, consider a Disney dinner show. Reservations are required and may be booked up

to 180 days in advance: call 407-WDW-DINE (939-3463), or visit *www.disneyworld.com/dining/*. Note that "tiered seating" has been introduced for the Hoop-Dee-Doo and the Spirit of Aloha. There are three categories from which to choose, with Category 1 providing the best views—and biggest prices. All perspectives on the shows are decent, so price is something to consider when making your reservation. Special dietary requests are honored with advance notice. Cancellations must be made at least 48 hours prior to showtime to avoid paying in full.

The most popular of the lot is the **Hoop-Dee-Doo Musical Revue**, held in Pioneer Hall at Fort Wilderness. The show incorporates whoopin', singin', dancin', and audience participation in a frontier hoedown.

Vittles include ribs, fried chicken, salad, seasonal veggie, and strawberry shortcake. There are three seatings, at 5 P.M., 7:15 P.M., and 9:30 P.M.; adults pay about $51 for Category 3; $55 for Category 2; and $60 for Category 1, including tax and tip. Note that Category 1 has the best views.

At the Polynesian resort, **Disney's Spirit of Aloha Dinner Show**—complete with hula skirts, ukuleles, and fire dancers—takes guests on a whirlwind journey from New Zealand to Samoa. The meal is served family style and features, chicken, spareribs, rice, veggies, and dessert. The show is presented in Luau Cove. It is an open-air, rain-or-shine affair and is canceled when temperatures drop below 50 degrees. It costs about $51 for Category 3; $55 for Category 2; and $60 for Category 1, including tax and tip.

It's not really a dinner show, but the daily Oktoberfest celebration at the Biergarten in Germany at Epcot's World Showcase makes for an entertaining experience. It features performers in lederhosen or dirndls yodeling and playing everything from accordions to cowbells. Seating is family style (8 to a table); the buffet includes bratwurst, chicken, spaetzle, red cabbage, and potato salad.

Adults pay about $30 for dinner, plus tax and tip; beer costs extra (though the beer selection is limited for a place that fancies itself a beer hall). The cost for lunch is about $20. Note that entertainment comes with lunch and dinner.

A lower-profile dinner show, **Mickey's Backyard Barbecue** is one of our favorites. Think of it as a Fourth of July–type picnic fortified by live entertainment. As an instructor gives line-dance lessons, a country band whoops it up Nashville style. Disney characters kick up their heels on the dance floor. The chow includes chicken and ribs, corn-on-the-cob, baked beans, corn bread, and other reminders of summer, plus as many cold drafts as you need to wash it all down. This seasonal show, presented at Fort Wilderness, costs about $45 for adults. For reservations, call 407-939-3463 up to 180 days ahead.

Notes

❤ Notes ❤

TERMS & CONDITIONS

- Must present coupon at check-in to receive discount.
- Discount applies to activities only, *not* merchandise.
- Call for activity restrictions.
- All activities are subject to availability.
- We reserve the right to cancel due to inclement weather.
- Terms and conditions subject to change without notice.
- Coupon not valid with any other discount.
- Coupon cannot be copied or reproduced.
- Coupon cannot be redeemed for cash.

  For more information, visit *www.sammyduvall.com,* or call 407-939-0754.

Expires 12/31/10